DATE DUE

Morality
and Its
Beyond

DICK WESTLEY

TWENTY-THIRD PUBLICATIONS
Mystic, Connecticut

Dedication

Whether this book be judged wise or foolish, I humbly dedicate it to all those men and women who were taught the traditional morality and were wounded by it, and who yet displayed nobility and courage in continuing the search for goodness and virtue on their own. They are our brothers and sisters. No—better—they are each of us.

Second printing September 1985

©1984 by Dick Westley. All rights reserved. No part of this publication may be reproduced in any manner without prior written permission of the publisher. Write to Permissions Editor, P.O. Box 180, Mystic CT 06355.

Library of Congress Catalog Card Number 83-51512

ISBN 0-89622-208-X
      0-89622-207-1 (paper)

Edited by Marie McIntyre
Designed by John G. van Bemmel
Cover photo by Andrea S. Carey
Cover design by George Herrick

Contents

Introduction

Some years ago, working from my own experiences, I attempted to give an account of the journey to adult faith in a book entitled *Redemptive Intimacy*. Many responded that their own journeys had led them to similar conclusions in matters of belief, but that they had been either unable or unwilling to express themselves publicly. They thanked me for having given expression to what was for so long locked up in their own minds and hearts. Those responses have encouraged me to write this companion volume, in which I want to attempt to give a similar public expression to the even more agonizing and ambiguous journey we adult Catholics have experienced in the matter of morals, that is, of sin and evil. In our journey, we have not always been helped by the traditional accounts of morality and the Christian lifestyle that have been presented to us. Now in adult life we find outselves still formed or, in some ways, deformed by what we were taught earlier in life, in many cases bearing unbelievable and unnecessary burdens of conscience. Still we find ourselves unable to shake loose from that pain because of fear. Our experience tells us that something is wrong, but we find it difficult to know how to set things right.

Looking back from the perspective of the mid-years, moral matters that were once crystal clear no longer are and things that were once judged to be selfish and evil suddenly look less so. That seems to be an inevitable result of journeying to adulthood and mid-life. For as we move through the various stages of life, our perspective invariably changes. To live is to grow and to change. So we come to hold things we once thought we could never espouse, and we give up as inadequate those things we once deemed eternal truths.

The problem, of course, is that such moves are not always the result of genuine growth, increased wisdom, greater faith, or authentic virtue. They may just as easily be the result of a certain weariness with self-denial and walking with the Lord and an increased need for self-indulgence. Or because of the disappointments and failures we have experienced in our relations with one another, we may just have finally become cynical about the practicality of Christian ideals in the "real" world. But regardless of what has prompted our change in outlook, we feel the need to give some sort of coherent account, both to ourselves and to others, of the new perspectives we have adopted in adult life. We know that the final judgment on those moral perspectives lies not with ourselves but with the faith community. It must judge whether our views stem from wisdom or folly. But let that faith community be mindful of one fact: *Truth has a strange way of continually reasserting itself until it is given its proper due.* In the end, of course, it is the risen Lord of history who will have the last word. In the meantime, we are called upon to do the very best we can. Most of us do.

I really believe that now, but I didn't always. Judging from my own experience, it probably takes half a lifetime before one recognizes how truly pervasive is the goodness and greatness of human beings. When I was younger and filled with self-righteousness, it was easy for me to condemn the conduct of others when they "broke the rules," especially when the rules they broke were the ones I either had no inclination to breach or no real opportunity to break. It is so easy for people who are serious about walking with the Lord to fall into self-righteousness and to become judgmental about those who do not share their faith or who act according to different values.

I am not myself a naturally guilt-ridden person. In faith, I gratefully accept the forgiveness of God and realize that one must get beyond past mistakes and not become obsessed with previous sins and transgressions. Still, in mid-life I continue to feel very uneasy whenever I recall those judgmental, self-righteous moments from my past when I closed my heart and mind to people (even to people within my own family) because they had not lived up to what I had been taught was expected of Christians. I would give anything to have the chance to undo all that, and to tell those I judged so harshly that it's really okay—and that I'm finally coming to understand. Better late than never!

Think about it. How many truly evil people do you know? I would be very much surprised if you couldn't count them all on one hand. And how many of those you've numbered as "evil" do you personally know? (Most of us will find that a good percentage of those we call "evil" are persons we've never met but only heard about on TV, in the newspapers, or in history books.) In any case, the number of people we'd be willing to call evil from personal experience is very small indeed. Oh, we certainly know people who do things that cause suffering and pain for others, but we seem more willing to say their actions are "evil" than to say they are. I think our instincts in this matter are correct. When people share their personal journeys and struggles with us and engage in the sort of sharing I have elsewhere called "redemptive intimacy," we soon discover the truth. In the face of life's pain and ambiguity, there is a courage, a nobility, an admirable toughness and survivability in us that bespeaks the presence of God and evidences that we are indeed and in truth made in his image. We lose sight of that fact when the seamy, low-life, vulgar, perverse, and evil side of us captures the lion's share of time and space in the electronic and print media. The stories of our failures, our insensitivities, our sins and our crimes seem to be judged more newsworthy. As a result, the truth about humankind is camouflaged; we become filled with fear and suspicion and the social fabric is weakened as we more and more come to lose confidence in one another. One of the joys of mid-life is that we are finally able to see through all that and come to recognize how incredibly good and truly remarkable human beings really are. No one would deny that the encounter with evil is real. But if the passage to adult life is as I have described it, it seems natural to assume that the account one gives of evil earlier in life will be radically different from what one thinks about it later on. It is not so easy, however, to give up one's earlier position, especially when it has been learned under Christian auspices and carries with it the weight of authority and tradition. We feel somehow guilty for not having been able to continue to see things in the same way. Still, when we see other Christians remaining rigid in moral matters and mouthing the same accounts they learned as children, as many fundamentalists, right-to-lifers, and moral majority so often do, we know we cannot go that route. Caught between our guilt on the one hand, and the unacceptability of the alternative presented to us on the other, we experience one of human life's special pains—ambiguity. As the expression goes, "We're caught between a rock and a hard place."

That situation is made even more painful when the magisterium in the church seems determined to "hold the line on moral matters" lest the institutional church appear weak and vacillating in the face of growing secularism. While we may have experienced renewal since Vatican II in many ways, the moral teaching of the church seems strangely unaffected. Moral theologians and scholars have made magnificent strides toward the light in the past twenty years, but the church's official position remains largely unchanged. Pope John Paul II is a courageous, faith-filled and loving man, but when he talks morality, he speaks a language foreign to the communally-funded experience of the adult faith community. Even though he is old enough himself to know better, when he speaks of moral matters, it is as if we were all back in grade school. He is so loving and charismatic that we feel inclined to want to agree with him, but we just can't because our experience tells us a different story. More ambiguity. More guilt feelings. More pain.

It is painful to have the institutional church so out of touch with the lived experiences of its people. I am not talking about the isolated and private experiences of individual Catholics, but of those experiences that are so indigenous to human life that they are shared by all of us regardless of our different social, educational, and economic backgrounds. The wisdom based on and derived from such universal human experiences may be said to be the "communally-funded" wisdom of humankind. In the past, the consensus derived from such experiences was recognized by our tradition as an authentic source of divine revelation. In our day, it seems to be the practice of the church to ignore that source of light from below in favor of a supposedly superior light from above. But it is painful for people to see the wisdom of their communally-funded experiences ignored and even contradicted by the official church. It tells them that what is revealed to them in their lived experience is suspect.

I have undertaken this book for one reason more than anyother, to assuage my own pain and that of so many of my brothers and sisters in faith. We can't go on like this. The Lord meant us to be at peace. We obviously cannot remove all the ambiguity from the present situation over morality among Christians, but perhaps it is possible to bring a greater clarity to the situation as well as to give an acceptable alternative account of Christian morality, one that does greater justice to our adult experience of evil.

Though I have written this book from the perspective of my own tradition, which is Roman Catholic, there is nothing in its positive assertions that could be labeled sectarian. Indeed, it would be my hope that Christians of various traditions, denominations, and communions would recognize their own faith-journeys in my account. We are, after all, attempting to walk in faith with the same Lord, committed to the same dream of his coming Kingdom.

When I talk to myself about how to characterize such an enterprise, I am inclined to call this book an exercise in pastoral morality. What do I mean by that? In the church in which I was reared, the pastor was the one who had the *cura animarum,* the "care of souls." Unfortunately, many pastors interpreted that to mean that within the confines of the parish they were boss, and that their word was law. Thankfully, there were always a sufficient number of priests who really understood what it meant to "care" for people; consequently, the dream of authentic priesthood remains a vital option to this very day. In the words of Milton Mayeroff (*Car-*

ing, Perennial Library, 1972, pp. 1, 5), "to care" for someone means

... in the most significant sense, to help him to grow and actualize himself. Caring is the antithesis of simply using the other person to satisfy one's own needs. In caring as helping the other to grow, I experience what I care for as an extension of myself and at the same time as something separate from me that I respect in its own right.

I take this to mean that an account of morality is "pastoral" when it takes as its central focus, not the commandments given by God, nor the natural law written in our hearts, nor the rules and regulations of the institutional church, but the moral development of the individual person. A pastoral morality 1) believes in the nobility and goodness of human beings, 2) is sensitive to the tremendous burdens we each carry for no other reason than that we are human, and 3) recognizes that as humans we experience a lifelong "passage" from stage to stage and that this development is a central factor in any moral theory. In a word, pastoral morality is not an abstract account of the "oughts" and "ought nots" of life, but a caring and personal involvement in another's groping for what is right. Pastoral morality aims not so much at presenting people with the correct answers to their moral dilemmas, as at helping to clear away the obstacles that keep them from seeing themselves for what they really are and hence judging the situation as it really is. As truly pastoral, it will try to delineate a "beyond" that transcends mere morality, a "beyond" that is incarnated in the Lord and remains the highest ideal of Christian faith.

In achieving those goals, it seemed convenient to divide the work into three parts. Part One is on the human condition as contemporary men and women have come to understand it. Too often, Christians talk glibly about what is morally evil and what isn't without taking into account the human condition as it really is. It is only after one gets clear on that issue that it is possible to discuss the origin of evil and the need for morality. Part Two is devoted to the "Christian" perspective on evil. That perspective will differ depending on whether one takes a "religious" or a "faith" view of the matter. This distinction is extremely important. There will always be a certain ambiguity about the Christian position and the role the institutional church plays in the conduct of its members. Having gotten clear on those matters, Part Three will attempt to take a contemporary pastoral look at what we mean by "sin" and "salvation," after which it will reflect on the issues most agonizing to the adult community of faith today: sexual, life/death, and justice.

As was the case with *Redemptive Intimacy,* this book makes no claim of having captured the truth. It was written from the perspective of one person's journey toward a mature Christian lifestyle. It may well have no wider validity than that. But in order to find that out, it was necessary to offer it as "gift" to the faith community, trusting the members to discern whether it be communally funded wisdom or individualistic folly. In any case, whether this book be judged wise or foolish, I humbly dedicate it to all those men and women whom the traditional morality we were taught has wounded most, and yet who displayed nobility and courage in continuing the search for goodness and virtue on their own. They are our brothers and sisters. No—better—they are each of us.

PART ONE

THE HUMAN CONDITION

Whatever else may be said for culture, in important ways it is the collective memory of humankind. It is the historical storehouse of what human beings have learned from their experiences and of the things they have thought worthwhile to hand down to future generations. It is because we have access to such a memory bank that we are freed from constantly having to "reinvent the wheel." Each generation is not condemned to start out from point zero, but can, as it were, stand on the shoulders of preceding generations. That is what makes human progress possible. Of course, that is not equally true for every area of human life, for in some matters we find that we cannot accept what the communally-funded experience of people reveals unless we experience it ourselves. And sometimes, we may even find that we can't accept it at all.

I suspect that this is the main reason that progress in science and technology, in know-how of coping with the material world, seems to be consistent and ever ongoing. Progress in things like morality, human relationships, and learning to love seems either non-existent or painfully slow and halting. When it comes to working with the world of things, it is senseless to "reinvent the wheel," but when it comes to things like the meaning of life, the encounter with evil, and intimacy in human relationships, each of us remains a novice and must begin at the beginning. This also accounts, I think, for the fact that while it is senseless to read the scientific treatises from past centuries for more than historical interest, the writings from the past that address the mystery of life's meaning continue to have value for us. In such matters we are all contemporaries, and history seems to have little bearing on the situation.

Perhaps the clearest indication of that comes from the experience of parents as they try to hand down a system of moral values to their children. Those values have been formed as the result of painful experiences with failure and evil and they are offered to the children in the hope they can avoid some of that. But the values and rules we present to our children strike them as just that, mere rules that they are not convinced they ought to follow. It is only after they, too, have corroborated their truth from bitter experiences that they come to see them as valid and worth handing down to their own offspring. Of course, they will run into a similar resistance. But to say that we are all novices and must learn from experience in moral and interpersonal matters is not at all to say that it makes no sense for us to attempt to formulate and perpetuate the wisdom of our experience on how best to live human life and walk with the Lord. The truth of what we have learned may not be immediately evident nor accepted at once, but by as much as our insights are true, they will be validated eventually. Life has a way of teaching us the truth, in spite of ourselves. Only after we have learned life's lessons do we come to treasure the words of wisdom from others who have made the same journey.

But if we are after truth about moral matters, we must first search out the truth about the human condition. Most of us suppose we already know the human condition. But do we? Perhaps it will not be fruitless to attempt to give an account of the great enigmas with which each of us must cope, just because we are human. The next two chapters will attempt to do precisely that.

CHAPTER ONE

The Human Context of Morality

Every age and every culture has a story it tells about what sort of beings we humans are. In the light of that story, it then goes on to fashion a second story or account that tells us how we ought to live our lives. Every story of "ought" depends on and is derived from a prior story of "is." Thus, some say we ought to grab for all the gusto we can, because it is a fact that we only go around once in life. (This is the contemporary version of: "Eat, drink and be merry, for tomorrow we die.") People soon come to understand that simply saying that one ought or ought not do something is not enough; they want to know why. And the "why" will always be found somewhere within an "is" story and sometimes within more than one of them. For example, when asked why one ought not murder another, the reason might be either because human life is sacred or because it is a fact that God forbade it. The point is that moral "oughts" are not as relative as people sometimes think. They always rest, if they are true, on some set of relevant facts. I

11

take that to be sufficient reason to begin this account of pastoral morality with a scenario of how it is, *really is,* with us human beings.

Whenever we are asked, "How is it with you?" we know the questioner doesn't have time for us to really tell her, so we answer simply, "Fine" or "Okay." By and large, the more accurate answer would be, "Very ambiguous, thank you." We all know that human life is never simply fine; it is always marked by an agonizing ambiguity. A main attraction of so many fundamentalist moral theories lies undoubtedly in the fact that they offer apparent relief from the ever-present ambiguity of human life. But only at a price —the devaluation of human dignity and freedom. Those who preach such unequivocal and rigid moral systems are usually those who feel most uncomfortable about human freedom. They contend it only leads to chaos and confusion and they try to convince people that God feels that way about human freedom, too. (This is a strange position if you think about it, since God is the very author of that freedom.) The fundamentalist posture is only one way to cope with ambiguity, but we should be sensitive to how important that way has become for some of our brothers and sisters. It is the only thing that works for them. No one really enjoys the ambiguity in her life, and yet it is definitely there and cope with it each one must if she would be truly human. In fact, ambiguity so permeates human life from start to finish that it could well be called the hallmark of the human. Animals don't experience it. It is unknown to the angels. Only humankind is stuck with it. Why?

Ambiguity 1: The Existential Dilemma

The primary source of the ambiguity in human life is the fact that we are neither straightforwardly animal, nor straightforwardly angelic, but as it were have a foot in each domain. As we watch people go through their daily rounds, this doesn't seem to be a very great problem; they rarely, if ever, allude to the fact that they are part spirit and part organic. The only way we would even suspect that there is any difficulty in "getting it together" is from our own inner experience. And even then only at certain key moments, since most of the time our coping mechanisms keep the matter from intruding too powerfully into our consciousness.

But even the most effective coping mechanisms cannot keep the problem at bay indefinitely, and so it is that in mid-life, if not before, we find ourselves unable to avoid confronting it directly. With the aging process, we are forced to admit that we have a body that is deteriorating and will inevitably cause us to experience death. We have known that for a long time, since the unavoidability of death was one of the first terrors we experienced in childhood. But we became distracted by the task of building a life, and though we knew we could not escape death, it did not seem important since it was such a long way off. Mid-life changes all that. Suddenly, our distractions no longer keep the problem at bay and we are over- taken with the ambiguity that has been present in our lives from the start.

How is it that someone like me, someone who dreams great dreams, whose mind soars to infinity recognizing limitless possibili- ties—how is it that someone whose symbolic mind is as vital and energetic as ever and whose sense of freedom is heightened is joined to a body that brings in its wake an unavoidable and ultimate de- struction? That is just not fair! Whose idea was it to join human consciousness to matter anyway? Being human may well be some sort of metaphysical joke, but it isn't very funny.

But of course, mid-life is not the only time or situation in which we are forced to feel the drag of matter on our spirit. The young man who struggles with erotic thoughts, wet dreams, and a growing habit of masturbation experiences the existential dilemma in its fullness. Driven by newly discovered urges, he doesn't feel good about himself if he succumbs to them, because he has a sense of his loss of freedom. A power is taking over in his life and his conscious self seems unable to control it. If he resists, he feels the dividedness of being human. If he succumbs, he experiences disap- pointment with himself for being out of control. Suddenly, the in- nocence of youth is gone, and an ambiguity he had never known before enters his life, never to go away.

A similar experience overtakes the young girl. Suddenly in the midst of her carefree life, a force begins to assert itself that por- tends that she is a woman and that nature has its own designs for her. Without so much as a "by your leave," she begins to have monthly periods, and she becomes conscious of the biological clock over which she has no control. Her will in the matter doesn't matter.

Illness or a disabling accident, when they strike, drive home the same enigma—the enigma of a spirit called to freedom being joined to a body, which is subject to the laws of physics, chemistry, and biology. Who among us has not had projects and plans thwarted and dreams and ambitions frustrated because of some physical disorder? Even when such episodes are only temporary, their significance is not lost on us. Should health return quickly, we soon forget and go our merry way. But for a brief time, we were face to face with the profoundest source of ambiguity and fear in human life. Of ambiguity, because we are never quite sure how best to bring the conscious self and the organic body together in our lives. Of fear, because we fully understand that because of our bodies we shall eventually experience death. Since the difficulty derives from our very constitution as human beings, there is no way to definitively solve or escape the problem; the best we can do is cope with it. By distracting ourselves and repressing our fears and anxieties we manage to continue on, knowing that at any moment something might happen to remind us once again of the fact that we are not in control and that our earthly destiny is determined by our biology. What an affront to a conscious self!

By what name shall we designate this fundamental tension or division between the organic body and the conscious self at the foundations of every human life? For convenience, let us label it humankind's Existential Dilemma: existential, because it arises from our very existence as human beings; a dilemma because it is not a problem that can be solved, but is a condition that can only be endured and coped with more or less well.

A Traditional Interpretation

While it may be true that it is only recently that we speak of this matter as our "existential dilemma," the experience of it is as old as the human race. The sages and religious leaders in every culture have had occasion to speak of it in one way or another. But undoubtedly the most influential of the pre-Christian sages for Western culture was the Greek philosopher Plato (fourth century B.C.). His views were adopted by the first Christians because they seemed to be so compatible with Christianity. Most of the Fathers of the Church were Platonic in their outlook. And to this day, the average Christian retains a decidedly Platonic interpretation of the human condition. That is unfortunate, because Platonism has often given rise to a very puritanical and un-Christian moral view.

As Plato interpreted the situation, he could do no other than to take as definitive the experience of the limitation of the conscious self by organic matter. For Plato, a human being is her conscious self or soul and the body is not an integral part of the person at all. It is merely the material husk that temporarily contains the soul for the brief sojourn of a human life. Indeed, the soul and its container are so foreign to each other that they are continually at war and the conflict ends only at death when the soul is freed from its imprisonment in the body. Briefly, this is Plato's rather straightforward account of the human condition and the Existential Dilemma, but one with significant implications.

To identify a human being with her soul is to say that humans are totally spirit. But if that is the case, then how to explain the presence of the soul in matter? Plato must give some reason why a spiritual soul would ever come to exist in union with a body, which is only a hindrance and a distraction, keeping it from easily pursuing its spiritual vocation. His answer was that the soul as spirit had pre-existed in a former, totally spiritual, life, and that through something like the story of the fall of Adam and Eve in Genesis, it fell and was punished by being immersed in matter. How ingenious! Plato explained the common experience we all have of the existential dilemma by saying that our bodies are the punishment and prison for our souls. In effect, this denies any real dilemma because the task is no longer how to integrate body and soul in our lives, but how to resist properly the body and all its accoutrements in this life so as to escape it eventually and completely in the next. The human agenda then becomes "to live centered on spiritual goods while imprisoned in the body until death can free us and we can return to the purely spiritual existence from whence we came."

That is simply marvelous! No wonder Christians have always been attracted to the Platonic account. He sounds the battle cry of spirit against matter and the things of the world, and one could cite passage after passage from Scripture that does exactly the same thing. But it would be a mistake to think, as so many have, that Platonism and Christianity are in the end really compatible. There are similaries, of course. For one thing, Plato speaks of a fall from an original state of spiritual privilege. For another, he gives total priority to the spiritual dimension of life, depicting body and material things as being counterspiritual. And perhaps most importantly for the average person, in the face of inevitable and certain death, Plato puts immortality and life after death on an absolutely firm foundation. But the truth is that the Platonic account not only flies in the face of our everyday experience, it actually undermines two foundational Christian dogmas, that of the incarnation and the resurrection.

Regarding our experience, it is certainly true that we all experience the tension between our symbolic selves and our bodies; we even named that tension the "existential dilemma." But that is a tension within one and the same human person. It will not do to make of it a tension between the human person on the one hand and her body on the other. My body *is* me in some mysterious way. At times I may say, "I *have* a body," but I know that I don't "have" my body the way I have a pen, a car, or a suit of clothes. There is always a distance, a real otherness, between me and what I only "have." I am one thing, and what I "have" is always another. But that is obviously not the case with my body. Rather than say, "I have a body," it would be far more accurate to say, "My body embodies me." There is no human self apart from body, because the human self, unlike the angels, is *always* an embodied self. Were that not true, we could not say things like, "I washed myself," "I see the rainbow," or "I have an earache." We would have to say, "I washed my body," "My eyes see the rainbow," or "My ear has an earache." Now while it is true that we can talk either way and be understood, the fact that it is perfectly legitimate to speak in the first way gives the lie to Plato's view. The bottom line, of course, is that the human body is not alien to the human person at all, and moralities that proceed on that assumption are Platonic and not Christian.

If the body is taken to be alien to the human spirit, then we can make sense out of neither the doctrine of the incarnation nor that of the resurrection. According to the Christian creed, Jesus is both true God and true man. If Plato's account were correct, Jesus would not have become human by taking on both a human soul *and* a human body but would have taken on only a human soul. Recall that in Plato's view souls are in bodies only because they sinned or fell. But Jesus is sinless. It is because Jesus was true man and took on both a human soul and a human body that Christians know that the body is an integral part of being human and not just a temporary prison for the human soul. On the other hand, Plato thought that the true human was all spirit. So we see that the incarnation would be a scandal to the Platonic mind. It not only reveals the goodness of matter but that matter is an integral part of the human person.

Furthermore, if Plato were right in his assessment, what possible sense could be made of the Christian doctrine of the resurrection, which holds that after this earthly sojourn our soul and body will be united in glory? Why would a soul or human spirit once freed from the body be again imprisoned in it after death? For Plato, life was to be lived in such a way as to cultivate the spirit and free it from the allurements of the body in this life, so that it might be forever free of such things in the next. The Christian doctrine of the resurrection of the body clearly shows that in the end Platonism and Christianity do not neatly mesh. Nonetheless, to this day the majority of Christians tend to take a Platonic view when coping with the existential dilemma. But being Platonic on those issues invariably means that one will continue to be dangerously close to some kind of puritanism in one's moral theory. The way a person understands reality influences the way a person acts.

If Plato's views are as flawed as we have suggested, what accounts for the tremendous popularity and influence of his position down through the centuries? It seems clear that the existential dilemma is something with which human beings have always had to cope, and they welcome help from any quarter in that struggle.

Whatever else may be said about the Platonic position, it not only recognized the centrality of the existential dilemma in human life, but went on to lay out a prescription for coping with it. It can honestly be said that even with all its dangers, Plato's excessive spiritualism is closer to the truth about the human condition than the contemporary view that we humans are merely more highly evolved animals.

Ambiguity 2: The Ontological Paradox

Having identified the source of the basic ambiguity in human life in the fact that we are embodied spirits, a strange amalgam of infinite possibilities and crippling limits leading to death, we may now turn to a second level of ambiguity no less real than the first, but derived from it.

Much has been said these days about the necessity of people feeling good about themselves. It has been suggested, and quite rightly, that unless and until people have a good feeling about themselves, they will be incapable of seeing good in others, of loving, of allowing themselves to be loved and hence of leading truly fulfilling human lives. That may seem to put an inordinately high value and priority on self-esteem, but if you have ever seen the total devastation visited on a human life by a neurotic inferiority complex, you will have no difficulty understanding that the case is not overstated. Self-esteem is an absolutely essential ingredient of a truly human life. Granted. But why all the difficulty? Because self-esteem, contrary to what the word might lead us to believe, is not something I can simply do for or by myself. It is precisely because my self-esteem is tied up with and depends on others that I have no simple and direct way of getting it.

Animals seem to be endowed by nature with an instinctive sense of their own worth. They are programmed to feel good about themselves. Not so with us. Because we are not animals, but rather embodied selves or incarnate spirits, our sense of self-worth is neither instinctive nor innate. It must be earned. What is more, it must be earned and then continually maintained—*symbolically*.

That sounds complicated, but it really isn't. We all experience it every day of our lives. Think about it. What is it that makes you feel good about yourself? Recall how fragile your own self-esteem is, and how easily it can be seriously wounded or even destroyed, the hunger deep inside each of us to be well thought of by others, the sometimes weird machinations we go through in an effort just to get affirmed, the various things we take to be the signs to others that we are indeed worthwhile. I have $40,000 in the bank—I am somebody. I have been a good and loving mother to my children—I am somebody. I drive a BMW—I am somebody. I have a master's degree—I am somebody. I can bench-press 300 lbs—I am somebody. I have been faithful in my marriage—I am somebody. I baked a birthday cake for my daddy—I am somebody. I am a permanent deacon—I am somebody. I finished the marathon—I am somebody. The everyday symbols of the self-worth of people is a virtually endless litany.

Although it may be true that we have self-worth simply because we are children of God, created and loved by him, that fact really does not satisfy our basic and fundamental hunger for esteem, because we had absolutely nothing to do with it. We had no say whatever in whether we would be or not, or whether we would be loved or not. Our just being and being loved by God strikes us more as a reason to affirm his self-worth than our own. To be convinced of our own self-worth, we must somehow incarnate it in visible signs and symbols. Those signs and symbols must then be recognized by others, who then must show us that they have recognized our personal worth and merit in them. Only then are we satisfied. How terribly convoluted. No wonder we, unlike the animals, have no simple and direct way to feel good about ourselves. As befits incarnate spirits, to feel good about ourselves we need to incarnate our intrinsic worth in the things of everyday life, and then await the response of our fellows. What agony! We're all waiting. Don't they know that? What's holding them back? Why don't they respond? Obviously, because they, too, are waiting in agonizing expectation for us to recognize *their* worth. A real stalemate.

Not if we can help it. We'll *force* them to notice us, *force* them to affirm our worth. We'll show them. In that effort to be recognized, we amass more money, love the kids even more, go on for a doctorate, run farther and faster, and lift even more weight—whatever our private heroism might be. Our need to stand out from the crowd, to be noticed, to be recognized as special, drives us to even greater efforts to escape in some way the faceless mediocrity of life. It is bad enough that like everyone else, I am condemned to finitude and am fated to go down the communal sink in death (the Existential Dilemma). At least while I live I *will* be noticed, I *will* be special, I *will* find some way to stand out from the crowd. Only by so doing can I convince even myself of my worth. As Ernest Becker once put it, "The debt to life has to be paid somehow; one has to be a hero in the best and only way he can—even if only for his skill at the pinball machine" (*The Denial of Death,* Free Press, 1975, p. 217).

The word "hero" may bother some of us because we have become accustomed to using it only for those who stand out the farthest and the most. The Gandhis, the Churchills, the Martin Luther Kings, the Mother Teresas—*they're* the heroes. We're just plain folks. But even as we say that, we know it isn't true. Granted, we may not have reached the pinnacle of heroism they have; nonetheless, each of us nurtures in her heart a secret account of how heroic we have been, and each of us has a story we tell ourselves about how we have lived our lives, a private scenario in which *we* are the heroes. As Rabbi Abraham Heschel has remarked, "In the eyes of the world, I am an average man. But to my heart, I am not average. To my heart I am of great moment. The challenge I face is how to actualize, how to concretize the quiet eminence of my own being" (*Who Is Man?* Stanford Univ. Press, 1965, p. 35). What makes this so important is the fact that how a person seeks to fulfill her natural desire for heroism greatly determines the quality of her life, the kind of person she becomes.

In that task of concretizing (incarnating) my self-worth, I am not left alone. Society with its various institutions stands ready to help. In fact, one of society's most important functions for its individual members is to present them with socially acceptable ways to answer their need to be heroic, that is, to be and to be recognized as special. Should a person choose one of her society's acceptable hero systems in which to excel, she is almost guaranteed the recognition of others in that society, because they all subscribe to the same cultural and societal values as to what counts as heroism. That should not surprise us, for if human beings have a deeper hunger for heroism, it would be expected that the human societies they set up would present them with codified and symbolic ways of answering so burning a human need. Of course, the fact that a hero system is societal and widespread is no guarantee of its intrinsic worth. Whole cultures have given themselves over to heroisms that were either ignoble (Hitler's Germany) or shallow and trite (American consumerism). As Ernest Becker has said, the debt to life must be paid; we all will be heroes one way or another.

I am sure that we can all recognize ourselves somewhere in that picture, but there doesn't seem to be anything particularly ambiguous about our need to be heroes. Aside from the fact that we don't like to admit to our need to stand out and try to appear more humble than we really are, the human hunger for self-affirmation is really rather direct and straightforward. True. Ambiguity does not come upon the scene until we realize that alongside that hunger, we humans have a second equally strong hunger that opposes it: the need each has to have done with competition and the alienation and separation it brings, to give up our pretenses of superiority and to feel the solidarity in weakness we share with all of humankind. Our strengths divide and separate us; it is in our finitude and weakness that we are one. If I push my drive for heroism too far, I become isolated and cut off from the rest of humankind and may fail to make the human connection I need as desperately as I need self-affirmation. But if, in the interests of unity and solidarity with my brothers and sisters, I submerge myself too completely in the community of others, I risk failing to become the fullest self I can. Heroism brings the isolation I abhor; solidarity bring the anonymity and facelessness I can't accept.

Once again, this may sound complicated, but it really isn't. We all have experienced the tension between working for our own self-fulfillment and sacrificing some measure of that self-fulfillment for others. In fact, every relationship, every friendship, every attempt at intimacy must come to terms with our desires for independence and self-fulfillment (heroism) on the one hand, and our need for dependence and self-giving (solidarity) on the other. Let us call that predicament, whenever and under whatever circumstances it occurs, humankind's Ontological Paradox.

The examples of this are all around us. Often we need look no further than our own homes. A man sets out to make his mark in the world for his family's sake and turns into a workaholic. He becomes a high achiever, very successful, and is well thought of and highly esteemed in the workplace. But in the process, he has become aggressive, insensitive, and unable to relate. So accustomed is he to have his own way at work that he alienates his loved ones because he cannot yield his heroic posture even in the bosom of his own family. His wife comes to look on him as a dictator, and his children flee from him as from an ogre. In the end, he is filled with remorse and recriminations for his inability to relate and his loss of solidarity. He pays dearly for not having taken seriously *both* dimensions of the ontological paradox.

The wife and mother whose life has been spent in loving service to her family feels the pangs of uneasiness because she feels totally submerged in others. She senses a loss of her very self, and so begins to yearn for a self-fulfillment that is solely her own. If husband and children are unable to adjust, she may have no alternative but to leave, searching for a life with a bit more self-affirmation in it. She too finds that she has not given enough attention to *both* sides of the human paradox. Nor does a one-sided feminism seem to offer women any better hope of escaping the pain of this paradox. Only a feminism mindful of both sets of needs in women, the need to achieve and seek self-fulfillment *and* the need to give themselves to others, has any chance of satisfactorily addressing the ontological paradox of contemporary women.

As is the case with the Existential Dilemma, so with the Ontological Paradox; balance is to be desired, one-sidedness to be avoided. There is no hope of definitively solving either predicament; the best we can ever do is to keep searching for more satisfactory and more balanced ways of coping with each.

The Significance of Coping

Dealing with the fundamental dilemma and paradox of human life is very much like the way we used to have to deal with our TV sets in the early days. Now we are told that the set electronically locks in the picture for the best balance of brightness and contrast, for the proper mixture of hues to give vibrant colors as well as authentic-looking skin tones. We have come to expect our TV sets to do such things automatically. Younger people can't understand why such a fuss is made over the TV capability of locking in the best picture. But some of us can remember. Before color, when TV was newly on the scene, it was a battle to keep your set finely tuned. You'd change channels and your picture would go out of adjustment. So they had a "fine tuner" knob on the set. This enabled you to fine tune the picture whenever it went out of adjustment. Sometimes the picture became distorted even when you weren't changing channels and you'd have to resort to the trusty little fine tuner. It seems to me that back then we used to be jumping up a lot to fine tune our sets, which at least was more exercise than one is likely to get with today's automatically tuned models.

Our lives are like those old TV sets. They demand constant vigilance and readjustment to insure the best performance under changing conditions. We don't have an electronic device inside us that automatically gives us just the right mix of conscious self and organic body, of self-seeking and self-giving. It is up to us to be constantly "fine tuning" the amounts of each of those things in our lives. But we are not born with that skill and know-how; we only learn it from experience. In that learning process we are bound to make mistakes, to temporarily overdo one or the other of the elements as we search for just the "right" mix. Just when we think we've found it, our lives change and we are back to adjusting the mix in the light of ever-changing circumstances. I noted earlier that ambiguity was the hallmark of a human life, but it is really more accurate to say that "*coping* with ambiguity" is what truly characterizes us as humans. Indeed, we might define the human person as one who copes, and those who do so most satisfactorily are the best of the breed.

What does it mean to cope? However enlightening the discussion of the Existential Dilemma and the Ontological Paradox may be in understanding the human condition, we must be careful not to be misled. It would be all too easy to conclude that we humans are driven by contradictory drives and impulses and that, in the end, human life is absurd, or, if not absurd, that human life is unbearably burdensome and beyond the reach of our freedom. Unable to transcend and get beyond the ambiguity we all experience, we are simply driven hither and yon aimlessly, unable to take control of, or responsibility for, our lives. Such conclusions would follow only if we were to make the mistake of taking the story as told thus far as the whole story. It is not. There is one more element to our story of the human condition, and it has to do precisely with our ability to cope in freedom with the givens of human life, for example, growth, change, ambiguity, sexuality, finitude, and death.

Ordinary language often reveals something significant by a simple change of a word. I don't think it is simply by chance that we usually say that plants and animals "adapt," "adjust," or "conform" to their environments, whereas we humans "relate to" or "cope with" ours. The "human" thing is not merely to adapt and adjust to the things of life as the animals must, but to "cope" with them, which means to create, in freedom, a relationship to them out of our humanness. What characterizes human beings is not the fact that we are besieged by ambiguity, but rather that we are able to take an attitude toward that situation and cope with it out of our freedom. For that even to be possible, there must be something about us that is not immersed in the contradictory drives and ambiguity. There must be something of us that can stand back and evaluate the contradictions of our lives and adopt a human stance toward them. That, after all, is what it means for a human person to be free. It is this "something" which distinguishes us from the animals, which makes morality possible, and which is quintessentially human. How shall we talk of this "something"?

Soren Kierkegaard, a nineteenth-century Christian philosopher, thought he found a way in a remark of St. Paul. It will sound strange to our ears, because we are accustomed to speaking differently, but it gives us a way to talk about freedom despite the ambiguities of the human condition. At least it is worth a try.

In the closing benediction of his first letter to the Thessalonians, Paul had written, "May the God of peace make you complete in holiness. May he preserve you whole and entire: *spirit, soul and body*" (5:23). Those of us who are accustomed to thinking of a human being as composed of only two elements, body and soul, simply identify or equate "soul" and "spirit" in Paul's remark. It strikes us as being unnecessarily redundant. Kierkegaard saw it differently. He preferred to take Paul literally and to base his whole philosophy of human freedom on that single remark. What emerges is an account that fills out and completes the scenario on the human condition we have been forging in this chapter (*Concept of Dread,* Princeton Univ. Press, 1967, p. 39).

Kierkegaard's exact words are:

> Man is a synthesis of the soulish and bodily. But a synthesis is unthinkable if the two are not united in a third factor. This third factor is spirit. Spirit is always present in man constituting the synthesis between soul and body. Man is a synthesis of soul and body sustained by spirit.

There is no hope of our understanding what Kierkegaard is driving at if we insist on thinking of humans as composed of three elements, body, soul, and spirit. Neither St. Paul nor Kierkegaard meant that. Following the custom of the ancient Hebrews, Paul was not thinking of the *parts* of the human person when he spoke of body, soul, and spirit. He was speaking of three different aspects or perspectives from which to view the *whole* person. Humans don't "have" a body, a soul, and a spirit. No. Looked at from one perspective, a human being "is" body; from another she "is" soul; from a third she "is" spirit. These are but three different ways of looking at the whole person.

For Kierkegaard, to look at a human person as *body* is to see her as subject to the physical and biological laws of nature, and as destined to feel the force of sexuality, physical limits, and death in her life. To look at her as *soul* is to see her as subject to the psychological laws of the ego or conscious self, along with all the dreams, anxieties, and fears that come her way. Finally, to look at her as *spirit* is to see her as capable of transcending and creatively synthesizing the contradictory physical (bodily) and psychological (soulish) aspects of her life, and of relating to the Absolute Power (God) that constituted her.

Kierkegaard found that in his day, as in our own, there was a tendency for human beings to concentrate exclusively on the physical, or on the psychological, or even on the conflict between them, but to flee from the integrating task of spirit. He accused his age of spiritlessness, not only for ignoring the spirit (freedom) dimension of the human condition, but also for actively striving to liberate themselves from the demands of spirit, which he took to be the demands of their truest selves. He warned: "The most efficacious means of liberation from the assaults of spirit is to become spiritless, the sooner the better. Spirit is often suppressed by an abortion, men having several self-serving devices for suppressing the embryo of their highest life" (*Concept of Dread*, Princeton Univ. Press, 1967, p. 104).

For Kierkegaard, spirit is not some other life humans lead apart from this one. When he says that the highest life of the human person is spirit, he is not thinking of some ethereal otherworldly life as Plato did. He is talking about that capacity of the human person whereby she "copes" *in this life* with finitude and body, with the dreams, anxieties, and fears of the conscious self, and does so humbly in the presence of God, the Infinite and Eternal One. It is because we are *spirit* that we cannot simply live, simply copulate, or simply die. As spirit we are called "to relate" to all of the physical and psychological things in our lives. Because we are spirit we can, and must, and so often do, relate creatively to the ambiguities of our lives rather than merely adapting to them. It is this ability "to cope" that is the infallible sign of our vocation, namely, in freedom, to become ever more human.

As was the case with the Existential Dilemma, and the Ontological Paradox, it is possible to give many examples from ordinary life that exemplify what Kierkegaard is talking about. The alcoholic that life's ambiguities has driven to drink acquires an addiction and seems to have totally lost control of her life. Still, any meeting of Alcoholics Anonymous gives witness to what can be done when we freely choose to see ourselves as "spirit." The edifying stories of people regaining control of their lives and easing their drivenness gives evidence of that "something" in each of us that is always there and can in freedom at any moment take back control of a human life. Call it what you will, that is what Kierkegaard meant by "spirit." Were it not for "spirit," questions of morality could never even arise. It is precisely because we are "spirit" that the human condition is the context of morality.

A final cautionary note. We must not allow Kierkegaard's account of human freedom to lull us into thinking that in the end there is no real ambiguity left about the human situation. To do that would be to once again travel down a Platonic road of some sort. No matter how well we cope, we humans remain a volatile and relatively unstable mixture. Our moments of authentic freedom are real, but they are probably neither as frequent nor as pervasive as we might wish. Though our coping does not totally dispel the ambiguity, it can introduce enough stability into the human mix to make becoming human, being moral and walking with the Lord realizable possibilities. The human condition can guarantee no more than that. Such human ideals are possible. Whether they are ever actualized depends on the choices and decisions of individual persons like you and me.

SUGGESTED READING

Gregory Baum, *Man Becoming,* Herder & Herder, 1970.

Ernest Becker, *The Denial of Death,* Free Press, 1976.

John Dunne, *Time and Myth,* Univ. of Notre Dame Press, 1973.

William Glasser, *Reality Therapy,* Harper & Row, 1975.

Abraham Heschel, *Who Is Man?,* Stanford Univ. Press, 1965.

Gail Sheehy, *Passages,* Bantam, 1977.

CHAPTER TWO

The Origin of Evil
and the
Need for Morality

The description we have given of the human condition in the preceding chapter was drawn from human experience alone, and it did not rely directly on any religious myth or story. In fact, in this whole first part of the book, we have deliberately chosen to lay our faith and religious beliefs aside, in an effort to get an experiential and natural (nonreligious) picture of the human situation. But up to this point, only half the story has been told. We have yet to give an explicit account of the origin of evil in human life, and the subsequent rise of morality to cope with it. This chapter is intended to complete that story.

As Christians, we have a rich and beautiful tradition concerning both the human condition and the origin of evil; it may be difficult for some to proceed as if we didn't. Still, it will prove helpful if we can put off the consideration of the Christian perspective on these matters until Part Two of this book. We have all experienced evil in our lives—both the evil we have suffered and the evil we have perpetrated. What might a natural (nonreligious) account arising from those encounters with evil look like? I suggest that it would look something like what follows.

Evil: A Spin-Off of Life

Judging from our experience, we certainly don't have to look very far before we are confronted by things we would all call evil. And it is this very experience that misleads us into thinking that evil is some *thing*, something out there, one of the pieces of furniture of our universe, so to speak. We interpret our experience with evil correctly when we conclude that evil is indeed one of the harsh and painful realities *of life*. We interpret that experience incorrectly when we conclude that this means evil exists independently of ourselves. A moment's reflection can clarify the matter for us.

Imagine a world devoid of all living things. We have all been privileged to travel by means of television to the moon. Our space satellites have given us magnificent pictures of lifeless planets, so we should be able to imagine that the whole solar system was that way. Of course, there would be no planet Earth teeming with life; in our imaginary universe it, too, would be totally lifeless. In such a universe what, if anything, would be called "evil"? Could anything in that imaginary universe be either good or evil? Obviously not. But why not?

Our imaginary universe would be neither good nor bad, precisely because it is lifeless. One planet might be beautiful to behold with clear, sparkling rivers, with glorious coloration, with magnificent sunsets, and fragrant atmosphere. Another might be barren and desolate, with brackish streams and oceans of dank and putred waters giving off noxious gases, filling its atmosphere with dark and foreboding clouds. Is the one better than the other? No. Each simply is what it is. In the absence of any living creature, neither would be good or bad, neither would be better or worse than the other.

Consider two pools, one of the clearest and purest water, the other toxic and poisonous beyond belief. In themselves they are neither good nor bad. But introduce a living creature who needs water to sustain its life, and suddenly everything changes. The pools, which in the absence of life were neither good nor bad, now become either life-giving or life-threatening, and hence either good or evil. What this reflection teaches us is that nothing is in itself evil, and that evil arises as a spin-off of life itself. Put another way, whatever we recognize as evil is so recognized only because it bears a harmful relation to a living thing, frustrating its vital needs, desires, and interests.

Scholars have a name for that sort of thing. They call it an *epiphenomenon,* which is an incidental or secondary occurrence that can only happen in conjunction with a primary occurrence, which is its prior condition. As we have just seen, life is the prior condition for evil, and so we may say that *evil is an epiphenomenon of life.* We capture that same thought exactly in our everyday language when we call evil a spin-off of life.

To better understand what this really means, and to identify exactly what it is about life that gives rise to that secondary occurrence we call evil, let us try another exercise of imagination. Suppose the world is populated by living persons much like you and me. Suppose further that these are rather strange and bizarre beings (not unlike Mr. Spock of *Star Trek*) who are rational but who have absolutely no emotions, no needs, no desires, no interests. Having no needs or wants, they are totally indifferent to the things of life. They may be rational. They may be able to reason and to distinguish the true from the false, but they are robotlike because nothing, absolutely nothing, matters to them. That would be a world in which there was not only life but rational life. Still, the question, "Would there be evil?" remains.

No, not really, because our robotlike beings don't care a fig about anything. They have no purpose, no goals, no desires, no interests. Everything is the same to them, which means there is no difference between life and death, pain and pleasure, sickness and health; each is all the same to them. In such a world, nothing would be or would be perceived as evil—or as good, for that matter. What does this reflection reveal to us about the relation of life to evil?

Since we just imagined rational life existing without evil existing, it is clear that evil is not a spin-off of life simply because it is rational. No. Evil is a spin-off of life because every life embodies specific needs, wants, desires, and interests. Life exhibits in every case, at least the drive for self-preservation. Life is itself a need, a desire, an interest. That is why it can and does give rise to the spin-off of evil. Robotlike life is completely imaginary; it cannot exist; it is a contradiction in terms. (Even Mr. Spock has a desire for the truth and for rationality, so he is not completely without interests.) To live *is* to have purpose and goals; to live *is* to have needs and wants; to live *is* to have an interest and a stake in what happens. It is precisely because life is *never* indifferent that in whatever environment it occurs there will simultaneously occur the possibility both of good and evil. What *fulfills* the vital needs, desires, and interests of living things will be looked upon as good; what *frustrates* those needs, desires, and interests will be viewed as evil. Better yet, given the actual existence of living things, what fulfills their vital needs, desires, and interests is *good,* and whatever frustrates them is *evil.* For as we have shown, neither good nor evil has any reality in the absence of life.

That conclusion may strike us as somewhat odd, because we have become so accustomed to thinking of things as good or evil in themselves. We may even find ourselves actively resisting it, because we are afraid that to accept it will eventually lead to saying that what is good and evil depends solely on human desires and interests. That sounds very much like saying that there is no objective good or evil; it is all subjective and relative, and that one person's meat is another's poison. Good and evil become matters of arbitrary personal taste, and concerning such tastes it is pointless to argue. No believer would ever want to move in that direction. Nor do I.

But there is really nothing arbitrary about saying that good and evil are real only "in relation" to life. To say that good and evil are relational is not at all the same thing as calling them relative. *Relational* says that good and evil are not absolutes but are objective spin-offs of life. *Relative* says that good and evil are merely matters of taste or personal preference, with no objective reality.

To make that point, we need only make up a list of the main evils of human life. It will be a list of those things our experiences tell us are the major frustrations of our vital needs, desires, and interests. One look at the list will show that there is nothing arbitrary about it at all.

1. Death
2. Pain
3. Disablement
4. Deprivation of pleasure
5. Deprivation of freedom and opportunity
6. Deprivation of worth and self-esteem.

These things are so universally and objectively evil in relation to human life that anyone who suggests that our trying to avoid them is simply a matter of personal taste would be laughed to scorn. Anyone who sought these things because she thought them desirable would be locked up as crazy. Those things are evil; that's just the way it is. But they are evil only because each of them invariably frustrates a vital human need, desire, or interest. No amount of wishing could ever make the situation otherwise. In fact, a good rule of thumb would be that these six items represent the major evils of human life, and that all of the other things we consider evil are thought to be so only because they introduce one or more of the six evils into our lives.

All other things being equal, no one in her right mind would desire any one of the items on our list. But sometimes all other things are not equal. Take death, for example. It is first on the list because it is the evil most destructive of vital needs, desires, and interests. Death puts an end to all all human projects or goals; it eradicates all interests, quiets all desires, and ends all relationships. (*Reminder:* we're taking a nonreligious view in this chapter and so cannot take into consideration belief in life *after* death.) It is therefore the supreme evil because it deprives us of every other good. But it is only the supreme evil, *all other things being equal.* A person can be in such unrelenting pain that death may be sought as a release from some other item on the list. That fact, however, does not make death a good to be sought in ordinary circumstances.

Similarly, we may submit to pain, disablement, and a temporary deprivation of our freedom in the form of cancer surgery, or limb amputation, in order to avoid death. Here again, we seek some of the items on our list in order to avoid others. This does not mean that those items we now seek have somehow suddenly become "goods." Not at all; they remain evils. That's what makes human life oftentimes so tragic. We are forced to embrace one or more evils in order to escape a greater evil. Once again we are brought face to face with the fundamental ambiguity of human life. Were the items on our list not actually, really and objectively evil, even when we are forced by circumstances to choose them, there would be no ambiguity, no tragedy for us humans in the choosing of them. But tragedy there is, and in abundance. All this demonstrates that the items on our list are objectively evil, and not merely matters of personal preference.

The Emergence of Moral Evil

From the preceding account, we see that evil is only possible because we humans are the sorts of beings we are. We can die and we don't want to. We can experience pain and we don't want to. We can experience disablement and we don't want to. We can be deprived of pleasure and we don't want to be. We can be deprived of freedom and we don't want to be. We can be deprived of our self-esteem and we surely don't want to be. Those things, and all the others that lead to them, are called evils because they *deprive human beings of what they need for their lives and for their growth and development as persons.* For convenience sake, let us call all such things *ontic evils.*

Why "ontic"? The Greek word for something real, something a being has because of its very constitution is *onta.* If we were to translate it most accurately into English, it would be rendered "real." But if we were to call those things that frustrate our vital human needs "real evils," that might give the impression that what we are going to call "moral evils" are in some way *not* "real evils." So to avoid any possibility of that interpretation, it seems better to speak simply of *ontic evils*. Whenever and under whatever circumstances a human person is deprived of what is needed for life and human development, we are face to face with ontic evil.

But ontic evils befall human beings in many different ways. We can be deprived of our vital needs by floods, tornadoes, epidemics, and other natural disasters, as well as by misfortunes such as industrial accidents and plane crashes. So the presence of ontic evil does not always indicate the presence of moral evil. But whenever such deprivation of persons is brought on by the free and conscious decision and action of other human beings, and in such a way as to be unjustified, then and only then are we face to face with *moral evil*.

This brings us to a very important truth universally revealed by human experience. Moral evil is a spin-off of the fact that we humans can suffer ontic evil. *Moral evil always involves an unjustified infliction of ontic evil.* If no ontic evil is unjustly intended or inflicted, then there is no moral evil either. You can have ontic evil without moral evil, but you can never have moral evil without ontic evil. That is because the very definition of moral evil is: *The free, deliberate, and unjustified intention and/or action of inflicting ontic evil on oneself or others.* Were it not for the fact that human beings are subject to ontic evil, moral evil would not even be possible. Consequently, actions that neither intend nor inflict ontic evil cannot be judged to be immoral.

One important consequence of this is that nothing is immoral simply because someone in authority says so. Ideally, it is because something is immoral that authority forbids it. But authoritative prohibition by itself is never sufficient reason to judge something to be immoral. To justify its prohibition, the authority in question must point out the ontic evil unjustly inflicted. Contraceptive love-making between spouses may or may not be morally evil. But if it is, that can only be because such acts inflict some ontic evil of some sort, and not because any group or institution says it is evil. It is precisely because all moral evil rides piggyback, so to speak, on ontic evil, that to talk of the former is necessarily to talk of the latter. In the case of contraception, for example, to prohibit it is to deprive spouses of the pleasure of engaging in sexual actions with peace of mind, which means the prohibition itself inflicts an ontic evil. That means that the prohibition itself is going to have to be justified. (More on that in Part Three, when we take up sexual issues.)

Nor do I mean by this to exclude divine prohibitions. Nothing is morally evil simply because God forbids it. God forbids it because it is morally evil, that is, because it perpetrates an unjustified ontic evil. To say otherwise is to hold that God can arbitrarily make evil whatever he feels like. No. As we have seen, evil is evil, is evil, is evil. By making us the way he did, God has already determined what would be evil, and he would contradict himself were he to say otherwise by direct command. This may be disconcerting to fundamentalist minds, but I am afraid that is just the way it is. Nor do I suppose that God would be offended by our saying so. He would be most willing and ready to point out to us *why* something is morally evil, and the reason will always have to do with ontic evil.

That is why it will not do to think of two separate and unrelated sorts of evil. Moral evil is a spin-off (epiphenomenon) of ontic evil, so in the end there is really only one fundamental evil, ontic. *Moral evil is the name we give to our voluntary and deliberate involvement in the spread of ontic evil.* What would cause us to become so involved?

Immorality and the Human Condition

If we recall the ambiguity that permeates human existence as described in the preceding chapter, it should not be too difficult to answer that question. As I try to get just the right balance of symbolic self and organic body, and the right mix of self-affirmation and self-giving, I am bound to make mistakes. And since we humans must *learn* to fine tune our lives, it is practically inevitable that in that learning process, we shall contribute to the world's ontic evil. Then too, my hungers for pleasures, for self-affirmation, for heroism, and just for more of life may make me insensitive to the ontic evils I leave in my wake. Add to that the fact that I myself am trying to avoid the ontic evils that befall me from others in the living of my everyday life, and you have a rather graphic picture of why I end up involved in the spread of ontic evil.

But we must make a clear distinction between our natural appetites and our symbolic ingenuity. Being organic, we share the needs and drives of all organisms. Some people think that we increase the ontic evil in the world primarily because of our animal drives. Ernest Becker thinks otherwise (*Escape From Evil*, Free Press, 1976, p. 1, 5):

> Existence, for all organismic life, is a constant struggle to feed, a struggle to incorporate whatever other organisms they can fit into their mouths and press down their gullets without choking. Seen in these stark terms, life on this planet is a gory spectacle, a science fiction nightmare in which digestive tracts fitted with teeth at one end are tearing away at whatever flesh they can reach, and at the other end are piling up the fuming waste excrement as they move along in search of more flesh...(But) in seeking to avoid evil (for themselves), humans are responsible for bringing more evil into the world than organisms could ever do merely by exercising their digestive tracts. It is human ingenuity, rather than animal nature, that has given our fellow creatures such a bitter earthly fate.

Becker's imagery is stark and his message is clear. If we were only organic, we would devour others in our immediate environment in order to fulfill our own organic needs. But we are also symbolic, ingenious in finding ways to satisfy not just organic needs, but human and personal symbolic ones—ways that shower ontic evils not only on a few individuals who happen to get too close, but even on the entire race. Who but ingenious humans could threaten the extinction of all life from nuclear holocaust? Who but symbolic beings could find ways to create and then bury radioactive wastes that pollute the environment and threaten the lives and well-being of their fellows? These things with their attending ontic evils are always done to make life better. It is our thirst for more of life, for a higher standard of living, and for escape from the evils done by others that so often accounts for our immorality toward one another. And so once again, life itself lies at the foundation of evil, especially of moral evil.

Becker's point is twofold. First, humans perpetrate more ontic evil on the world and their fellow humans because of the needs of their symbolic selves than because of their animal nature. And second, evil comes from a thirst for life, which means that evil comes from good. That is difficult for us to comprehend. We seem to want to insist that evil can come only from evil. It seems wrong-headed to us to say that we commit moral evil because we are filled with the desire for more, and a fuller, life. We prefer to say that the reason we wreak such ontic evils on the world is because we *are* evil. But even that seems inadequate at times.

Sometimes the ontic evils we cause are so horrendous and so demonic that we think they can only be explained by an evil being superior to ourselves, namely, the devil. Thus we convince ourselves of the truth of our principle that evil begets evil. But experience gives us no real evidence that such is the case. The longer we live, the clearer it becomes that such a view is mistaken. Evil comes from basically good people like us, whose hunger for more of the good of life for ourselves causes us to rationalize the infliction of ontic evil on others. That seems to be a much more accurate description of the human condition than saying either that we are ourselves depraved, or that we are the playthings of diabolic powers.

Ambiguity 3: The Moral Predicament

And so, once again, we are brought face to face with a fundamental ambiguity of human life. We are basically good, and yet we invariably cause unjustified ontic evil for those around us. We may call this situation our Moral Predicament. It takes its place with the other ambiguities of human existence, the Existential Dilemma (that we are part spirit and part organic) and the Ontological Paradox (that we yearn for individual recognition of our specialness while at the same time yearning for solidarity with the rest of humankind) as major perplexities with which we must learn to cope if we would be fully human.

I have already admitted that it was not until mid-life that I became convinced of the fact that people are basically good. I am now firm in that conviction, even though I know case after case could be brought up against it. Indeed, opposition to that view comes from all sides. Fundamentalists and puritanical Christians never tire of telling us that we are basically evil and were it not for the blood of Christ shed for our depravity, all would be lost. Freudians tell us of the innate perversity of humankind, driven by unconscious lusts and primal desires. I have a Freudian colleague who insists that I must be living in a different world from the one in which he lives. The litany of our inhumanities to one another certainly tends to give credence to that view. Still, I would submit that our experience more than corroborates the truth of the assertion that we humans are basically good.

As one gets older, it becomes clear there is another and longer litany of our kindnesses, generosities, and acts of love, a litany not as well publicized as the first. God knows, we are capable of choosing to live our lives like the organisms so graphically described by Becker, devouring and laying waste everything in our path just to enhance our own lives. But when we do that, we do so at the expense of frustrating several equally important needs—to be well thought of by others, to give ourselves to something other than our own sweet self-interest, and to live in solidarity with the rest of humankind. Unjustly inflicting ontic evil on others is bound to frustrate all those other needs. Symbolic needs thus constitute a kind of natural inner check on rampant immorality. Immoral acts (those that unjustly inflict ontic evil) always involve a trade-off within the person between conflicting or paradoxical human needs. Were we not basically good, such trade-offs and ambiguities would not be a part of human life. Of course, because they are only a part of every human life, none of us is totally good either. No matter how hard we try, the ambiguities of our lives and the human condition seem to preclude avoiding all immorality. We must use our liberty (spirit) to try to find just the right mix in every situation. This mix will satisfy our own need for more life with the minimum infliction of unjustified ontic evil on others.

Why Be Moral?

Once it is seen that being moral requires restraint and the free acceptance of limitations on one's own needs, desires, and interests, the immediate question arises: Why would anyone ever choose to be moral? Religious people and people of faith have ready answers to give to that question, answers not available to us now because our account is intended to be nonreligious. Still, we are not totally without responses, though they may not be the definitive ones.

Every society and every culture must, for the sake of right order and in order to avoid chaos, provide its people with reasons for being moral, that is, for not inflicting the major ontic evils on one another. Thus it is that every state has laws against the unjust infliction of death, pain, and disablement, as well as against the unwarranted deprivation of freedom, self-esteem, and a certain number (not all) of important human pleasures. To motivate people to obey those laws, the state threatens to inflict one or more of those six ontic evils on offenders by way of punishment. This provides us with a first answer to our question. We should be moral, that is, avoid inflicting the major ontic evils on others, because if we aren't, society will inflict such evils on us. This is a self-serving answer, but a potent one nonetheless, especially so in small and close-knit societies where the likelihood of being caught is great.

But there's the rub. If the only reason I am moral is to avoid the punishment society metes out to me if I am caught, then what answer can we give to the question, "Why be moral?" when the likelihood of being caught and punished by the authorities is relatively small? Even in that situation, I still run the risk of having ontic evil inflicted on me by my victims. They may take revenge on me and themselves act outside the laws of our society. So it is still in my best interests to not inflict evil on others.

A third version of that same answer might be put this way. I should be moral and obey the laws of my society because if I do I am less likely to be the victim of ontic evil perpetrated by others. If we all agree to accept limits on our own freedom, pleasures, and our need for self-esteem, we may well have less of those things than we would otherwise wish, but we shall also be less likely to suffer severe losses of those things at the hands of others. So we see that the superficial first-line answers to our question are all motivated out of self-interest, out of a desire that we ourselves avoid as much ontic evil as we can.

Is that the best that can be said in response to the question, "Why be moral?" No. There is a deeper, nobler, and more profound answer that arises out of human experience and marks us off as more fully human. William James said, "The nobler thing tastes better to us, and that's all that can be said about it." In that vein, to say we should be moral out of fear of reprisal or out of self-interest just doesn't measure up to our higher expectations of ourselves. There must be some better reason for being moral. There is, one that answers the human need to be at once heroic and self-giving (the Ontological Paradox). Unfortunately, it depends on a certain kind of experience, and unless and until one has this sort of experience, it may be difficult to understand what we are talking about here.

Most of us don't begin by actually having the experience ourselves; we usually read about it before we experience it directly. (If TV programs weren't so unrelentingly awful, we might get the experience that way, but too much of the current fare is trash.) Who can forget being deeply moved by reading Charles Dickens' *A Tale of Two Cities?* This is the story of Sydney Carton's life journey from being totally and unscrupulously self-centered, to that heroic moment at the end of the novel when he uses his tremendous wit and talent to substitute himself for a man destined for the guillotine. After a life of self-willed indulgence that spread ontic evil on all around him, he makes the supreme sacrifice by freeing the man loved by the woman he loves and taking his place on death row. His words (*A Tale of Two Cities,* Bk. III, Ch. 15) as he climbs the steps of the guillotine are unforgettable:

It is a far, far better thing that I do, than I have ever done; it is a far, far better rest that I go to, than I have ever known.

Or was it Fr. Chisholm in A.J. Cronin's *The Keys to the Kingdom,* or Atticus in Harper Lee's *To Kill a Mocking Bird,* or Olan in Pearl Buck's *The Good Earth,* or one of the hundred other characters from the world's great fictional literature who precipitated the experience for you? Perhaps it wasn't fiction at all that first introduced you to the foundational moral truth. Perhaps you first encountered it in one of the *Lives of the Saints,* or in the biographies of some of the world's great people: Mohandas Gandhi, Albert Schweitzer, Miguel Pro, Dorothy Day, Martin Luther

King, Jr. No matter; the truth is the same, however one comes to see it.

Sometimes that truth is preserved not in print, but in our oral tradition, in the stories we tell of the nameless people who unmistakably incarnated it. There is the oft-repeated story from World War II about a German soldier in the army occupying the Netherlands. He was ordered to form a firing squad to shoot innocent women and children who had been rounded up and condemned simply because they were Jews. He refused, saying that it was wrong to kill innocent women and children who were noncombatants. His commanding officer told him that if he did not do as he was ordered, he would join the women and children and be shot himself. He quietly took off his helmet, laid down his rifle and walked over to the wall and stood silently with the innocent victims. His death that day eloquently proclaims the basic moral truth of the human condition.

The problem is that truth has to be experienced and personally appropriated somehow. It cannot be proven, or taught to others by simply telling them what it is; it must be personally experienced if it is to be known at all. And what is that truth? It is that human persons are precious, unique, and worth suffering or undergoing ontic evil for. It is the sort of truth one knows only by "feeling" it. Of course, feeling it is not enough; I must then act upon it. This means I must so conduct myself so as to show that each human life is precious, unique, and unprecedented, and I will resist *all* attempts to reduce it or gamble away its inherent meaning. In the absence of that experience, all moral cogitations become either empty rationalizations, or self-seeking sophistries.

This is all in keeping with a basic truth every parent knows or soon learns. It is not enough to get children to do what is right. The real goal is much more difficult than that. I can usually get my children to do what is right if I make it worth their while either by promising them goods or threatening them with ontic evils. (At least, that is true until they reach the teen years.) But that means I am actually educating them to self-interest. It gives them no basis for doing what is right when I am not there either to reward or punish them. The herculean task of parenting in those early formative years is not to get the children to *do* what is right, but to get them to *want to do* what is right. We want them to feel an attraction for what is truly good and right so that when they leave home they will not only know the rules for right conduct, but will also be disposed and attracted to what is right.

The fundamental first step in that enterprise is to create an environment in which they are most likely to experience the foundational moral truth for themselves. Obviously, it does not hurt to *tell* them about the preciousness of others, but until they have that experience for themselves, they will not have really learned that truth, and will remain unable to give anything but self-serving answers to the question: Why be moral?

A Concluding Overview

Some final thoughts as we come to the end of Part One on the human condition and prepare to take up next section, a Christian perspective on evil.

We must resist the temptation to see moral evil merely as an inevitable by-product of human life, one for which we bear no real responsibility. We should not lose sight of the main point of Chapter One, namely, that although human life is filled with ambiguity, we are spirit, and hence capable of transcending the human condition enough to take a stand with regard to it. Indeed, were we not free (spirit), we would not even be capable of moral evil, much less responsible for it. Of course, to see ourselves as spirit is bound to bring us into conflict with our culture's prevailing views of the human condition. Some hold that we are mere by-products of our genetic codes. Others think we are merely more highly evolved animals. Still others see us as mere pawns of the environment or of unconscious drives and mechanisms, fated to seek the ultimate meaning of our lives in some sort of psychological therapy. We must resist such erosions of our human dignity.

We would do well to recapture the attitude of Soren Kierkegaard in this matter. He wrote in 1844 (*Concept of Dread,* Princeton Univ. Press, 1967, pp. 70, 85):

Although there have lived countless millions of "selves," no science can state what the self is. And this is the wonderful thing about life, that every man who gives heed to himself knows what no science knows, since he knows what he himself really is. . . . There is only one proof of spirit, and that is the proof within oneself. Anyone who requires another proof is already classified as spirit-less.

Put simply, Kierkegaard was asking, "Don't you know you're spirit?" If not, there is absolutely no way anyone else can prove it to you. Don't become so confused or intimidated by the data of the sciences that you give up what is only revealed to every human person in the private depths of her own being. We are essentially spirit, capable of transcending and relating freely to all of the things of our lives.

While there may be no proofs, the "signs of spirit" are all around us. Whenever we encounter fear, selfishness, greed, envy, self-sacrifice, intimacy or love, we are not encountering things of our lives, but rather *relationships* to the things of our lives, relationships that bespeak freedom (spirit). That means that moral evil is itself a "sign of spirit." It is not something we merely find in the world. It is not something animals are capable of. No. Moral evil is a certain way we humans have of relating to our world. We know that is the case from our own experience, or we don't know it at all.

But the work of spirit is complicated by the fact that our lives are not static. We grow and develop, we learn from our experiences and make progress of some sort in the art of living. In short, we are on a journey; we have a history. Our lives are marked by certain identifiable stages or passages. And so, at each stage we must begin again to integrate our lives, to put it all together, and to relate to the self we are becoming. That means that human life is marked not only by ambiguity, but by the fact that nothing is ever quite settled, as we must learn anew the lessons of life at each stage. Adolescence, young adulthood, mid-life, and old age—each contains a new lesson to be learned, a new skill at being spirit, a new challenge to be moral. It is new and yet it is the same because at each stage we are asked to do the same work of spirit, but only in different circumstances. All of this becomes clear if only we give heed to our lives and live long enough.

Perhaps the most important of the works of spirit is love. It is, after all, love that lies at the base of the foundational moral experience. At every stage and passage of life, the call to love can be heard sounding within us. I have found that in mid-life this call takes on very special dimensions. It is the same, and yet not quite.

Mid-life is the time for facing limits. Such limits are a deprivation of freedom and opportunity and so are ontic evils—evils experienced as losses. One loses one's vigor. One loses one's looks. One loses one's hair. One loses one's figure. One loses one's teeth. Bifocals become the order of the day. One loses one's parents to death, and one's friends begin to die in greater numbers and with greater frequency. We might cope more easily with such blows experienced singly, but when they are experienced in rapid succession, their cumulative effect can be devastating—like several hammer blows to the temple. But as spirit, one notices a side effect of such losses; they make one mindful of one's finitude. They begin to soften a person, to cause him to melt and become aware of his oneness with all that is and with all that is good. The losses of mid-life reveal the human condition better than anything else. One becomes sensitized to the burdens others carry. Trapped in prisons not of their own choosing, suffering untold pain, one's heart begins to expand to embrace them all. The focus of one's love goes out beyond the family, beyond immediate friends to all who share with us the human condition. Compassion for the whole of humankind overwhelms one's soul. At such times, one cries out in hopeful love the words of *Godspell:* "When will God save the people? O God of Mercy—when?" And suddenly, one feels called not only to morality, but to its beyond.

That is a typical mid-life manifestation of a call that may be experienced at any stage of life, under any circumstances, and in many different ways. It indicates one final and very important dimension of the human condition: *humankind's openness and receptivity to the beyond of morality, which, in the end, means the openness in each of us to the God of faith.*

Suggested Reading

Mortimer Adler, Chs. 9-15 of *Aristotle for Everybody,* Macmillan, 1978.

_____.Chs. 9-13 of *Six Great Ideas,* Macmillan, 1981.

Ernest Becker, *Escape From Evil,* Free Press, 1976.

Bernard Gert, *The Moral Rules,* Harper & Row, 1973.

Daniel Maguire, *The Moral Choice,* Doubleday, 1978.

Milton Mayeroff, *On Caring,* Harper & Row, 1971.

Richard Taylor, *Good and Evil,* Macmillan, 1970.

PART TWO

THE CHRISTIAN
PERSPECTIVE OF EVIL

Adherents of every religion have difficulty seeing what evil is in itself as revealed by human experience because they cannot help but interpret that experience from the perspective of their own beliefs. That is why I thought it helpful to begin this book with an account of evil arising out of our everyday experience with the human condition. It may have been difficult for some readers to lay aside their Christianity that way, and for them it must be a relief to move now to more familiar ground. (Some may even have skipped Part One, and are beginning the book at this point. Although not recommended, that should not prove detrimental since each of the first two parts is a unit in itself.)

Most of us Christians have had our understanding of evil formed (or deformed, as the case may be) by our early understandings of the book of Genesis, which begins with the words, ''In the beginning...,'' giving every indication that it is going to "tell it like it was." In every culture there are accepted ways to distinguish fiction or storytelling from an account that claims to be based on historical memory. In English, we know immediately that we are into a "story" when the account begins, "Once upon a time ..." We certainly could have avoided a lot of confusion if only the book of Genesis had begun that way. At least then we would have known that Genesis isn't telling it as it was at all. Still, one might have expected readers to catch on anyway, especially when they got to the part about the talking serpent. That should have tipped them off to the fact that Genesis is an attempt to rewrite the ancient myths about the origin of things from the perspective of the faith of the ancient Hebrews. But the urge and need to take sacred books literally has blinded many to the mythic dimensions of Scripture.

Among other things, that means that there will be a very clear division between those Christians who take the Genesis account of the origin of evil literally, and those who take it as a mythic attempt to interpret the human condition and our experience of evil. Consequently, when it comes to talking about evil, there will not be a single, uniform, universally accepted account among Christians. The main cleavage will be between those who take Genesis literally, and those who do not. I have arbitrarily called the account given by the former a "religious" account, and have named the one given by the latter a "faith" account. There are many variations within each account, but I have been satisfied in these chapters to delineate only the main outlines of each. (On the distinction between "faith" and "religion," see my *Redemptive Intimacy,* Twenty-Third Publications, 1981, "Faith vs. Religion," pp. 47-62.)

That fundamental cleavage among Christians can be made another way as well. Catholics in both camps hold Thomas Aquinas as an authority, but I think he really belongs in the camp of those who give a "faith" account. This is evident to me from the very first words of the moral part of his great *Summa Theologica.* He writes (I-II, Prologue):

> The subject matter to be considered in this part is man, inasmuch as he is God's image, which is to say: Inasmuch as he, like God, is the

principle of his own actions, having the power of free choice and the authority to govern himself.

And in case there is any doubt as to what that is supposed to mean, later on in that same treatise he leaves no doubt at all when he says (I-II, 91, 2, c):

All things are subject to divine providence, but rational creatures are so in a superior way. For they are under divine providence by participating in it, for they are called to in some way *be* divine providence for themselves and for others.

Aquinas clearly affirms the grandeur and autonomy of humankind, and does not say that such autonomy is only valid under God. He says instead that our autonomy makes us *like* God; we are his image. This is contrasted to all those Christian moral doctrines that insist on humankind's littleness and smallness *under* God.

It is not by chance, then, that those who present a "religious" account of morality are most likely to take Genesis literally, and to see human beings as called to strict, if not blind, obedience to God. Those who prefer the "faith" account are generally those who understand that Genesis is mythic and not to be taken literally, and who also espouse the view of Aquinas that we are made in God's image precisely because, like God, we have authority over our own actions.

The chapters that make up Part Two will be devoted to a consideration of these two major perspectives found among Catholics and other Christians, and of the proper role of the church in the moral life and decisions of its members.

CHAPTER THREE

A "Religious" Account of Evil

I suspect that there has always been something very attractive about good people who strive to keep the law. Whether it be the Essenes of first-century Israel, the Lamas of Tibet, or the Puritans of early America, wherever such people have gathered together in communities, they have laboriously liberated a small corner of their world from ambiguity and chaos. That is no small accomplishment, and wherever and whenever it occurs, it deserves our respect. So it is not at all my intention to make light of good people who keep the law. They are the backbone of any stable culture. They create enclaves of order by setting down simple and very clear ways of coping with the Existential Dilemma, the Ontological Paradox, and the Moral Predicament. Given the human condition, there will always be those who, having found the ambiguity of life and its inherent immorality painfully destructive, seek to establish a viable alternative by turning to law and order.

While good people striving to keep the law are admirable, history has shown us that they can all too easily be transformed into a people who think they are good *because* they keep the law. Once that move occurs, woe to anyone in their midst who deviates from the established norms. Deviation from the law becomes the epitome of evil and must be dealt with harshly. Maintaining the purity and integrity of the group becomes paramount; deviators are ostracized and excommunicated lest they contaminate the rest. Harsh ontic evils are meted out for even minor offenses. Suddenly, those who, out of their goodness, withdraw a little from the booming, buzzing confusion of life to create enclaves of order and goodness find they are themselves the agents inflicting the six major ontic evils on one another: death, pain, disablement, deprivation of pleasure, of opportunity, and of self-worth. That is a sure sign that something has gone wrong. But instead of seeing that, people have usually tried to justify that situation by having recourse to some sort of story that speaks of the need to undergo such trials and tribulations here, in order to achieve a glorious happiness in a hereafter.

When Christians are caught up in that predicament, they have little difficulty finding a model to justify what they do, for it seems at first glance that is exactly the way the God of Genesis acted. Made in his image, it would seem that we are called to do likewise—in his name, of course.

Sin: Our Earliest Understanding

The story of Genesis is known to even the youngest of Christians; indeed, most of us came to know it when we were very, very young. One of the wonderful things about the Adam and Eve story is that it can be understood so easily; its message is clear and uncomplicated. It looks like a simply marvelous way to introduce children to the notion of moral evil. That is so true that once one has been introduced to the notion of sin in the story of the fall, it is virtually impossible to get that account out of one's consciousness. It is easy to learn but most difficult to unlearn. Witness the fact that so many of us in adult life have still not unlearned it, and the more fundamentalist people castigate those of us who have.

Taking Genesis literally is about all a little child can do. It would be unrealistic to think a child could do more. When you consider the context in which most of us first came to learn about moral evil, you can readily understand why Genesis was a godsend to our teachers of religion. The problem of moral evil is formally raised for Catholic children, most generally, at the time of their first confession, usually when they are about eight years old. Now consider the problem facing the religion teacher: how to bring to consciousness the notion of moral evil (called sin when viewed in a Christian context) in children who are generally quite innocent and who have very limited experience with evil?

For most of us, the problem was solved this way. We were being prepared for our first confession, but we had gotten along for almost a decade without it. We didn't really have a felt need. We were doing just fine without it. So the first step was to convince us that we really did need the sacrament of penance (now more appropriately called reconciliation). The teacher had a solution—the sacrament—for a problem we did not yet have. So the only thing to be done was *to give us the problem!* How ingenious. With the best intentions in the world, religion teachers took second graders with little or no consciousness of moral evil, and made us suddenly terribly aware of such things. They did it because they were confident that having once given us the problem, they were also in a position to give us the solution as well.

Genesis played an important role, then, in the systematic effort to bring moral evil to consciousness. But when we reflect that moral evil was being brought to consciousness in the minds of second graders, we can see that the notion of moral evil brought to consciousness could not help but be very simplistic. As I recall, the two Scriptural foundation stones of the effort to introduce moral evil into our consciousness were the story of God's having given the ten commandments to Moses as recounted in Exodus, and the Genesis story of the fall. The scenario went something like this:

Boys and girls, we all know that God created the world and everything in it. And when he did, he set down certain laws which everything in nature must obey. So the rain falls down, not up. The sun comes up in the east and sets in the west. The planets move in their prearranged orbits, and we have the four seasons following in orderly succession each year. So it was that God created and ordered the whole universe.

Now, when God created human beings, he did the same thing. He gave them a law they had to follow if things were to be rightly ordered. And what do we call that law, class? (We all eagerly replied in unison: the ten commandments!) That's right. And whenever we break one of those ten commandments, or laws given us by God, we dirty the beauty of our souls, and commit what we call...Class? (Again with enthusiasm: "Sin!") Right again. My, you're doing wonderfully well this morning, children.

Thus it was that most of us came to understand what a sin was. We were not only given the problem—breaking God's law besmirched our souls and made us unpleasing in his sight—we were being set up for what I now like to call "the car-wash view of confession." Remember?

Sin is a terrible thing, children. Each time we knowingly break God's law, we are committing a sin and disobeying God. And with each act of such disobedience, our souls get dirtier and dirtier, more ugly and more defaced. This makes God very angry. You remember what happened to Adam and Eve when they violated a command given them by God. They were punished, and expelled from paradise. Instead of having food for the taking, Adam had to work the land and struggle to get food by the sweat of his brow. And Eve had to be subject to Adam, and from then on, she would suffer the pains of giving birth. Adam and Eve listened to the devil and disobeyed God, and so they were punished. Children, never listen to the devil. He is always trying to trick you into sinning, just the way he did Adam and Eve. They thought God wouldn't find out. But we know that God is everywhere, and he sees everything you do. I mean *everything*. And each time you sin it leaves a mark on your soul.

Well done! The children now have the problem. They know that God is always watching them and is ever vigilant lest they break his laws. They know that breaking those laws disfigures their souls and makes them dirty in God's sight. They know there is an evil force loose in the world, working hard to get them to break God's law. And they know that they are liable to punishment should they die with a "dirty soul." Marvelous. Next time, all we have to do is give them the solution.

So effective was this strategy for bringing sin to consciousness that many never break free of it. To this day, we find adults who still feel themselves caught between the eternal vigilance of God on the one hand, and the wicked machinations of the devil on the other. Even those of us who have managed to break free of it still have residual effects from time to time as we find ourselves reverting to our second-grade consciousness in moments of moral crisis. That should make us reluctant ever to doubt the power of stories/myths when told to the very young. Of course, the solution came in the wake of their having given us the problem. The solution went something like this:

> Children, God so loved the world that he sent his only-begotten son, Jesus, to die for our sins. And Jesus set up the church and the system of the sacraments to save us from our sins. One of those sacraments, which you will be receiving soon, is the sacrament of penance, in which your sins are forgiven and your soul is restored to its original beauty. The priest has Jesus' own power to forgive sins. And when you confess your sins to the priest, it's like confessing them to Jesus, himself. When the priest gives you absolution, it is the Lord himself who is forgiving you. God so loved us that he gave us this great sacrament. Our job is to do the best we can to avoid sin and the temptations of the devil. But if we fall we know we can always go to confession and be forgiven. Isn't God great, children?

He is. But I wonder if there weren't some children then who thought God would have been a whole lot greater if only he hadn't let the devil loose on the world, and if he didn't become so very threatening every time we sinned.

Let me be clear about this whole situation. I do not for a moment want to be taken as being critical of those good men and women who did their best to form us in the "faith of our fathers" back then. They had an impossible task. They did as well as could be expected. The lesson that emerges is not that they somehow deformed us due to their stupidity or ignorance, but rather that it would have been far wiser to put off the discussion of moral evil until we were a little older. If one attempts to bring moral evil to consciousness in small children, then one cannot avoid giving them a very primitive view of moral evil. We should face up to that fact, and put off reconciliation until after eucharist or when individual children can understand, which may be as long after as junior high. By then, we can be sure young people can grasp the significance of moral evil in other than the most primitive terms.

Implications and Effects of That Early Understanding

Obviously, one cannot teach people about sin without at the same time teaching them something about God by implication. In fact, if a particular view of sin gives rise to a caricature of the God of faith, or to a view of him that contradicts the revelation that Jesus is, that is *prima facie* evidence that it is erroneous and wrongheaded. Statements about sin are always simultaneously statements about what sort of being God is and what he is about in the world, what sorts of beings we are or ought to be, what the ultimate significance of human life is. Sin-talk always implies tacit statements about all three of those things.

What did our childhood view of sin say about God? For many of us, it said that he is something of an ogre. He's very concerned that we obey his rules and regulations for the world, and he gets pretty darn sore if and when we don't. In fact, our obedience seems to be something of a top priority with him; it may even be his main concern. When we are disobedient, we become repulsive in his sight, for sin defaces and defiles our souls. We then become objects of his special wrath and our very eternal salvation is in jeopardy. That's the view of God implied in our childhood understanding of sin; God is primarily lawgiver and punisher.

Of course, this rather negative picture of God was softened a bit by saying that he was our loving father, that he loved us so much he sent his son to save us, and gave us the church and the sacraments to help us stay out of sin and in the state of grace. But, for many, the talk about how loving God was came too late in the game. We already had a rather ominous picture of him from Genesis. In fact, if the truth be told, that rather fearsome picture of God is to be found not only in Genesis but throughout Scripture. From time to time, God kills off those who disobey him, sends plagues and famines on the ancient Hebrews when they aren't obedient to his will, sends his own son to the cross, and threatens all kinds of ontic evils in this life and eternal damnation in the next. So if God is a lover, he has some rather strange ways of showing it, to say the least.

Unfortunately, since Scripture is filled with such stories, which do God no credit, it is little wonder that many have decided it was easier simply not to believe in him at all. Sadly, goodly numbers of those who continue to believe in him are convinced he is a Monstergod with a quick temper and a short fuse.

What does our childhood view of sin say about the sorts of beings we humans are, or ought to be? It says little or nothing about the ambiguity that we have seen marks all of human life. We are fully responsible for our actions and the expectation is that we will obey the law. When we do not, because we are fully responsible, the guilt is clear and the punishment deserved. The fact is, we are to be obedient to the law, period. No exceptions. Put in another way, we were created by God; we owe our lives and everything else to him. We are his creatures, creations of his will, and that means that our ultimate reason for existing is to serve and obey the will that created us. We are his subjects. If we are good subjects, he will reward us. And if we are not, we may escape his punishment here, but we cannot hope to escape it hereafter. So it is definitely in our self-interest to be docile and obedient servants of God. Only in that way can we be sure of unending and eternal happiness in heaven.

Of course, as creatures we are weak. From time to time we find that we are ourselves outside the law. In such circumstances, our best hope is to quickly repent, make amends, do penance, and reaffirm our commitment to God and his law. Unrepentant sinners are in terrible jeopardy. Since association with them might be construed as our condoning their conduct, and since they themselves constitute a serious temptation to us, they are to be shunned. By obeying the law and avoiding unnecessary contamination, we are pleasing to God and fulfill his will.

Our childhood view of sin also implies a certain view of the significance and ultimate meaning of life. Our situation is at best a perilous one. We are caught between God the lawgiver, and the principalities and powers of the devil. The devil and his minions prowl the world seeking the destruction of souls. So we are in constant danger of succumbing to his allurements, thus breaking the law of the good God. Why are we situated so precariously between good and evil? Why would God put us in this predicament? Why, to test us, of course. That should not be surprising to anyone who has read the story of Abraham who was tested by Yahweh and asked to sacrifice his only son, Isaac. God is into testing, it seems. He tests us to see if we are worthy of heaven.

This life, then, is a test. God gives us our life on earth as a time of trial, a time to work out our salvation by keeping his laws. The task is to keep our purity and not become defiled in the process. To help us in that regard, the church has standard rites of purification (baptism, penance, the last rites), which it puts at the disposal of believers. To strengthen us against the assaults of the devil, the church has other rites of spiritual strength and power (eucharist, confirmation). In a word, then, our situation is one of warfare. Besieged by the power of the devil, we are upheld and strengthened by the power of God, and our eternal salvation is in the balance. It depends on how well we fight the war, and whether after the last battle we have managed to retain the grace of God in our souls.

Obviously, this life is not what is really worthwhile. It is war, struggle, a vale of tears, and a time of perilous dangers. But as with all wars, it comes to an end. What matters is the life we are to live after the war. We yearn for everlasting peace, but only those who have kept the commandments and died in the state of grace will have proven worthy of so great a prize.

Clearly, our childhood view of sin, if not given up somewhere along the line for a more mature and realistic view, leads us inevitably into some such view of our lives as given above. Many in adult life, even after Vatican II, continue to hold this rather impoverished view of the situation. This can only be because it continues to answer one of the primary needs we have, making some coherent sense of our lived experience. Since it does so with such certainty and without ambiguity, it continues to remain attractive to many. The "religious" account of evil has been so effective in helping people cope with life and feel close to God that it should only be done away with in favor of an alternative that does even greater justice to human experience while at the same time putting one in touch with God.

A Concluding Assessment

Our childhood view of sin, which I have called a "religious" account, manifests itself in adult life in various forms. Some are more modified than others. What they all have in common is that they make of Christianity primarily a "morality play." That is to say, the central issue in Christianity is avoiding moral evil. No one would deny that avoiding moral evil is an essential element in Christian life, so there is no quarrel there. The disagreement comes over whether that is the central issue.

Second, as we have already noted, any account of sin will involve statements about God, and in the "religious" account, quite frankly, God comes off pretty badly. He deserves better of us. We Christians really ought to be friends of God. We usually don't allow people to say horrible things about our friends in our presence. Yet we seem to stand by and allow people to say terrible things about God just because they are part of the traditional "religious" account. As God's friends, we should strongly object. "Hey, wait a minute—it's not fair to talk about God that way." Unfortunately, we seem to think that God can pretty well take care of himself, that he doesn't need us to defend him, and so we remain silent in the presence of some of the most malicious and offensive remarks imaginable. Perhaps we are reluctant to speak because those who make them are merely repeating, without thinking and reflecting, what they have learned from official church teaching.

Experience has taught me that some of the most offensive remarks about God occur whenever we are confronted with evil, ontic or moral. "I've got cancer. God must be punishing me for my sins." "God will send you to hell for one mortal sin not repented." "God tested Abraham's faith by ordering him to kill his son, Isaac. We know that's true because it is in the Bible." "God lets the devil prowl about the world seeking the destruction of souls." "Why did God take my four-year-old son in that automobile accident?" And so it goes. When we remain silent in the face of such malicious gossip about God, we show that God is not very blessed in having us for his friends.

Third, once Christians take the "religious" account as normative, there is no real possiblity of growing out of it; to do so would be tantamount to losing the faith. Many years after Vatican II there seems to be a concerted effort to undo the council. There is a growing conservatism in the Catholic Church, as if we were suddenly repenting Vatican II because it meant treating lay Catholics as adults called to minister to the world in the name of the Lord. When that posture is assumed by people in very high places in the church, the pressure increases to give up the advances made in the past generation and to return to our childish ways. Simultaneously, around the world, conservative fundamentalism in all religious sects seems to be on the rise. Prophetic voices are stilled or repudiated, and we are told our life journeys must become circular as we return whence we came. True in matters of doctrine, the trend is even more oppressively true in matters of morality. The cry is: We've gone too far—we must go back!"

For my part, I can't go back. I think we must go on, led by the Spirit. We are called to create a whole new array of moral (life-giving) alternatives in the name of the Lord. There is a kind of moral cowardice in simply returning to the established ways at this point. That would be not to understand the process in which we humans are all caught up; that would be not to distinguish "religion" from "faith"; that would be not to walk with the Lord of history into the future. But if we are ever going to become prophetic people in moral matters, we are going to have to give up the "religious" account of evil and open our minds and hearts to a more adequate account. It is to just such an account that we turn next.

SUGGESTED READING

Tad Guzie, *What a Modern Catholic Believes About Confession,* Thomas More, 1974, esp. Ch. 4.

Louis Monden, *Sin, Liberty & Law,* Sheed & Ward, 1965, Ch. 1.

Dick Westley, *Redemptive Intimacy,* Twenty-Third Publications, 1981, esp. Chs. 2 and 3.

CHAPTER FOUR

A "Faith" Account
of Evil

Had the book of Genesis begun "Once upon a time...," we would not now be fighting against those who insist on giving it a literal interpretation, and the creationist vs. evolutionist battles of the last century would never have arisen and would not still be raging. Had the opening words of Genesis not been "In the beginning...," we might also have had a better chance of seeing Genesis in its proper perspective. As it is, Genesis became the first book of the Bible, leading us Christians to think of it as the controlling book of the Old Testament. It is not. That honor goes to the book of Exodus, as any believing Jew could tell us.

Most of us Christians have had our understanding of evil formed by the interpretation of Genesis we received when we were in school. It now seems pretty clear that we would have been better served had our understanding of such things been derived from the book of Exodus. For as we have now come to understand, Exodus controls the content and meaning of the book of Genesis. Just how does that work?

If the New Testament is controlled by a single event, the Jesus event, his life, death, and resurrection, then the Old Testament is likewise controlled by a single event—the exodus. To put that in some sort of historical context, the exodus of the Jews from Egypt occurred in the thirteenth century B.C., say around 1280, during the reign of Ramses II (1292-1225 B.C.). But the oldest parts of the Old Testament date from about 950 B.C., which means that the whole of the Old Testament, as we know it, was written *after* the exodus, and that includes Genesis. Why is that so significant?

It seems that Israel's first historical awareness of God's dealing with them as a nation in history was the act of deliverance in the exodus. It was at the time of their deliverance that the Hebrews, however tenuously, became one nation with one God. Before that, it is even thought that they were disparate tribes with many gods. That great act of deliverance brought them to a new consciousness, and started them down the path of history that was to culminate in Jesus of Nazareth with whom we now walk. It was only natural, then, that they remembered that deliverance and passed down the recollections of it by word of mouth from generation to generation. So we read in Deuteronomy (26:5-9):

> Then, Israel, you shall declare before the Lord, your God: "My father was a wandering Aramean who went down to Egypt with a small household and lived there as an alien. But there he became a nation, great, strong and numerous. When the Egyptians maltreated and oppressed us, we cried to the Lord, the God of our fathers, and he heard our cry and saw our affliction, our toil and our oppression. He brought us out of Egypt with his strong hand and outstretched arm, with terrifying power, with signs and wonders; and bringing us into this country, he gave us this land flowing with milk and honey."

What the Declaration of Independence and the Constitution are to the United States, the account of exodus was and still is to Israel. That was their first conscious recorded encounter with the living God, and forever after whenever they spoke of Yahweh (God), no matter what the context, it was taken for granted that everyone knew it was the God of exodus of whom they spoke. No Jew could ever have thought otherwise. To this day, at the Jewish Seder, which is the annual celebration of the Passover, that text from

Deuteronomy is recited by the youngest child so that Jews will always remember that their God is "Yahweh"—the God of freedom.

What, you may ask, does this have to do with Genesis? After the exodus, Israel then reinterpreted its previous pre-exodus history in a new light, in the light of that deliverance event. They rewrote their history in the light of Yahweh's manifestation of himself in the exodus. So we have the account of Yahweh's faithfulness and the infidelities of their Hebrew ancestors, the stories of the patriarchs Abraham, Isaac, and Jacob, and even the Genesis account of the primitive beginnings. Now if one is unaware that that is how the process worked, then it is all too easy to interpret the God of Genesis as Israel's first and definitive understanding of Yahweh. After all, what could be more natural? The Genesis account comes at the very beginning of the Old Testament. But that is to miss the central point of the Old Testament. God is then seen primarily as creator, lawgiver, and punisher and only occasionally and incidentally as liberator. This is a cruel distortion of the revelation. No wonder so many of us Christians have missed the true meaning of the Genesis account of creation and the fall. To remedy that situation, we would have to have an Exodus interpretation of Genesis. What might such an account look like?

An Exodus Interpretation of Genesis

As we have seen, the central theme of the Old Testament is "liberation," the liberation of a whole people as described in Deuteronomy 26:5-9, but that means that "liberation" is the central theme of Genesis as well. We can only understand Genesis if we remember that. It, too, is about God moving in a people and freeing them, thus making it possible for them to share the most intimate relationship that can exist in this world: the relationship between God, humankind, and the earth.

The Christian image of creation is that somehow God is there all by himself and suddenly he gets a notion to create, and bang, things start to appear out of nothing. If you read Genesis carefully, that is not exactly the way it is described. *Creation is the first act of liberation.* Prior to the intervention of Yahweh, everything was formless chaos, terribly mixed up and disordered. So creation in Genesis is described as the process whereby God separates various things from the primordial chaos. God is the separator and orderer. He liberates all of creation from disorder by separating things and putting them in their proper places.

The Jews were a people who in their history had experienced chaos and order. They knew the difference, and after the exodus they clearly understood that God prefers order. The creation story of Genesis was to remind believing Jews that as Yahweh's people made in his image, they are to dedicate themselves to separating/liberating the things of life from chaos and to putting them in proper order. When things are disordered, when they are not the way they are supposed to be, then the people of God have to act against that particular chaotic and disordered situation and bring about a world the way God wants it.

Genesis finally comes to the story of the creation of humankind. Fittingly, Genesis 1 speaks of Adam and Eve being created simultaneously and together. The human race came to be in the relationship of two, not in a single individual. Humankind is in relationship to one another and to God; that is the ordered way; that is the way it is supposed to be. As we shall see, this fact has great importance when we come to discuss the origin of evil from the perspective of Judaeo-Christian faith.

Yahweh, having introduced the proper order into all of subhuman creation, and having made humankind in his image and constituted them relationally, he looked at it all and saw that it was good, indeed very good. There was neither ontic nor moral evil in creation. And so, on the seventh day, he rested.

If you want to see sin and evil in a Scriptural way, then you have to accept this starting point: a perfectly good world, ordered by God, separated out from darkness and chaos, and hence absolutely good. There is nothing in it that is spoiled, disordered, or out of joint. It is marvelous. It is magnificent. It is totally gift! Given that starting point, what are we to say about the origin of evil?

Evil is possible in the situation described in Genesis precisely because creation is gift. What are the prerequisites for a gift? First, there must be someone to give the gift, and this someone must be at liberty to either give or not give it. Second, there must be someone to receive the gift, and that someone must also be at liberty to accept or reject the gift. Obviously, freedom is an essential ingredient on either side of the giving. Gift-giving and gift-receiving are marked by gratuity and graciousness, which means they are activities of freedom. Finally, what is given and received must be some sort of good. It must be something befitting beings endowed with freedom. We usually don't consider gratuitously inflicted harms or burdens as "gifts." We only feel "gifted" when that which is bestowed is a good, a good that somehow benefits us.

Once one understands the nature of "gift," one has all that is required to account for the emergence of evil in a creation put in order by God. Evil is a possibility because there is someone who receives the gift. One can take the gift, see its beauty and goodness, and say, "Wow, this is great; it is really something; it is truly gift!" Or one can take the gift and say, "What the hell is this? I don't want it." There is someone who can take the gift and throw it away, or crush it or spoil it. There is a reality in the world capable of doing that, not because that reality is bad, not because that reality is evil or deformed or comes into the world a little bit twisted, but simply because that reality as presented in Scripture is a "response-able" reality, a reality free enough to be able to respond. That reality is us—it is humankind. Genesis makes clear that we are the source of evil in God's perfectly ordered creation.

Humankind is constituted not so much as a *rational* creature whose task is to dominate and control the rest of creation, as a *relational* creature called to live in redemptive intimacy with one another, thus affording the God who is love a suitable dwelling place. We are meant to relate; we receive the gift exactly in the relating, or better, living relationally *is* the gift. Living relationally *is* eternal life. It is life as it should be lived, that is, relationally. *Life is to be lived in solidarity with all of humankind.* That's the proper order for human life and to reject it is to sin.

Sin, then, is alienation, division, not living in solidarity, not living life in a relational fashion as a gift to be shared. The sin that

Jesus fought to overcome is precisely that situation in which there is no solidarity in humanity. That is the fundamental sin. It was that sin that moved Yahweh to liberate the Jews from Egypt by the exodus; it was that sin that caused him to call Israel to be his own relational people; it was that sin that was the occasion for raising up the prophets of Israel to call the people back to the dream; it was that sin that the Lord came to eradicate from the face of the earth.

Genesis presents Adam as the first one of our breed to say, "No, I won't live relationally. I don't want to be one with all of this." Notice how Adam and Eve are themselves divided from each other at the time of the fall. Adam exclaims, "It's not my fault; she made me do it!" And Eve blames the talking serpent. So much for solidarity. But Adam was also the first to realize: "If I'm not truly human, if I'm not truly one with all those who suffer, with those who die, what am I? What can I possibly be? Isn't that what being human means?" And Jesus, the second Adam, right from the start said, "I will be completely human. I will live my life relationally as gift. I will be one with all of them. I freely choose it!"

How about us, who claim to walk with the Lord? Can we in like fashion say, "I will live my life as a gift—regardless of the difficulties that come my way, despite all the ambiguity and pain I experience in coping with the Existential Dilemma, the Ontological Paradox, and the Moral Predicament?" Can I, like the Lord, *choose* the life before me, with whatever it holds, for example, loss of loved ones by death or alienation, the wrenching agony of starting over to put it all together as I move through the various stages of my life, the pain, the tears, the spirit, the laughter, the limitations, the joys, the celebrating—and live it *relationally?* Can I take all that and say, "It is my life. I'm going to live it as a gift. I'm going to transform it until it becomes an expression of eternal life"? Can we freely choose to be human, that is, to be relational, in the face of all that? That's the point. And what we find in Genesis is the ancient authors saying, "That's what God chose for us; can we choose it, too?" In the final analysis, the heart of evil from the faith perspective, in fact, *the* paradigm of sin, is not to choose freely to be human.

Caught up as we are in the Ontological Paradox, this may seem too high an ideal for us to aspire to. But that can only mean that we still think of ourselves as individuals, and have not fully accepted the revelation of faith about human solidarity. Our faith tells us that we were constituted by God *in relation,* and to reject that gift ultimately leads to the loss of our selves. John MacMurray (*Persons in Relation,* Faber & Faber, 1961, p. 211) put it this way:

> *It is only in relation to others that we exist as persons;* we are invested with significance by others who have need of us, and borrow our reality from those who care for us. We live and move and have our being not in ourselves but in one another.... Here is the basic fact of our human condition; which all of us can know if we stop pretending and do know in moments when the veil of self-deception is stripped from us and we are forced to look upon our own nakedness.

Human beings either freely choose to live relationally or they cease to be fully human. That is why sin is not merely or primarily breaking a divine law. It is first and foremost a self-mutilation, a freely chosen dehumanization whereby I cease to be what I am, what God made me, by saying no to human solidarity.

The Real God of Exodus-Genesis

As we have seen, sin-talk always involves some sort of God-talk by implication as well. What sort of a God emerges from the view of sin we have just seen? A God markedly different from the one we saw emerge from a literal interpretation of Genesis and Exodus. That was the Genesis-Exodus God of religion, a God who scourged his people and seemed determined to frighten them into keeping his laws. Even St. Paul felt obliged to explain to the Corinthians why so many such horror stories occur consistently throughout the Old Testament, never suspecting that his explanation just compounded the difficulty (1 Corinthians 10:5-6, 11):

> We know that God was not pleased with most of our fathers, for they were struck down in the desert. These things happened as an example to keep us from wicked desires such as theirs.... The things that happened to them serve as an example, and they have been written down as a warning to us.

Obviously, a person is always at liberty to interpret the horror stories of Genesis and Exodus as St. Paul did, but to do so yields a "religious" picture of God—a God attempting to bludgeon us into submission, who rules through fear instilled in his people by constant threats and reminders of what will happen to them if they don't obey. If one takes a nonliteral approach to those first two books of the Bible and centers on their overall meaning, the horror stories become irrelevant, and a vastly different picture of God and what he wants for the world emerges, a picture much more compatible with Christian faith.

Clearly, the Exodus-Genesis God is primarily a liberator; the liberation of all of humankind is what he is really about. Just as in the beginning he liberated the whole of creation from the primordial chaos, so now his main concern in history is to free humankind from the disorder they have created for themselves by refusing to live relationally. To that end, he himself has entered into a relationship with humankind, one so intimate that he has chosen to dwell in us. We have trouble grasping that, and even when we say we believe it, we don't realize what it means. Strange as it seems, and incredible as it sounds, the Exodus-Genesis God takes delight in being with the "children of men." His dwelling place is not in some far-off heaven, but in people, down deep in our noblest parts. As a sign and guarantee of that unfailing presence, he covenanted himself to the whole human race through the ancient Hebrews. They were the first to come to understand the marvelous ways of this God of faith. Our God is not a God of law, but of the covenant.

It all began when the Lord Yahweh called Abraham out of his own land. "Look around, Abraham. Things are really bad, not as they should be. Humankind is hopelessly divided. Everything is out of joint. *It is not my dream because it cannot speak my presence.* Why, they don't even know I'm here. Leave it all! Let's start anew! Come, mount the dream of my presence. It will be your new homeland. And if you do, I shall be your God, and you shall be my people." So begins the most remarkable story in all of human history—the story of the covenant. This is the story of God's loving presence to all of humankind and that special people he forms in every age to be the living signs of his redeeming presence and of the transformation of the world into the Kingdom that it effects.

The dream of Yahweh was, and is, that the world be so transformed in all its aspects that it bespeaks the presence of the loving God of faith. Ancient Israel did not always understand that, and so the Lord Yahweh raised up the prophets of Israel to retell the story of the covenant and to call the people of God back to their essential mission: working for the transformation of this world into a place where God's presence will be obvious, a place where he can truly feel at home.

There was always a remnant in Israel, a small group of people who were not misled into thinking of God in "religious" categories, but who had somehow gotten the revelation of faith straight. They strove to keep the dream of Yahweh alive, despite the fact that their world continued to be out of joint and did not speak the presence of the loving God of faith to humankind. It was from this faithful remnant that the Man came. For Jesus was not only born into and bred on this great dream, he enfleshed (incarnated) it. He was God-with-us, which is to say, Emmanuel. He inaugurated by his coming the reign of God, the coming of the Kingdom, that ancient dream of Yahweh first revealed to Abraham. That dream was so important to Jesus that he never tired of proclaiming it up and down the dusty roads of Palestine. And when his disciples asked him to teach them to pray, he told them to pray for the realization of that ancient dream: "Thy Kingdom come...."

To walk with the Lord means to share his commitment to that dream of his Father, the dream of a world where things will be right between us, where we shall live in intimacy and solidarity with one another so that God's presence will be clearly evident and not just a matter of belief. That dream is so important to faith-filled people that they can't wait for its *full* realization. So they freely decide to start to live the dream *now* as a sign of hope to others, a sign that the Lord's dream is not a daydream or a pipe dream, but a reality they can actually see coming to be in us.

Some day this world of ours—the world of drugs, violence, and pornography, the world of greed and lust, the world of injustice and exploitation—will so bespeak God's presence that it will be itself transformed into the Kingdom. That is our faith. That is the promise made to Abraham. That is the promise the fulfillment of which Jesus incarnated and proclaimed. That is the authentic meaning of Judaeo-Christian faith. Alongside that ancient dream, to religiously turn Christianity into some kind of insurance policy to guarantee personal salvation is just too mean, too little, too self-serving, and too egotistical to be taken seriously. Christianity so understood and so lived rejects the ancient dream of Yahweh, cuts itself off from its Jewish roots, and betrays its founder as well.

There is no deep division, then, between the Old and New Testaments. The God of faith is ever and the same in both accounts. Sometimes we think that Jesus came to put an end to the Old Testament, but he really came to fulfill it, and to establish the ancient dream as the ever ongoing enterprise God works within humankind. It will not do to think of the God of the Old Testament as a vengeful, wrathful, angry God, and the God of the New Testament as the loving Father of us all. We had best take to heart what was revealed to the Hebrews of old: "Hear O Israel, the Lord your God is One." There is no other, none besides him. He is the only God we have. And his dream for the world has remained constant from the beginning. So has his *modus operandi*. He dwells with humankind, and by living in us transforms us and our relationships into witnessing signs of his presence. As that process becomes more perfect, the reign of God becomes more evident, and the coming of his Kingdom closer at hand.

An important conclusion follows from all of that. Christians are not *primarily* concerned with being moral, that is, with avoiding the unjustified infliction of ontic evil, but rather with bespeaking God's presence in the world and heralding the coming Kingdom. That is the "beyond" to which, in faith, each believer dedicates herself. Being moral may be a necessary first step in that enterprise, but it is only the humblest of beginnings. Obviously, to the degree that I am inflicting ontic evil on others, to that same degree I am denying the incarnational presence of God in myself and in my fellow human beings, and I become an obstacle and hindrance to the coming Kingdom.

But I can be moral simply by doing nothing at all. When I am asleep, for instance, I am not, except in the most bizarre circumstances, inflicting ontic evil on anyone. I am, therefore, being moral. That should be reason enough for Christians to see that the Lord has called us to morality *and* its beyond. We are covenanted to be signs and witnesses of God's salvific presence and of the Kingdom that presence effects. In order to accomplish that, *we must give ourselves not only to morality but to its beyond as well.* We must become now a people of the coming Kingdom. Christians are not only to be moral, they are to adopt a Kingdom-lifestyle, that is, to be themselves like the Lord.

Understanding the Ancient Dream of the Kingdom

Carl Sandberg, the American poet, wisely observed, "Nothing happens unless first—*a dream!*" How true. For many of us, the dream of Christianity has traditionally been to instill in people a desire for salvation. To help us acquire that desire, many who taught us leaned on scaring us with the horrors of the alternative—eternal damnation. That works rather well, up to a point, because when the dream is presented in that "religious" way, it capitalizes on the natural dynamism of self-interest. This, after all, is the engine of most of our actions.

But that dream was bound to go stale. It ignored the ancient dream of Yahweh, a dream incarnated in the Lord Jesus who was "the man for others." Vatican II addressed itself to this situation, and if Carl Sandberg is correct, then the first priority of the post-Vatican II church is to fashion an acceptable contemporary articulation of the ancient dream. Without the dream, nothing is going to happen! We'll be stuck with the *status quo.*

As we have seen, put most simply, *the dream is the coming of the Kingdom of God.* Until recently that hasn't meant much to Catholics, but that is itself very instructive, since the coming of the Kingdom is the central theme in the whole of the New Testament. I sometimes get angry when I reflect on that fact. Having gone to Catholic schools all my life, why did I have to wait until I was approaching mid-life before I came to understand the importance of the Kingdom? Obviously, those who formed me in the faith didn't think it was very important. But to have been raised in the Christian faith without ever encountering its central theme is nothing short of scandalous. I hope the advent of Vatican II has definitively put an end to that sort of thing, which is one very important reason why I resist so fiercely any thought of repealing Vatican II and going back to things as they were.

For most Catholics, the word "kingdom" signifies the place that you go after you've lived your life well here. It is the "after life," "being with God"; it is "going to heaven." We got that impression from the episode recounted in Luke between Jesus and the good thief on his right. "Lord, remember me when you come into your Kingdom." "Amen, amen, I say to you, this day you shall be with me in paradise" (Luke 23:42-43). What more need be said? The Kingdom was the reward we were to receive for being good.

That understanding of the "Kingdom" also coincided with the obvious fact that in English, the word "kingdom" is a space-word. If I said that the King of Spain surveyed his kingdom, you would image him in crown and full regalia walking around the Iberian peninsula. From the Pyrenees down the west coast to the Straits of Gibraltar, up the east coast back to the Pyrenees. There. He would have circumscribed his kingdom.

So naturally, when we read the Scriptures and run across the expression the "Kingdom of God," we immediately translate it in our imaginations into a place where the blessed dwell with God in everlasting glory. But that is not what the ancient Hebrews meant by the "Kingdom of God," nor is it what the New Testament means either. We all know that the ancient Hebrews were very careful in their use of language when they spoke of Yahweh. They never spoke his name directly and out of reverence would prefer not to talk about him directly. Indirection seemed more appropriate to them. So instead of saying, "God spoke to Moses," they would be more comfortable with saying, "The word of God came to Moses in the desert." It just seemed to be more polite and respectful to put "God" after the preposition rather than to assume to put "God" as the subject of the sentence.

One result of this is that there are nouns used in Scripture to designate what would properly be expressed by verbs. So "the word of God" replaced "God speaks" in their vocabulary. If we don't understand that, then we will fail to see that "the Kingdom of God" was a similar noun-use, and that what they are really talking about is a divine activity—the activity when "God reigns," "God governs," "God manages," or "God directs." Having missed that significance until very recently, no wonder we Catholics misunderstood and took the Kingdom of God for a place. It is the situation, the state of affairs that obtains when God reigns and his Spirit rules. That is the Kingdom! To pray for the coming of the Kingdom is to pray for a situation in which God will reign in our lives and his Spirit will rule the relations between us. *It is not to pray to go somewhere; it is to pray that our world exist in a certain way.*

Once we understand that, it becomes clear how the New Testament can speak of the Kingdom in two seemingly incompatible ways. Some texts indicate that the Kingdom is now (Matthew 12:28, 11:11-13; Luke 11:20; 16:16; 7:28; 17:21), while others speak of it as not yet but as coming (Matthew 5:20; 6:10; 22:12; 25:10; Mark 14:25; Luke 22:30). That represents accurately the present state of things, doesn't it? To some degree, God reigns and his Spirit rules in our lives, but not so fully that the presence of God in humankind is a matter of fact and not still a matter of belief. The New Testament is not contradicting itself, therefore; it is merely "calling it like it is," and up to that point in human history (as up to our day as well) things remained ambiguous, even concerning the coming Kingdom. But we hope we are all still working on it!

When God Reigns and His Spirit Rules

What is it like when God reigns and his Spirit rules? What are the "signs" that bespeak that state of affairs? One way of putting it is:

When God reigns and his Spirit rules:
1. No individual rules.
2. It means the end of injustice.
   a. God determines the agenda; we don't.
   b. Humankind relates in terms of absolute equality; there is no domination among us.
   c. Matter does not dominate us.
3. Unconditional love prevails.

1. When God reigns and his Spirit rules, no individual rules. Not pope or bishop. Not king or president. Not pastor or priest. Not the local politician, the corporation president, the labor leader, the shop steward or foreman. Not the president of the women's guild. Not the choir director. Not the biggest benefactor of the parish, nor those in the highest social positions. (And just so we're sure that everyone's ox gets gored, not even college professors, the writers of spiritual books, or their publishers!) The Lord rules.

This is not, as it might at first blush seem, a diatribe against authority. Far from it. It is the best way I know of beginning to understand what real authority is. Some examples may help. For some years in my parish, we went without any female eucharistic ministers although the surrounding parishes all had them. The pope had said it was all right. Even the Cardinal, our bishop, said it was all right. But our pastor said that there would be no female eucharistic ministers in the parish. When asked why, he said simply, "I don't want them." That ended the matter for a couple of years, but eventually the pressures were too great and he acquiessed—reluctantly.

Such examples are not restricted to the local level in the church. A similar situation occurred in the universal church with regard to Pope Paul VI's decision on the birth-control controversy of some years back. Ignoring the advice of his own international study commission as given in their report, he reaffirmed the traditional prohibition against contraception. After issuing *Humanae Vitae* on July 25, 1968, Paul VI was questioned about the matter because there had been great expectations that he would change the discipline of the Catholic Church in the matter of contraception. When such turned out not to be the case, he was asked for an explanation. He said that though it was true that the church's teaching on the issue was not infallible and that another pope at another time might well change the discipline of the church in the matter, he himself could not in good conscience be the one to do it. So it was that *his* conscience became the norm for all. That seems to be an almost classic example of what happens when an individual rules. Of course, we have seen the results. (More of that later, when we discuss contraception in Part Three.)

The point to be made is that those in authority in the church are not at liberty to exercise that authority in any way they please. In ancient Israel, when the leaders of the people rose to speak to them authoritatively, they would gather the people and stand before the Ark of the Covenant to address them. And when they spoke authoritatively they would always begin, "In the name of the Lord, I say to you...." Whatever comes after that initial phrase can only be something in accord with the Kingdom. Whatever cannot come after that initial phrase without contradiction cannot be said authoritatively. Finally, whenever what comes after that phrase is a contradiction to, rather than an expression of, the coming Kingdom, that is when the individual speaking is trying to rule in his or her own name. That is why we said that when God reigns and his Spirit rules, no individual rules.

If the key factor of our faith is that the Lord dwells in us, then only those statements can be authoritative for faith that mirror what the risen Lord of history is revealing and effecting in us. That is why one cannot say, *"In the name of the Lord, I say to you...* there can be no ordained women." It is like saying "square-circle"; it is a contradiction in terms. As such, it is not authoritative, nor can it ever be, no matter who says it, no matter what ecclesiastical office that person holds. (On the birth-control issue, at least Paul VI was honest enough to admit that he was speaking in his own name. Unfortunately, he did not put that into the encyclical *Humanae Vitae* itself, but only admitted it when questioned afterward.) As we go on to describe the other "signs" of the reign of God, it will become clear why that statement is contradictory, and also why the fact that we'll ordain women someday is as inevitable as the dawn. The Kingdom can't fully come until we do.

2. *When God reigns and his Spirit rules, it means the end of injustice.* We North Americans think that "justice" is when we get our fair share, when we get what's coming to us. Justice to the Western mind is when things come out even. The ancient Hebrews had a much different understanding. Justice is not when things come out even, but when they come out "right." That is why the Jews always thought of the Kingdom of God as a kingdom of right-

eousness. Recalling what we said about creation as putting things in order, we can see that for the Jews, justice was when everything was in proper order and things were working together the way they should. That is justice.

We experience that sort of thing in many different ways in our everyday lives. We have a dinner party and we invite people who, at first sight, look as though they could never be compatible. We expect the worst. As things turn out, the dinner conversation was scintillating, the guests were fascinated with our another, and when they left, all said they couldn't remember when they had had such a good time, and they hoped they could do it again sometime. That's justice.

In every family there are periods (all too brief) like that, too. We can recall times in our family when everything was together. The younger children related as they should to the older children. The older children were solicitous of the younger ones. All related to their parents idyllically, and the parents related to one another and to the children in just the right way. It was marvelous. That is justice. Of course, it did not last. Family members each proceeded on their own journeys and moved to the next stage. Things were no longer quite right, they were "out of sync," and everyone once again coped with the situation as best she could. But for a time, like Camelot, it was right; it was good; it was the way it was supposed to be; it was justice.

When God reigns and his Spirit rules, things are right between us. We live relationally as gift; we are in solidarity with all our brothers and sisters. When the Kingdom comes, it marks the end of injustice, the end of destructive and evil relationships, the end of division and alienation, the end of lust and abuse, the end of domination and exploitation. It means that humankind will be ordered and related as they should be, as they were meant to be, that is, in ways that evidently bespeak the covenant and the presence of God among us. But for that to occur, we have to put certain of our relations in order, our relation to God, to one another, and to the world.

a. When justice prevails, God determines the agenda; we don't. In these days of rampant individualism, people everywhere claim the right to be free, which means they see it as an inalienable right that *they* determine the meaning of their lives. Of course, in practice, it does not quite work out that way. Only the rich and the powerful, only the "in" people, seem to get to do it. They then impose that on the rest of us. Our God is good, incredibly good, and he knew that sort of thing would happen. So to protect our sanity and for justice's sake, he reserved that task to himself. "*I* determine the meaning of life," says Yahweh. "I reserve that to myself, not because I am a chauvinistic and dominating God who wants to force it on you, but because I know that if I didn't do that, one of you would try to do it to the detriment of others." That is the message contained in that episode from Genesis: "Of all the trees in the garden you may eat, except of the tree of the knowledge of good and evil" (2:16, 17). "That's *mine,*" says the Lord. "I have already determined life's meaning. Life is a gift to be lived relationally, remember? The response to that gift is *yours!*"

When, in the fullness of time, Jesus came, he showed us how to set that relationship straight. It is as if God saw us trying to establish life's meaning on our own, and said, "Oh, no. You poor creatures. You've misunderstood. You'll never be truly free that way. Wait, I'll come and show you. Watch me, this is what you have to do." Jesus incarnated the right relationship in his very person. By living as he did, he tried to show us that there can be no real liberation until there is justice, and there can be no justice until a people accepts the fact that *they* do not determine life's meaning, they do not determine what is right and wrong. That is God's job. All the texts in the New Testament that speak of the Lord's obedience to the Father should be read in that light.

b. *When justice prevails, humankind relates in terms of absolute equality; there is no domination among us.* Here too, Jesus shows the way and incarnates the right relationship. He never dominates. Though he is the Lord of history, he relates to other people on a basis of equality, not privilege. He mounts the dream of human solidarity, and always offers the gentle invitation, "walk with me," "be like me." When they come to make him king, he disappears from their midst (John 6:15). Though he is the Son of God, he will not lord it over anybody. The message is clear. If we are serious about the coming of the Kingdom, we too must give up on power as the way to achieve it. Jesus reveals for all to see the fact that power and domination are disorder: *they corrupt everything they touch.* We find it so hard to give up on power. We find ourselves trying to dominate and work our wills on one another. We turn a deaf ear to those who call for an end to the domination of women, of migrant workers, and of minorities in our society and in our church. Justice cannot prevail so long as men continue to harbor thoughts that they are better than women, Whites that they are better than Blacks, Hispanics, and Asians, clergy that they are better than lay persons. For the Kingdom to come, all that has to go!

c. When justice prevails, matter and its spin-offs don't dominate us. The third relationship Jesus came to set straight for justice's sake is humankind's relationship to the world of matter. All the stories of the miracles are meant to make it clear to us that Jesus would not be dominated by matter. He walked on the water, changed water into wine, raised people from the dead, and cured them of all manner of physical ills. Matter was no match for him. His message again is clear: the Kingdom of righteousness can only come if we do not let matter dominate us.

And what about us? We not only want to determine life's meaning for ourselves. We not only want to dominate one another. We get heavy into matter, allowing it to get its hooks into us, and we are no longer free but addicted. Addicted to sex, alcohol, drugs, money, power, prestige, pleasure, or whatever, we lose control of our lives; we have a monkey on our backs. More than that, we reject the message of the Lord and actually insist that human freedom really means the right to choose for ourselves the sort of enslavement to matter we prefer.

So we see that justice requires a certain kind of order in our relationships to God, to our fellow human beings, and to the world. For us, the reign of God began with Jesus, for he was the one who set all those relationships in order and showed us what it means to be fully human and living signs of the coming Kingdom as well. But that Kingdom requires something else of us.

3. When God reigns and his Spirit rules, unconditional love prevails. How could it be otherwise? God *is* love, as John's first epistle so eloquently tells us (4:8 and 16). The reign of God could not help but be a reign of love. Jesus is the love of God, enfleshed, incarnated, made visible for all to see. But that does not quite tell the whole story. God is not only love—he is *unconditional* love. That is something we believers are very reluctant to accept. To love someone, for example, only on the condition that she change her ways is to deprive her of the best means of doing so. The rule of love is to believe in the beloved, to trust in the beloved. It does not demand. To love someone is to have faith in her; it is to hope in her forever. The incarnation is all the proof one could ever need that God loves us and has confidence that we can break out of our egoism, expand ourselves to include others, and can change not only ourselves, but our world as well.

To say that God is love, in the light of the fact that he has freely covenanted himself to dwell in all of humankind, means that love is at the center of things. Just as the earth is molten matter at its center, and just as that molten matter breaks through the crust from time to time to explode into our atmosphere in volcanic eruptions, so from time to time the God who is love bursts forth in flashes of radiance that reveal his presence and confirm our belief that at the heart of all reality there is love.

Each of us has had experiences that reveal the truth of what was just said. There we were, living our lives on the surface, the crust of life, believing in our heads that love is at the center, but having forgotten it. At least it was not operative as we went about our daily rounds. Busy about the mundane business at hand, we had lost sight of the central truth of our lives. And then suddenly it happened. Love burst forth into our lives with a splendor and power that almost knocked us off our feet. Preoccupied and harassed by the trivia of life, wrapped up in ourselves and convinced that everyone was either hostile or indifferent to us, we were suddenly brought up short by a loving glance, an unexpected kindness, an unmerited show of generosity. However briefly, the curtains parted and we caught sight of a truth we had forgotten, a truth that had become crusted over by the cares of our everyday lives. The truth is that love is really all that matters, that love is at the center of it all, and that our vocation as persons is to human solidarity.

As a result of such an experience, we suddenly became more alive. Our humdrum daily lives were animated with a new energy and vitality; our hearts were filled with a joy beyond the telling. We suddenly realized what caused Julian of Norwich to cry out in ecstasy: "All will be well, all will be well. All manner of things will be well." And why not? At the center of it all, there is love.

Of course, that bright and shining moment passed all too quickly. Too soon we were immersed once again in the humdrum, trivial crust of life. The exaltation did not last. Indeed, in a world marked by time and the human passage, it could not last. But we would be wrong to conclude that because of that the experience was really hallucinatory, and that we didn't experience anything real at all. In that precious moment, love revealed itself to us, and called us to respond to our vocation as persons.

The moment is gone now. But notice that even the recollection of it after the fact has the power to change our lives, if only we respond. However humble and fleeting the gesture that incarnated it, in that moment the transcendent power of God himself touched us and called us to reorder our lives in the image of love. That is how God works most often in our world. For in encountering one another in love and intimacy, we encounter God. The loving person, whose humble glance or act began the whole thing, translates the exuberant and vibrant life of God into human terms for us. Thanks to that person, we glimpsed the unconditional benevolence that sustains human life at its center, and that threatens to erupt anew at any moment to further herald its Kingdom.

Morality and Its Beyond

Having looked at the origin of evil from three different perspectives— from the "human" point of view, from the "religious" point of view, and finally from the "faith" point of view—it should now be possible to draw some modest conclusions. We hope these will clarify the situation and create a context within which to approach, in Part Three, the specific issues that are currently causing so much pain in the adult faith community.

Up to this point, we have chosen to speak of "moral evil" and have avoided talking about "sin." It seemed better not to talk of sin until we had finished the "religious" and "faith" views of moral evil. Sin is a religious or faith category, in as much as it assumes the existence, or better, the presence, of God. If we keep God out of the picture, it is really inappropriate for us to speak of "sin" at all. Something is a moral evil because it is an offense against human beings, unjustly frustrating their needs, desires, and interests. Something is a sin because it is an offense against God, frustrating his desires and interests. "Sin" is part of the language of belief.

Still, most of us use the two words interchangeably, and manage to make ourselves understood quite well. The reason that works out so well is because, as we have seen, God wants us to live our lives relationally as gift. When we unjustly inflict ontic evil on our brothers and sisters, we are acting not only against their interests but also against his. So moral evil becomes sin when viewed in the light of God's desires and interests. Speaking religiously, frustrating divine interests is described as our breaking God's laws. That's "religious" sin. From a faith perspective, frustrating divine interests is described as our not witnessing God's incarnational presence in our actions and not living our lives in solidarity with humankind so as to be signs of the coming Kingdom. Breaking the covenant is the sin of *faith*. But however one wishes to take that word "sin," it is always a theological term, a way of talking about human conduct as done "before God."

Clearly, in the religious view where sin is disobeying divine laws, the goal of Christianity is for each of us "to be good." What does that mean? We have all known what it means from our earliest days of childhood. Our mothers would send us off to school each morning with the admonition, "Be good!" It didn't take us very long to discover exactly what she meant. Translated freely, she was saying, "Do as you are told. Obey the teacher. Don't break the rules. Don't create disturbances. Don't make waves." That's what "being good" meant to us as children, and to this day that is usually what it still means. But is that what Yahweh, the Exodus-God of freedom, is calling us to—to be good? Is that what walking with the

Lord and being living signs of the kingdom means? Hardly. Unlike our mothers, *our God has never told us to be good!* Think about it. When has that ever been his message to humankind? Never. We have only gotten that message from those who, speaking religiously, claim to speak in his name.

Being good is just too mediocre to be worthy of the Lord and of those who truly walk with him. It lacks any sense of the heroic, which we have seen is so important to us as humans. We want to do something great, something significant, something beyond the mediocrity of the crowd. When we tell young people that Christianity calls them to be good, they don't experience a call to greatness; rather, they are grade schoolers once again with their mothers telling them to "be good." They find it not only too small a dream, but an insult to their young womanhood and manhood. As Ernest Becker has written (*The Denial of Death*, Free Press, 1975, pp. 6-7):

> The crisis of modern society is precisely that the youth no longer feel heroic in the plan for action that their culture has set up. We are living a crisis of heroism that reaches into every aspect of our social life. ...And the crisis of society is, of course, the crisis of organized religion too: religion is no longer valid as a hero system, *and so the youth scorn it.* If traditional culture is discredited as heroics, then the church that supports that culture automatically discredits itself. *If the church, on the other hand, chooses to insist on its own special heroics* it might find that in crucial ways it must work against the culture, recruit youth to be anti-heroes to the ways of life of the society they live in. This is the dilemma of faith in our time.

We wonder why our young people are attracted to the cults and to the most fundamentalist of Christian sects. The answer is obvious. Those things offer them a concrete plan for heroism. They feel special. They feel saved. In many cases, they pay a high personal price for that brand of heroism, but they would not be attracted to all that if they had only been given to see the faith of their fathers as an heroic enterprise instead of an insipid call to "be good little girls and boys." No wonder so many of them have bolted and run.

What makes that all so tragic is that it was totally unnecessary. When Judaeo-Christianity is understood from the faith perspective, it offers the brightest, noblest heroism the world has ever seen. In this heroic enterprise there is room for everyone. More than that, such heroism cannot be judged trivial or insignificant because it plugs one into the cosmic dream of Yahweh and of the Lord Jesus. To become a Kingdom-person is to be involved in the most important and significant movement in all of human history. It joins one to the ranks of those gallant and noble women and men of faith down through the ages who have kept the ancient dream alive by incarnating it in their own lives.

Now it is our turn. We're on stage. Will the ancient dream die with us? We have only the time of our brief sojourn to make our contributions to the dream and hand it down to the young, thus advancing the day when the Kingdom shall fully come and all of humankind will live relationally in peace, in justice, and in love. To contribute to the realization of that dream makes one very special indeed, and makes her life far more meaningful than were she simply to settle for being good and working for her own salvation.

But once again, as with all things human, there is an ambiguity in the center of all of this that makes us pause and gives us reason to wonder whether it is realistic for us to think we can become people of the Kingdom. How can I think of becoming a sign of the Kingdom when I can't even manage to be moral? How can I possibly entertain the call to greatness in the Lord when I can't even manage to be good? It seems so hopeless.

Discouraging perhaps, but not hopeless. Where does it say you have to be able to avoid moral evil completely before you can be a Kingdom-person? Were that the case, as we have seen, the Moral Predicament would make being a Kingdom-person beyond the reach of any of us. Leaving aside for the moment the matter of God's forgiveness (to be taken up in the next chapter), what does our experience tell us? Aren't there truly great people you know who are "gift" to their fellow humans, who are signs of the Kingdom, but who haven't managed to avoid moral evil in every respect? When we look at other people, we seem to be able to see their greatness and their sign value, because whatever faults they have, whatever residues of moral evil remain in their lives, they pale to insignificance in the light of their overall lifestyle. Now if we can view other people that way, why can't we accept the fact that other people and the Lord may well view us in that way, too?

Human life, even for believers, is a passage, a journey, a growing experience whereby we slowly and painfully learn life's lessons. We should not expect either ourselves or others to reach perfection quickly. It is an arduous task of years, even of a lifetime. While we are on the way, there will be moments when we are caught up in activities and situations that are destructive, are morally evil, and hence are really contrary to the dream and to our own heart's deepest desire. Experience shows that it takes us time to work through such situations as we struggle creatively to find ways to bring our lives back into accord with the ancient dream of faith. At such times, the most we can do is perhaps that we not give up on the dream, that we not lose our will to find our way back. The Lord understands that and so should we. This does not give us license to play games with our lives, and pretend we are serious about the dream when in reality we have given up on it. But it does mean that we shall most likely all experience times when we find it impossible to be our best selves, and we should not think that those times of ambiguity disqualify us forever from walking with the Lord and being Kingdom-people. It is at such difficult and painful times that one's friends and faith community can be a strong support and bulwark against the temptation to simply walk away.

Summing Up

As we have seen, morality is essential both to living human life and as a first step in becoming a Kingdom-person. But Christianity is not primarily a morality play, and being good enough to be saved is not the primary Christian agenda. Beyond morality, there is the realm of the ancient dream of Yahweh, the realm of the coming Kingdom. To that dream incarnational faith calls us. Unfortunately, we do not believe in ourselves as much as the Lord does, for we think we are too little, too small, too insignificant to be involved in so grand an enterprise. We take more comfort in a Christianity aimed at making us worthy of salvation than in one that covenants us to be signs of God's transforming our world into the Kingdom.

Nonetheless, faith calls us to a lifestyle that bespeaks God's presence and heralds his Kingdom. Moral evil need not destroy that lifestyle completely, so long as we retain our fundamental option for and commitment to the dream. Perhaps we are not totally to blame for so often misunderstanding the agenda of faith. Some portion of that blame belongs to the institutional church that too often has presented us with a view of God that negates the dream and makes of morality the central Christian issue. Ultimately, it is our ambiguity about who this God of ours really is that causes our confusion and vacillation between the "religious" and "faith" accounts of Christianity. So before we go on, we had best grasp clearly who the God of faith really is, and what his fundamental message to humankind contains.

SUGGESTED READING

John MacMurray, *Persons In Relation,* Faber & Faber, 1961.

Louis Monden, *Sin, Liberty & Law,* Sheed & Ward, 1965.

National Conference of Catholics Bishops, *To Live In Christ Jesus: A Pastoral Reflection on the Moral Life,* United States Catholic Conference, Nov. 11, 1976.

John Shea, *What A Modern Catholic Believes About Sin,* Thomas More, 1971

_____. *The Challenge of Jesus,* Thomas More, 1975.

Dick Westley, *Redemptive Intimacy,* Twenty-Third Publications, 1981. See esp. Chs. 4, 5 & 7.

CHAPTER FIVE

The Yahweh-God
of Love

As Christians we were always thought to have a very special vocation. First, we were supposed to come *to know personally the God
of love* as revealed in Jesus and then we were to *make that God and
his love known to the world.* A noble vocation, but one with which
we struggle and have great difficulty. As I hope to show, it is not
just our own personal sins and weaknesses that account for our inability to really know and witness the God of love. Some share of
the blame for that must be borne by the inspired writers of Scripture, by the church itself, as well as by our parents and teachers, all
of whom bequeathed to us an incredible view of God which, quite
simply, was not to be believed.

Be that as it may, it is now long past the time when we can
legitimately blame others for our distorted views of God and how
he works in the world. Though there may be certain reasons why we
have come to hold what we do, there are no excuses for our still be-

ing so far off the mark. But even if we were among those who
didn't quite get it right back in our school days, we have now lived
long enough so that our own experiences reveal God to us as he has
always been trying to reveal himself to humankind. If we still don't
know him at this stage of our lives, it can only be either because the
revelation he makes of himself in our lives is such "good news"
that it is, quite literally, unbelievable, or because we are so wedded
to the erroneous view of God from former days that we lack the
will to give it up despite all of our experiences to the contrary. The
fact remains, however, that until we really know him as he reveals
himself in our experience, we cannot fulfill our vocation as Christians.

Obstacles to Our Knowing God

One might imagine that knowing God would be relatively easy and
one of the most natural events in human life. When you add that
God is constantly attempting to reveal who he really is to
humankind, then the fact that there is so little "knowledge of
God" in the land becomes something of a paradox. Nor is that
paradox of recent origin. The prophet Hosea marked it as a central
problem in his own times, around 750 B.C. (4:1):

> Hear the word of the Lord, O People, for the Lord has a grievance
> against the inhabitants of the land: there is no fidelity, no mercy, *no
> knowledge of God in the land.*

And a century later things were still pretty much the same, which
caused the prophet Jeremiah (4:22) to put these words of frustration into the mouth of the Lord Yahweh:

> My people are fools, *they know me not.* They are senseless children
> having no understanding of me.

Nor after the coming of Christ, which was specifically aimed at
remedying that situation, have things much improved. In every age,
there seems always to have been a small remnant of believers who
got it right, but *the fact is that the majority of Christians have in
the past said, and continue in the present to say, things about God*

that would correctly be judged to be slander or defamation of character in any court in this land. The worldwide resurgence of fundamentalism and the revitalization of a pre-Vatican II conservatism in the post-Vatican II Catholic Church seem to indicate that the misrepresentations of God will continue to be widely preached in our lifetime. Unfortunately.

Now if we are not to be taken in by such nonsense, we must take seriously our vocation to become part of the faithful remnant for our age, that relatively small number of believers who have somehow gotten the revelation straight and who attempt to keep the dream alive by witnessing the truth about God to their world and to their fellow Christians—regardless of the cost.

In that effort, it is only natural that one would turn to the Bible and to the institutional church for help, it being assumed that each is a most likely source for authentic knowledge of God. Although that may be true, surprisingly it is also true that each has historically been the source of major distortions and misrepresentations of who God is, where he dwells, and how he operates in our world. More often than not, it is so-called believers who undermine the correct answers to those questions and labor tirelessly against acceptance of the God of faith as he is actually revealing himself to us, preferring instead a religious idol, that is, a god of human fashioning.

One does not have to be a believer in order to know the meaning of the word "God," just as one does not have to believe that unicorns actually exist in order to know what the word "unicorn" means. What does our world take the word "God" to mean? As everyone knows, "God" is that invisible being who sits on a throne somewhere up there, watching us, testing us, punishing us if we're bad and rewarding us if we're good. He is the eternally vigilant lawgiver who is no respector of persons, making heavy demands of obedience on all of humankind, threatening them with eternal damnation should they not keep his laws and walk in his ways. That is God as most of the world knows him. And where did the world get this horrible caricature of the God of Judaeo-Christian faith? From the Bible and from the church, of course.

In Genesis 22:1-2, which is entitled in Christian Bibles the "Testing of Abraham," we read:

> Some time after these events, God put Abraham to the test. He called to him, "Abraham!" "Ready!" he replied. Then God said: "Take your son Isaac, your only one whom you love, and go to the land of Moriah. There you shall offer him up as a holocaust on a height that I will point out to you."

And in Genesis 38, we are told of how God deals with those who disobey. Judah ordered his son, Onan, to have relations with his brother's wife, Tamar, after she had been widowed by the death of his brother, Er. Genesis 38:9-10 tells us what happened next:

> Onan, however, knew that the descendants would not be counted as his; so whenever he had relations with his brother's widow, he wasted his seed on the ground, to avoid contributing offspring to his brother. What he did greatly offended the Lord Yahweh, and so the Lord Yahweh took his life.

And the God depicted in these episodes is celebrated and praised in song in the Book of Psalms, with the result that many of the psalms depict God as the chauvinistic God of Israel who is a scourge to the rest of humankind.

Nor are such shocking accounts restricted to the Old Testament, as many believe, for we read in the fifth chapter of the Acts of the Apostles how God mercilessly dispatched Ananias and Sapphira without a second thought, because they lied about some financial transactions. In that same place, St. Peter is depicted as insensitively entrapping Sapphira with all the dexterity of an FBI agent in an undercover operation. And the blood-letting does not end there, for in Revelation 2:21-23 we are treated once again to a view of a heartless and threatening God:

> I have given her a chance to repent but she refuses to turn from her lewdness. I mean to cast her down on a bed of pain; her companions in sin I will plunge into intense suffering unless they repent of their sins with her, *and her children I shall put to death*. Thus shall all know that I will give each of you what your conduct deserves.

So from the first book of the Bible to the last, we can always find the ever-present caricature of the God of faith. That should be warning enough for us against any attempt to take Scripture literally. For to do so involves us in ratifying what the world thinks of God and necessarily separates us from that faithful remnant who knows otherwise.

If the Scriptures can be used to promote so distorted a view of God, then it should not surprise us to find that the institutional church has too often used its good offices, prestige, and power in behalf of that same distortion. With impeccable logical consistency, the church has in the name of that God threatened eternal damnation for such things as missing Mass on Sunday, eating meat on Friday, remarrying after divorce, masturbation, extramarital sex, and the teaching of heretical doctrine, to name only a few. Is it any wonder, then, that the world got the impression from *us* that God, if he existed at all, was something of an ogre? That view of a chauvinistic and jealous God even found its way into Vatican Council II when in the *Constitution on the Church* (14) it declared:

> . . . whoever knows that the Catholic Church was made necessary for salvation and still refuses to enter her cannot be saved.

That same sort of thinking surfaced with a vengeance in that classic case when, in the name of the Lord, two priests from the Joliet diocese refused a young paraplegic the right to marry in the church because of his disability. Evidently, everyone in the world knew that was silly except those two priests. Fortunately, their bishop quickly intervened to put an end to the insanity. For two days, though, the world thought it had been right all along about God and about those who claim to speak in his name.

My point in all this is not to suggest that we should somehow repudiate both Scripture and the church, but rather to indicate that it is by no means an easy thing for us to come to know God and his ways, precisely because we are freighted with so many erroneous notions about him arising from the Christian tradition itself. Still, the existence in every age of a faithful remnant gives us reason to hope and indicates that our tradition can also be the source of an *authentic* knowledge of God as well. The trick is not to allow oneself to become depressed at the majority view, nor to succumb to it simply because it is traditionally held or authoritatively proclaimed. The first principle of the remnant people in every age of the church has been not to confuse the God of "faith" with the God of "religion," which is God as the world sees him.

It is the manufactured god of religion who threatens us with hellfire and damnation; who visits his wrath on the children of Adam; who is so insecure that he demands constant affirmation from his creatures; who forgives only grudgingly but does not forget. It is the chauvinistic god of erroneous legend who saves only Christians and views all others as infidels; who inflicts suffering on humankind in order to test their allegiance; who views women as inferior members of the human species, unworthy of leadership roles in the ecclesial community. Despite the fact that such a God is often depicted in Scripture or invoked by the church to validate inhuman decisions (especially in the area of morality), that is not the God of Judaeo-Christian faith, that is not the God who reveals himself fully in the Lord Jesus, and in the intimacy of every human heart.

The God of Faith

For some strange reason, people have always found it easier to believe in the Monster-god, and have over the centuries found the God of incarnational faith to be absolutely incredible. Indeed, whenever anyone gets even close to describing him or depicting the way he works in our world, people take off as if frightened by something awful. How sad.

If we would be persons of faith and fulfill our Christian vocation to make known to the world the immense love of God, then it is imperative that we get straight in our faith the answers to some very important questions. Who is God? (And therefore who is God not?) Where is God? (And where is God not?) The answers to those questions are clearly and consistently given throughout the Old and New Testaments. In the Old Testament, they are especially clear in Exodus.

Now the God of Exodus is obviously a liberator; liberation is his main agenda. But more than that, time and again in Exodus we read of the covenant whereby he pledged himself to dwell with us. In *Redemptive Intimacy* (pp. 82-83), I tried to capture that thought when I put it this way:

> For centuries, the Jews and their ancestors had been the laughing stock of the ancient world. Their neighbors always thought them

particularly strange and irreligious because they carried around the Ark of the Covenant and thought that God actually dwelt with them. After centuries of such ridicule, their faith was at long last validated as the Word became flesh and dwelt among us. With the coming of Christ, we now know definitively where God is. He is not in religious images, laws or rituals; he is not in Jerusalem, Mecca or even Rome. He is *not* in some far-off heaven. No, he is where he has *always* been, with, among and in his people, especially in our noblest parts where justice and charity dwell.

Although I would not want to take back a word of that, it adds an interesting dimension when the question of God's presence is viewed from the perspective of Exodus.

Perhaps no Old Testament text has been the source of so much speculation as Exodus 3:14, in which God is supposed to have revealed his name to Moses. Moses had asked, "If they should say to me: What is his name? What shall I say to them?" And God said to Moses, *"I am who am."* He said, "Thus shall you say to the children of Israel: *I am* sent me to you." Some scholars have suggested that God was really putting Moses off, not giving him a name at all, because to know another's name for ancient peoples was to have power over him. So God was saying to Moses, "You don't have to know my name. *I am what I am.*"

A second interpretation is that God was saying that he was the creator, the giver of life and being itself. But for various reasons scholars have come to think that a better rendering of the riddle would be (Remember, this is an Exodus text.): *"I am the one who will be there.* Which is to say, when they ask you who I am, Moses, tell them to be not afraid—for they will find me in the liberating events of their history—*for I will always be the one liberating them."* That liberation may take many different forms in the course of history, but whenever and however people experience it, *that's what I am.* And it is from the Hebrew of this riddle in Exodus 3:14 that we get the name *Yahweh.* To call God Yahweh is to accept him as the God, Lord of history, liberating humankind by forming and fashioning a people in whom he can finally and fully both *be* and *dwell.*

What that really means for us is that we find the Yahweh-God best when we look ahead, when we discover where the transformation of the world is leading, when we see where it is that the Kingdom is coming to. That poses an important question for every believer. For as we look ahead, read the signs of the times, we must attempt to discern where we find the humanity that God wants to walk with and dwell in most. Where is that humanity a-borning? Where is that humanity threatened? *That* is where we should be. Somehow, if we would truly be where God is, we will have to be where the liberation is occurring, where the new life is unfolding, where humanization is happening. To walk with the Lord is really to be in on that, and not just a disinterested spectator of it.

So the God of Exodus is the God of life-giving future possibilities. To turn to him, to be "converted" to him, is to struggle to turn ourselves away from the comfortable present with its temptations to leave the *status quo* unchanged, thinking we have done enough, and to turn toward life-giving possibilities for all. To turn elsewhere is in a way to turn away from God as Yahweh. At the very least it is to seek him where he isn't.

Many think that "conversion" is a category of personal salvation. I am converted away from sin in order to be a better person, deserving of salvation. But that seems woefully inadequate in the light of Judaeo-Christian history. *I am to be converted so that I may become a factor in the moral decisions of my time.*

What Yahweh was telling Moses was that he was to be found not only in the depths of people, but also in the liberating events of their history. Whenever and however a people experiences authentic liberation, that is, when they feel freer, walk taller, think nobler, love better, sing more joyfully, and are more alive and human than they ever were before, whether they know it or not, they have encountered the Yahweh-God of freedom. Dan Schutte, in one of his songs (*Here I Am, Lord,* North American Liturgical Resources, 1981) gives us a glimpse of this Old Testament God of "faith":

I, the Lord of sea and sky, I have heard My people cry.
I, the Lord of snow and rain, I have borne My people's pain.
I have wept for love of them, I will speak
My Word to them.
I will give my life to them.

The message of faith is clear. Contrary to what you may have read elsewhere, the truth is that God is so taken with humankind, so smitten with love of us, that he graces us, loves us and forgives us—*unconditionally!* That's the secret that the faithful remnant has always known, and the majority of Christians and the institutional church simply cannot accept it. All too often, the church fails to give witness to this divine graciousness. It dispenses with anything but graciousness the spiritual goods that have been entrusted to her. Conditions are set on almost every good the church dispenses, some of them harsh, unfeeling, and even spiritually lethal.

As a consequence, the institutional church has, as often as not, enslaved or wounded human beings rather than liberated them, and many have simply walked away to find life-giving help elsewhere. The church may have done a lot of evil in its history, but inflicting ontic evil is not its purpose. The church is primarily concerned with love. Despite its many sins, its incredible institutional stupidities, its love affairs with power, and the unbelievable amount of unnecessary burdens it has laid on the back of its people, what is truly good about the church continues to shine through. The church is one of the few remaining institutional symbols of God's unconditional love in our fragmented and hate-filled world. Were it not so, we, like so many of our contemporaries, would have left it long ago.

So now I think we can see more clearly why it is not so easy to be a person of faith these days and to fulfill our vocation as Christians. With the rise of fundamentalism, many more things now militate against an easy acceptance of God's unconditional love. People have been taught to think of themselves as sinners who therefore have something to fear from God. That fear enslaves them and keeps them from the freedom of spirit the Lord intended—the freedom of spirit required if one is to be a sign of the coming Kingdom. It is the task of those who wish to be remnant Christians to somehow get through to those people that they are loved, they are precious, and no matter what they may have done, (I repeat, *no matter what they have done*) *they have nothing whatsoever to fear from God.*

If you had a drinking problem, God does not look at you as a reformed alcoholic. If you committed adultery, defrauded a business partner, got into drugs, exploited minorities, and even murdered someone, he does not treat you as a repentant sinner with a sinful past. No. That's all obliterated. It's all forgiven. It's all gone. And he says to us, "Sure you died, but you rose again, and in my eyes you are a new creation! In my presence you are entirely new without any guilt whatsoever. It's gone—it's forgotten—I love you. If you had a bad experience last year, forget it. If you've been going through bad times, it's over. You can be your best now, because I am with you and I shall never, never abandon you."

Down through the centuries that has been the primary message of the Yahweh-God to humankind. Yet, only a small number of people have ever heard God described that way, and an even smaller number have accepted that description as true. What about ourselves? Have we accepted the unconditional love and forgiveness of God in our own lives? Have we been reluctant to accept it, and even more reticent about proclaiming it to others? Perhaps we are carrying a lingering burden from our past. When others proclaim the unbelievable graciousness of the Yahweh-God to us, through fear and guilt, do we say, "Yes, I know, but..."? There are no "buts." It is time for us to turn that whole thing around. We shall never be vital and vibrant signs of the Kingdom if we cannot accept the words of love and forgiveness of the Yahweh-God, whose dream that Kingdom is. Those words are directed not to others, but to each of us.

Once we bring ourselves to a heartfelt acceptance of the Yahweh-God in our own lives, then we can begin to witness him and his unconditional love to others. In the words of Jim Griffin (*Proclaim,* 1978), we shall fulfill our vocation as Christians and be able to:

Proclaim the God of Abraham, believe his love for *all.*
A God who dreams with us, forgives us when we fall.
Proclaim that Jesus lives in us, believe that Spirit shines.
Proclaim a God of love—the risen Jesus-Sign.

Let your life *be* that Sign, trust your life and mine
Can show the world his Kingdom's here and now.
We live forever not alone, his people living free.
In faithful love of God—in these things we believe!
Proclaim what we believe!

Naming the Beyond: A Reflection on Unconditional Love

If we aren't quite sure that the Yahweh-God really does love and forgive unconditionally, then we don't have any hope at all of understanding his call that we do likewise with one another. What are we to say about *our* loving unconditionally? That seems clearly out of the question. Or is it? Remember, we are spirit!

Certainly, love is one of the central issues of our faith. In truth, it may be the most central such issue. Scripture speaks of it over and over. Christianity is unthinkable without it. And however else one may be lacking in spirituality, one can be said to have a deep and profound spirituality if only she be busy about the "works of love."

Nor should our expectations of the church surpass our expectations of ourselves in this matter of love. How could they? We are the church! But we all know that many times we do not do things that are really representative of who we really are. Similarly, our best friends do negative things that are not representative of our friendship. But we couldn't keep our friendship going unless we were free enough and gracious enough to overlook those things, knowing they do not really represent our friend's deepest heart. Were we to identify those negative things with our friend, our friendship would be doomed. So it is with the church.

Once we no longer see that what makes the church sacred is what it is trying to do with its believing members, once we lose sight of the incredible amount of love the church has lavished on us and the equally incredible amount of love it has managed to coax out of us, our church affiliation is doomed. The great value of the church, despite everything, is that Jesus' call to love has not been lost down through the centuries. It continues to sound in our day, thanks primarily to the church. We are simply rationalizing when we allow the defects of the institutional church to blind us to the light so that we can justify our own self-centeredness and indifference, and allow this to deafen us to the Lord's call. From the beginning, down through the corridors of time and history, that call resounds in the depths of the human spirit: Be in love! Be in love! Be in love! Yet humankind finds it so difficult to respond. Why?

Because! (Careful here, this gets a little like an Abbott and Costello routine.)

"Yes, I'm listening. Because...why?"

"I thought I told you just now. Because!"

"I guess I just don't understand. Could we start over? Let me see. You said that human beings have difficulty responding to the Lord's call to be in love! And then you asked...why? And ever since I've been all ears. So please tell me...why?"

"I already did. Because!"

"No, you didn't! I was listening very carefully and you stopped in mid-sentence, and after 'because' there was not another word out of your mouth."

"I didn't have to say another word—I had already told you

why—because!''
"I'm confused."
"Obviously!''
Soren Kierkegaard makes that same point with brevity and wit in his *Journals* (2416):

> To love someone *because* is egotism. To love without further qualifications is higher in the sense that a general is higher than a major-general. To love *because* is like "major" added to "general"—it diminishes!

Well said! But perhaps we can get clearer on it. In this matter of love, a human person can position or posture herself in one or more of several different ways. They might be represented thus:

1. Not-Love
   a. Not caring about anything...(Indifference or Despair)
   b. Caring only for oneself...(Blatant Egoism)
2. Because-Love
   a. Caring for another, but only as a means of caring for oneself...(Masked Egoism)
   b. Caring for another but with conditions...(Conditional Love)
3. To Be-in-Love
   a. Caring for another without conditions in an unrestricted way...(Unconditional Love).

Quite clearly, because-Love may be really only masked egoism (2a) in which the beloved is loved because of what she or he can do for me. One speaks very loosely to even call such a thing love. But because-Love may also be a genuine caring for the other, but on conditions (2b), and it is this sort of love that Kierkegaard spoke of as "diminished." He then went on to add, "It would be nonsense, yes, an insult, if instead of loving unconditionally a person offered, say half a dozen, *as if one could love to a certain degree,* and if in this matter of love a four-shilling down payment were possible." Such ridicule is quite understandable, for each of us yearns to be loved unconditionally. This led Leo Buscaglia (WTTW-TV, "Speaking on Love," Aug. 20, 1980) to remark:

Under the guise of love, oftentimes, comes the greatest violations of the person, because our loves are always *with conditions*. I'd like to think that there is at least one person who would say to you: "I love you, period." One person? That's not asking too much, is it?

One is tempted to immediately respond to Buscaglia, "Of course not!" It is not too much to ask that every man, woman, and child have at least one person who cares for them, who shares with them, and is "gift" to them. But that is not exactly what Buscaglia was asking. He asked whether it is too much to ask that each have at least one person *who loves her unconditionally*. That is an entirely different matter. Leaving the Yahweh-God out of it for the moment, reflect on this: Do you know *anyone* who loves *you* unconditionally?

Is unconditional love a realistic expectation of mere human beings? Is a finite creature coping with the Ontological Paradox capable of giving that sort of love to another? Evidently Buscaglia thinks so, because he added the injunction: "Become that sort of person to somebody else!" In the face of so positive an attitude, one appears foolishly timid should she ask, "But how? How does a finite creature come to the point that she can love without restriction or reservation?" However it appears, that is a valid question deserving a response, if not an answer.

The Two Most Frequented Paths to Unconditional Love

It should be admitted straight out that we fight against such love, and no wonder. It transforms us, changes us into another sort of person, and we resist change. We like ourselves just the way we are, with our Because-loves. So whatever else may be said, it is clear that whichever path one takes toward unconditional love, it will be a way of the cross; it will involve pain. In my own reflections on the matter, there seem to be two paths leading most directly to the goal. They are connected but clearly distinct routes: faith/religion and life.

The person of any of the major religions sets out knowing full well what the goal is and what is involved in achieving it. Of course, for the Christian the Lord is the model of unconditional love. The Christian knows that to walk with him is to espouse that ideal, however imperfectly. Asceticism and the various spiritualities are the usual means she employs on that journey, and one sees the striking results of such efforts in the lives of Pope John XXIII, Teresa of Calcutta, and Martin Luther King, Jr., as well as in those more anonymous lives of Christians we know who grace each of us with the gift of "unconditional" love.

But what faith consciously seeks, life also inexorably reveals. As expected, it is more difficult to describe how that path works, because not all who live life come to know its message of unconditional love. One has to have "eyes" to see it and we are all born blind, blind in the sense that we have a third eye, an inner eye, the eye of love that must be awakened before we can see the real beauty of the universe and the glory that is in people. William Johnston (*The Inner Eye of Love,* Harper & Row, 1978, p. 131) describes what happens once that eye of love is awakened:

> ...there can be an experience of enlightenment in which all the barriers which separate me from others collapse and I discover that I am one with the human race, that no one is excluded from my compassion and love, that no rancour exists in my heart.

As we have seen, it is just that sort of experience that grounds the foundational moral experience and answers best the question of why we should be moral. Because of experiences like that, believers take as evidence that the Exodus-Genesis account of human solidarity is correct. The truth of that experience explains those sudden bursts of love into our lives, reminding us that love *is* at the heart of reality after all. That kind of experience gives us confidence that the Lord's promise of the coming Kingdom is in the process of being realized. Clearly, all of the world's great religious seek to gain that sort of experience for their members. But life can with equal effectiveness, though perhaps in a less disciplined way, precipitate such an enlightenment. Rollo May (*Love and Will,* Norton, 1969, p. 102) suggests how life accomplishes that feat if only we are open to its lesson:

> When a friend or family member dies, we are vividly impressed by the fact that life is evanescent and irretrievable. But there is also a deeper sense of its meaningful possibilities and an impetus to risk ourselves in taking the leap. Some, perhaps most, human beings never know deep love until they experience, at someone's death, the preciousness of friendship, devotion and loyalty.

The loss of a loved one brings each of us face to face with the Existential Dilemma and the inevitable realization of our own finitude and weakness, our own vulnerability. Along with that comes the realization that I am one with all my sisters and brothers—precisely in my weakness. People who appear so self-possessed and sure of themselves suddenly appear gallant and noble as they cope with the human condition. Those who stumble and fall under the weight of the burden of their humanity are no longer seen as failures but as fallen comrades. The bizarre conduct and idiosyncracies in others, which I had been unable to understand and unwilling to tolerate, suddenly take on meaning in the light of the loss and vulnerability I experience. Such an experience of enlightenment in the midst of my own losses puts me on the threshold of "unconditional love." It is a frightening experience because of the response it requires. The challenge is always not to pull back from it, but to immerse myself ever more deeply in the experience, letting it transform me as it has so many before me.

Obviously, it is possible for finite, limited creatures such as ourselves to experience the call to unconditional love at some time in our lives. Because we are spirit and because love itself dwells within us, it is also possible for us to answer that call. We may not be able to sustain that kind of love at all times or in each and every circumstance of our lives, but we are capable of loving unconditionally intermittently and sufficiently often that we can become witnesses of the Yahweh-God's presence, and heralds of his coming Kingdom—even if we say we are nonbelievers.

SUGGESTED READING

John S. Dunne, *The Reasons of the Heart,* Macmillan, 1978.

William Johnston, *The Inner Eye of Love,* Harper & Row, 1978.

Soren Kierkegaard, *The Works of Love,* Harper & Row, 1964.

Rollo May, *Love and Will,* Norton, 1969.

Elizabeth O'Connor, *The New Community,* Harper & Row, 1976.

John Shea, *Stories of God,* Thomas More, 1978.

L. John Topel, S.J., *The Way to Peace,* Orbis, 1979.

CHAPTER SIX

The Role
of the
Institutional Church

I keep having this fantasy. Although it shocks people when I share it with them, I am convinced that its message is true. My fantasy goes something like this. Some year or other on the Sunday before Ash Wednesday, after the lenten regulations of the diocese are read to the congregation, I fully expect the priest to continue on as follows:

> My dear people, there is going to be a very important change in the Catholic Church starting on Easter Sunday. And we are all going to do our best to be prepared for it by using our Lent this year to get ready. The Chancery has ordered that all the homilies during Lent be devoted to the topic so that our people will have a real understanding of the significance of the new change. We have been given special

banners, banners which, starting on Ash Wednesday, you will see hanging over the main doors of all the Catholic churches in town. They shall remind each of us and all passers-by of the upcoming change.

So when you come to church next Sunday, you will see our banner. It has a red background with white lettering, and the words in block letters large enough to be seen across the street say it all: Going Out of the Salvation Business as of Easter Sunday!

I know that is going to shock you, and that at first hearing you can't believe your ears. So I invite you to participate as fully as you can in this year's lenten programs; it will help you understand what this all means. I know you are hurting right now, so I ask you to be patient. Trust in the Lord. And pray, pray for those of us who must try to explain all this to the people. It is not going to be easy for any of us. I guess we'll all be doing "real" penance this year!

Of course, once you let you imagination run as wild as that, it is quite easy to carry it further. Imagine parishes having "Going Out of Business" sales, as it were: "Last chance to insure your eternal salvation!" "Step right up and get your final plenary indulgence!" "We're selling out, right down to the fixtures. Bargain prices on holy water fonts, altar stones, purple stoles, and other vestments!" The possibilities are endless.

The Church as Gift

I suspect that this fantasy stems from my conviction, expressed in *Redemptive Intimacy,* that the Catholic Church will, if not in my lifetime at least soon afterwards, finally be forced to admit officially to one and all that it is going out of the salvation business. Whatever it is that the institutional church is concerned with, causing, effecting, and guaranteeing salvation is not its task. *God* saves. Thanks to be God. (We have seen in the preceding chapter what kind of a God our Yahweh-God really is.) That happens to be the way it is, despite all the talk about "binding and loosing" to the contrary (See Matthew 16:19; 18:18).

A key element in the confusion in the minds of many Catholics today is the survival in the post-Vatican II Church of the pre-

Vatican II view that somehow the institutional church is necessary for salvation, that it is needed. We are reluctant to give that notion up because to do so seems to require us to hold that the church, therefore, has no importance. But we have a sense that the church is very important to our lives. So to make the point, we think we have to continue to say it is necessary. But we are wrong. The real importance of the institutional church rests not on the fact that it is "needed" by the world, but rather on the fact that it is "given" to the world. For some reason we think that to say the church is God's "gift" to the world is somehow to decrease its importance. But as Gregory Baum (*Man Becoming,* Herder, 1970, p. 128) has observed:

> Some things can be produced by will power or merited by personal effort, but the important things just happen to a man. ... *The profound things in life are always gifts.*

It should have dawned on us that since the institutional church is one of those profound things of life, it too was gift.

As we have seen, the Yahweh-God graces us, loves us and forgives us—*unconditionally.* His relations with humankind are always marked by gratuity and graciousness, not by necessity and obligation. When Jesus came, he could not give witness to the absolute graciousness of the Yahweh-God toward humankind had he given it only a conditional expression. If the incarnation means that suddenly we shall be graced by God only on the condition that we are baptized, join the church, and conform to its regulations, then the coming of Jesus is a step backward, away from the Kingdom, and not its opening shot. We would have every right then, with the Herod of *Jesus Christ, Superstar,* to say to Jesus, "You're not the Lord! You're nothing but a fraud!" To be the Lord, Jesus must both *be* and *announce* to the world the unconditional gratuity of the Yahweh-God to all of humankind.

But if that is the context of the Lord's coming, then his founding of church must be viewed in that same light. As we all know too well, the church has not always been as gracious and gift-giving as its Lord. One cannot help but be reminded of the story of the unforgiving steward who when he was graciously dispensed from his large debt by his master, turned around and put those of his fellow stewards who owed him a pittance into jail (see Matthew 18:23-35). It has taken us Catholics far too long to finally ask the question why it is that God's world and God's relations with humankind are marked with an unconditional gratuity, whereas God's church isn't. Just to ask that question is already to be on the way to answering it. The church is not marked by gratuity because it still has a way of presenting itself and the Christian life as an obligation. If you don't accept it and live it, you're lost, you're finished, you're evil, you're out!

As we have already seen, that is not at all how the Yahweh-God works, and it must not be the way the church, acting in his name, works either. We must come to understand that *there are no Christian obligations, since the whole faith enterprise is from start to finish a gratuity.* Graced and gifted by God, our only appropriate response is to gift back, that is, to become "gift" to our world, thereby becoming signs of his gracious presence. Christ did not come so that the Yahweh-God could begin to give himself to human beings, nor even as the precondition for the gifts of salvation and forgiveness to be given. No. All those things were given and available to all of humankind right from the start. *The human race has never been without them.* The coming of Christ was to make the unconditional nature of God's love for us and the unbelievable extent of his graciousness toward us visible in our very flesh, thereby giving all of humankind reason to hope. Since the church is the post-resurrection continuation of that enterprise, it is only logical to conclude that this is her main mission as well.

In view of that mission, it no longer seems rightheaded to say either that the church is the cause of salvation, or that salvation occurs only within it. God offers his gifts to all without discrimination. As for the keys of forgiveness given to Peter, they should not be understood to mean that the church of Rome has the exclusive sacramental franchise on forgiveness, but rather to indicate in a public-sign way that forgiveness is available to all and that to lay hold of that gift one need only want it, *really* want it. (This means turning away from whatever inflicts ontic evil and/or contradicts the reign of God, that is, *metanoia.)*

Put bluntly, the world doesn't *need* Christianity. The world did quite well without it for a very long time. (Humankind is roughly a million years old—Christianity a mere two thousand.) The reason it did so well was because the Yahweh-God has always been present, gifting humankind, calling us out of our own homeland (egoism), and inviting us into his (solidarity and the Kingdom). From the perspective of the history of human life on the planet, the Jesus-event and the church are important but very recent gifts of God. Jesus is "given" to the world and so is his church, which means that we must stop viewing the refusal to become a Christian as something of a tragedy. Maybe some people aren't meant to be Christians; the Yahweh-God seems to deal with them pretty well. (For example, Socrates, Buddha, and Mohandas Gandhi.) Anthony Padovano (unpublished lecture at Mundelein College, Chicago, July 14, 1980) sums this all up with sensitivity and beauty as follows:

> We are meant to be gift-bringers, not authoritarians. What you and I have witnessed to in our lives are all the things people don't need. We, Christians, are like singers in the darkness or poets in the desert. And you really don't need songs in the darkness, but how nice it is if someone sings. And in the desert and wilderness of our own lives we may feel we don't need poets. But what a pity if there were no one who saw life with the beauty and grace of a poet. If you never had someone to say words that made you wordless because what was said was so beautiful, and so true. People don't *need* singers in the darkness or poets in the desert, but the song and the poetry bring unexpected beauty. *And when you have heard it you are haunted by something unforgettable.* So we Christians *can* be dispensed with—*but not forgotten.* We can be dismissed, but not without the loss to the entire human family of a vision, and a song, and a poem without which the human heart remains empty wherein it might have rejoiced.

With joy and graciousness, the church and its members are by their lives to sing of the Kingdom and recite the poem of the reign of God, thus bringing unexpected beauty into life—a beauty that frees, gives hope, and haunts the hearts of those it reaches.

Church and the Morality Game

Unfortunately, the institutional church too often shunned its giftedness for a role it mistakenly deemed more important, that of being the guardian and protector of the moral order. No wonder the world took for granted that morality was its main concern. Since being moral was a necessary prerequisite for eternal salvation, it was only natural that the church would be concerned with it and that society would more and more look to the church for help in its own task of maintaining social order. By responding to that call, Christianity was converted into a religion, became a police system with its own penal code and list of penalties, for example, excommunication, hell-fire and damnation. As is the case with all law-enforcement agencies, the church found itself more and more resorting to threats and subtle kinds of force in order to achieve its goal. In the minds of many, this made the church an obstacle to the ancient dream of authentic freedom rather than its troubadour. Of course, throughout it all, there always could be heard the faint strains of the Kingdom-song in the background, but it was drowned out by the brass section of the church tooting the morality song *fortissimo*. Vatican II muted the brass, and now the haunting melody of the Kingdom-song has finally begun to be heard in the land and is becoming the dominant tune for Catholics.

So we see that the church too, as any human enterprise, faces the ever-present polarity and the consequent ambiguity as we search for the right blend or mix or opposing elements. Should the church stress morality too much, she becomes a harping mother yelling at her children to "be good" and threatening to tell their father, who will mete out severe punishments when he comes home. In such circumstances, it is always possible to rationalize that things are so bad that proclaiming the ancient dream of the Kingdom will just have to wait. But should the church really mount that dream, and give itself fully to proclaiming and witnessing the reign of God, then people will think that God is an easy mark because he loves and forgives unconditionally. Knowing they are forgiven, they will have no real motivation to "be good." Their salvation and the whole social order would thus be put in real jeopardy. And then the rationalizations go the other way but with the same effect. It is dangerous to proclaim the unconditional love of God; it is dangerous to preach the gratuity of it all because such things will be misunderstood by our people. The dream is just too radical, too dangerous, too open to misunderstanding and misuse; we'd better not make too much of it.

The ancient dream comes out badly in either case. Either it is viewed as something of a luxury that will be faced up to later, but right now we have to really concentrate on helping people become moral. Or it is seen as revolutionary and radical, a threat to the existing social order, and just too open to self-serving interpretation on the part of individual Christians to be indiscriminately proclaimed. And so it was that up until Vatican II, the ancient dream was kept alive among us by a kind of whisper campaign, while publicly the institutional church invested herself ever more heavily in the morality game.

Before going on to describe how the morality game works, I would like to avoid a possible misunderstanding. I am not at all disturbed about the situation as I have described it up to this point. It is hard to see how the institutional church could have gone any other way under the circumstances. Morality is a very important dimension of human life, and it is a good and helpful thing to promote it. We should be proud of the church for its commitment to morality. Then, too, we have to agree that we humans are capable of taking the most noble of dreams and prostituting them to self-interest. So the fear that we might do just that is certainly not groundless. Part of the agony of the contemporary church is that the Spirit seems to have judged it is now time to give top priority not to morality but to the ancient dream, and to live with the consequences, trusting in the presence of the Yahweh-God.

Human life is marked by passages and stages, and we seem to have arrived at that moment in our history when the dream of the coming Kingdom must replace morality in the top spot in the priorities of the Catholic Church. This does not mean the end of our commitment to morality. Just because it loses the top spot doesn't mean it isn't important and essential to Christian life. What it does mean is that the institutional church can no longer focus on morality; it is being called to center on the ancient dream of the reign of God. I am not disturbed so much over the fact that the church put morality in top spot for so long, as over how it eventually came to play that game. It is one thing to downplay the dream and pursue morality; it is quite another to pursue morality in ways that actually inhibit the coming of the Kingdom.

The morality game is a spin-off of the game of life, as we saw in Part One. Just as we had no say in whether we would play the game of life, so also we are automatically involved in morality simply because we live and are the sorts of beings we are. If we had no needs, desires, and interests, if we could not suffer death, pain, and disablement, or if we could not be deprived of freedom, pleasure, or our sense of self-worth, then and only then would we be exempted from playing the morality game. As it is, we are born into it. And we have also seen that the object of that game is to avoid and prevent the deliberate and unjustified infliction of ontic evil. Morality is primarily aimed at preventing ontic evils.

The rules of the morality game, the "moral rules," are derived by taking the ontic evils that most frustrate human needs, desires, and interests, and putting "Thou shalt not..." in front of them. Don't kill. Don't inflict pain. Don't maim. Don't deprive another of freedom and opportunity. Don't deprive another of pleasure. Don't deprive another of esteem and self-worth. Those are the six primary moral rules, but there are other secondary ones derived from these. Don't lie, is an example of such secondary rules. Lying is immoral because it causes pain, deprives people of opportunity, pleasure, or self-worth. So a "moral rule" is one that prohibits the infliction of the six primary ontic evils or prohibits certain other things because they invariably lead to the infliction of one or more of the primary evils. Of course no moral rule, primary or secondary, is absolute, because circumstances may arise when breaking the rule causes less ontic evil than keeping it. So the morality game is one in which the rules are at best "rules of thumb," rules that apply as stated only generally, all other things being equal.

Traditionally, the ten commandments are thought to be "moral rules." A moment's reflection, however, should make clear that not all of them are. Only the last seven are moral rules, because the first three are aimed at promoting some particular good, not at preventing ontic evil. Strictly speaking, then, the first three of the commandments are not moral rules at all. Not keeping the Sabbath may well fall below the level of the ideal presented in Judaeo-Christianity, but that act is not and should not be labeled immoral. If in the process of not keeping the Sabbath, I deliberately and unjustly inflict ontic evil, then my not keeping the Sabbath is immoral, but not because I did not keep the day holy, but because in not keeping it holy I did something else that was immoral. Nor should missing Mass on Sunday or eating meat on Friday have ever been called immoral. They inflict no ontic evil. They are breaches in achieving or promoting some good; they are failures to live an ideal, but they are not thereby immoral. As we have said from the start, where there is no infliction of ontic evil, there is no moral evil either.

Thus from the beginnings of our Judaeo-Christian tradition, from the time of the ten commandments, there has been confusion because the impression was given that failure to promote certain goods was immoral. The result of that has not been insignificant. This misunderstanding opened the door to allowing those in authority arbitrarily to label certain things immoral that have no foundation in ontic evil. What that comes down to, of course, is that in some instances things are said to be immoral for no other reason than that the church said they were.

If that sounds extreme, one need only reflect on what we were all taught about mortal sins. A mortal sin was a grievous matter, done with sufficient reflection and full consent of the will. So far so good. But we still don't know what a mortal sin is until we know what grievous matter is. Murder, rape and such things were obviously grievous matter; they were not slight matters at all, and still aren't. The horrendous ontic evil they inflict is obvious. But missing Mass on Sunday, eating meat on Friday, and all, I repeat *all,* violations of the sixth and ninth commandments (all sexual violations) were grievous matter. They were grievous *simply because the church said so.* This means that a mortal sin is whatever the church stipulates is a mortal sin. If that is not arbitrary, what is? But that was bound to happen, once moral evil was unhooked from its mooring in ontic evil.

Church and Kingdom Ideals

Although the confusion over moral evil occurred in good faith (after all, we find that confusion in the ten commandments themselves and throughout the whole of the Bible), it forced the institutional church to adopt some rather embarrassing positions throughout its history. In every age this reduced its credibility with nonbelievers and large numbers of believers as well. Moral evils that inflict ontic evil and personal failures that do not were treated as equivalent and punished as such. That in itself is an embarrassing posture to take, since human experience reveals that it is in the nature of things that actually inflicting ontic evil is much more malicious and destructive than failing to promote some good. In an effort to soften that embarrassment, it was suggested that the personal failures in question were really contrary to the will of God, and therefore were tantamount to disobedience, which was seen as an ontic evil. And so was born the "religious" view of moral evil.

As we have now come to understand, the Kingdom requirements are really of two sorts. First, there are those that require us to cease and desist from inflicting ontic evils, for example, the call to justice. Second, there are those that call us to personal growth as we walk with the Lord, for example, the call to greater intimacy and unconditional love. Obviously, all of the first sorts of requirements are also moral requirements. To violate them is not only to act against the Kingdom, but also to break a moral rule and to commit a moral evil. As already noted, moral evil always runs counter to the Kingdom because it unjustly inflicts ontic evil and hence violates the solidarity and justice requirement. We may call the first sort of requirements *Kingdom Rules,* to indicate that they are not only requirements of the Kingdom but of the moral rules (morality) as well. As used in this context, "rules" always attempt to regulate and prevent the infliction and spread of ontic evil.

The second sort of Kingdom requirements do not center on evil and its control at all. They center rather on promoting some good, on achieving something more of humankind's infinite potential in the face of everyday finitude. Violations of these requirements do not inflict any ontic evil; they simply mean I am not my best self; I have not responded to the fullest degree of my potential; I have failed to live up to the highest standards; I have not grown as much as I might have. We may call this second sort of requirement *Kingdom Ideals,* to indicate that they are not included in morality's struggle to control evil, but rather are precisely what we mean by morality's beyond, what promotes Yahweh's ancient dream, the good of the coming Kingdom.

Kingdom Rules and Kingdom Ideals have one important thing in common. The violations of each are obstacles to the ancient dream of Judaeo-Christianity, and when viewed from that perspective, both kinds of violations can be called sins. "Sin" is a religious and faith category, and as such is wider than the category "moral evil." *All moral evils are sins, but not all sins are moral evils.*

Sins are then of two sorts: 1) violations of the Kingdom Rules, which also happen to be moral evils; and 2) violations of the Kingdom Ideals, which are "sins" for believers even though they are not moral evils. It is because they were so keenly aware of their failures in living the dream of the Kingdom Ideals that so many of the great saints insisted on calling themselves "sinners." We find that impossible to understand if we restrict the terms "sin" to moral evils.

The fundamental difference between the Kingdom Rules and Kingdom Ideals is this: Apart from those tragic situations in which I am forced to choose between two evils and cannot avoid inflicting some ontic evil, it is generally possible to keep the Kingdom Rules reasonably well, if only I really want to. I am always at liberty, in the name of the Lord, to act morally, that is, to keep the Kingdom Rules. It is altogether otherwise with the Kingdom Ideals.

Endowed with a symbolic self with limitless potential, in the course of a single lifetime I can only realize a limited portion of that potential, never fully, always to this or that degree only. The Kingdom Ideals incarnated by the Lord and presented to us Christians as our highest vocation and aspiration always beckon us to more and more, and we die with the sound of that "more" still ringing in our ears. That is the way it is with ideals. They are *never* fully realizable. While such infinite possibilities excite and attract us as spirits, because they offer such spiritual promise, our organic and finite side shudders at the thought of trying to realize them. Kierkegaard, once again (*Journals,* 1823) puts that human ambiguity into words:

> Man naturally loves finitude. The introduction of ideals is to him the greatest agony; of course if it is introduced very poetically as

fascinating make-believe, well this he accepts with pleasure. But when the ideal is introduced as a requirement, a demand of faith, it is the most terrifying agony for man. . . . It shows him his own wretchedness. In the most painful way it keeps him in sleepless unrest; whereas finitude quiets him down in a life given over to enjoyment.

This means that ideals are also subversive, that is, they undermine our complacency that things are fine the way they are. They call us forth to a better future radically different from the way we are living now. And yet, without such terrifying ideals, human life would be devoid of all hope. We would be fated to live forever exactly as we do now and we would become spiritless.

As we can see, ideals capture perfectly the ambiguity of the human condition. They give us hope and hold out a better future. They attract and still frighten us because of the uncompromising nature of their demands, and simultaneously fill us with awe and sadness because they are at once so beautiful and so beyond our grasp. When it centers too much on the avoidance of evil, the institutional church misses the opportunity to do what she was established for, namely, to raise the ideal of the Kingdom to human consciousness and to help those who answer the call to cope with the ambiguity that ideal introduces into human lives. As a result, we are greatly impoverished.

We are truly impoverished when, instead of mounting the ancient dream and with loving compassion helping us cope with the added ambiguity that introduces into our lives, the institutional church chooses instead to play moral policeman. We really don't need all those silly threats of eternal damnation; life is difficult enough for us without them. By cajoling and engendering fear, by making us feel small and inadequate, by treating us like idiot children whose only task is to obey because Mother (church) knows best, the church becomes herself a countersign of the Kingdom.

The father in the Prodigal Son story (Luke 15:11-32) is a model of how the institutional church should treat its wayward (immoral) members. The father doesn't threaten or impose severe penalties; he forgives, unconditionally. He never even allows the wayward son to get his apology speech out of his mouth, but rushes to him, puts his arms about him, assures him of his love and forgiveness, and thereby incarnates the Kingdom dream right there for his wayward son to see. If only he has eyes. Nor does he act otherwise with the righteous son. When faced with the criticism that he had been made a fool of by the wayward son, and that by taking him back he is not showing sufficient appreciation for all that the righteous son had done, the father resorts to his only strategy. He mounts the dream for the older boy as well. Without criticism he assures him of his love and respect and says simply, "But he is your brother!" Again the dream is incarnated and brought to consciousness, and the father then leaves it to the freedom of his sons to determine how each will respond. Oh, to have such a church! Oh, to be such a church for others!

Church: Its Essential Ministry

The institutional church has fallen on hard times. It is often suggested that this is because of the secular, pagan, and hedonistic tone of our present culture. But the truth of the matter is that the hedonism and paganism of today are far less brutal, far less cruel, far less intense than before the coming of Christ and his church. No, if the institution has fallen on hard times, it must be because it has not been as fully "church" as it was meant to be. It has not pursued with vigor and enthusiasm its primary essential ministry. So it is that most of the young and growing numbers adults have simply come to the conclusion that if the institutional church were lost to us, nothing of great value would be missing from human life. I have tried to suggest that this is because the institutional church continues to view herself as "needed" and not as "given," and has opted to play the morality-song to the world rather than the much more beautiful and haunting Kingdom-song. Neither the drop in priestly vocations nor the defection of hundreds of thousands of its members has been sufficient to get it to change its tune.

All of this caused Avery Dulles to give this candid expression of the present situation in the United States (*Imaging the Church for the 80's,* a paper for the New York Province of the Jesuits, Fordham University, June 1980):

In America today there is lively interest in prayer and a widespread quest for transcendent experience. ... Yet for some reason the Catholic Church seems unable to capitalize on this yearning for spiritual experience felt by so many of our people. In the minds of most Americans, Catholic and non-Catholic, the prevailing image of the Catholic Church is highly institutional. The Church is understood in terms of dogmas, laws and hierarchical authorities which impose heavy demands of conformity. One may say that many think of the Church as a huge, impersonal machine set over against its own members. The hierarchy themselves are prisoners of the system they impose on others. Following the in-built logic of all large institutions, they do what makes for law and order in the Church rather than what Jesus himself would be likely to do.

I do not think the difficulty Dulles identifies is the result of the fact that the church is institutional, but rather because it has institutionalized the wrong dream, the wrong ministry. It thinks it is in the salvation business, and that its role as moral policeman is to interfere in people's lives to see whether they are pure enough and good enough to get to heaven. Thinking that, it has institutionalized itself to effectively carry out that mission. It is a mission and ministry that people not only don't need, but are more and more telling us they don't want.

If we look at church in its noninstitutionalized form, as the people of God, what do we find? *Church is, or should be, a movement of change in the world,* an attempt to transform the institutional relations within the world so that they can better express the Lord's dream of the coming Kingdom. *Church is, or should be, a movement of truth in the world,* challenging the world to see itself, in part at least, as a world of hatred, war, bitterness, poverty and bigotry. *Church is, or should be, a movement of light in the world,* a light enabling us humans to see ourselves in solidarity with one another, with *all* others, be they Christians or not. *Church is, or should be, a movement of freedom in the world,* a movement to free humans from irrational fears, unredeemed guilts, oppression and injustice. In effect, church is a movement to free us—*to love.* Church, then, *is* the risen Christ acting among and within human beings through his Spirit.

Do we have church today? Have we ever had church? Not really. We are always *becoming* church, becoming the Christ present to the world. Once we think of ourselves as *being* church, we are no longer church but a poor facsimile of it. As Kingdom people we are always becoming rather than being, for we are challenged to incarnate an ideal and dream we can never fully realize. But even though we are always in process of becoming church, we still can never give up trying to *be* church. For when we stop trying to be church, we say to the world that we are satisfied with things just as they are. We give up on the ancient dream. We are no longer a movement of change, truth, light, freedom, and love.

Where is church today? Look around and see for yourself. See where there is church and unchurch. Look at your family, your parish, your diocese. Look at any group of Christians with whom you share and with whom you work. Look and decide for yourself. For only you can answer in your own environment where there is church and where there is unchurch. *You will find church wherever a group of people, believing in Christ, and trusting in one another, are striving to move the world and transform it into the Kingdom.* That must be what we mean when we say proudly that we are the church!

If that is the way it is with the people of God, then the *essential ministry of the church that we "have" is to institutionalize the church that we "are."* That means that the institutional church must somehow encourage, foster, unify, orchestrate, and celebrate the Kingdom Ideals especially as incarnate in its own members, but also wherever they occur throughout humankind. It must do all that in such a way as to witness itself the presence of God, his unconditional love and forgiveness, the lordship of Christ, and the coming of the Kingdom. The first step in that task is to really believe in the people. Let us see why that is so.

Think back in your own life. What led you to walk with the Lord and become a person of faith? No one ever felt empowered to become a Kingdom-person because someone told them they were no good, or pointed out their faults, or put them down. No. We only find the courage to move forward toward love because people affirm us, trust us, and believe in us, and we just can't bear to disappoint them. People count on you, trust you, and see the greatness that is in you and you just can't let them down, because you want that vision they have of you to be true, to be justified. The most powerful force for conversion to Kingdom Ideals we have is the fact that people affirm us and believe in us. That is what strengthens our resolve to be converted out of egoism, greed, dishonesty, and self-indulgence, and opens us to the possibility of freely choosing to make the values of God's Kingdom preeminent in our lives. When we are believed in and affirmed, we find ourselves able to take on the Lord's own attitude toward life, that is, an attitude of mercy, forgiveness, love, poverty, compassion, peace, and joy. The church we "have" must begin by institutionalizing the Lord's own affirmation of and belief in his people.

That same truth can be put another way. We know that God is love (I John 4:8), but we take as a proof of that all that he does for people. If God is love, and if God really loves all of humankind as he professes, then we expect that he will show that love by doing great things for us, and giving good things to us. But is that really the epitome of love? If we look at our experience we find that quite often when people do things for us or give us things, it is for some ulterior motive. Even when I act from the most noble motives in the world in doing good for others, it is always possible for these people to resent it and to interpret my act as an attempt to make them beholden to me, or as some sort of a personally satisfying ego trip.

In any case, others can just as easily feel put down as enhanced by the gifts of my love. If love is to be judged by the things it does for or gives to others, it will always be open to a sinister interpretation. There is only one act of love that can never be so misinterpreted. It is so obviously an act of genuine love that the recipient cannot help but feel and be graced and enhanced by it.

The greatest of love's gifts is none of the good things it does or gives, but rather the fact that love really believes in the beloved. To believe in the other is the greatest thing love can do for them. It is the one thing love does that can never be distorted. (Recall how you feel, how buoyed up you are, when someone really believes in you. What a gift!) Well, as one might expect, God deals with humankind in precisely that way. Unlike the *religions* of the world, each of which is based on humankind's belief in God, the Judaeo-Christian *faith* is not; it is based on God's incredible belief in us. The Father did not intervene with power and strength to save Jesus from the cross, but he pledged himself to be with him as he suffered through it. More than that, the Father believed in Jesus even when from all appearances his life and mission appeared to have failed. And so it was that the Father subsequently raised him up.

The essential ministry of the institutional church is to publicly incarnate God's incredible love for us and belief in us. When it incarnates that love and belief, *something happens to us.* By what name shall we call this happening within us when the church that we "have" loves and believes in us? We feel ourselves "built up" by it; in short, we are edified. A detailed examination of that experience reveals that we detect a build-up of love within ourselves. We become more loving and more selfless than we might otherwise have been. Nothing else in life produces this same effect. Worldly success, no matter how splendid and ego affirming, is loveless and therefore cannot build up love in us. Take away love and belief and there is no one to build up and there are none who are built up.

When the institutional church opted to invest itself so heavily in the morality game, it was bound to look on us in unedifying ways, in ways that did not empower us, but rather paternalistically reduced us to passive recipients of spiritual goods. Small wonder that we so often lost heart and courage, were unable to grow toward love, and failed to more adequately respond to our vocation as Christians to become *signs* of the Kingdom. By clinging to its self-image of being "needed," it assumed a position of privilege, and ended up dominating rather than edifying us. Its moral theology became the domain of experts, and turned bookish and academic and out of touch with life, if not always rigid and inflexible. Once it gives up its privilege and power, admits it is not in the salvation business, the church will be more in touch with the experiences of its faith-filled members and will itself be empowered to run a pastoral morality for Kingdom-people. It is to one person's version of that kind of pastoral morality that we now turn.

Suggested Reading

Vincent Donovan, *Christianity Rediscovered,* Fides, 1978.

Louis Evely, *If the Church Is to Survive,* Doubleday, 1972.

Robert Fuller, *Adventures of a Collegial Parish,* Twenty-Third Publications, 1981.

Hans Kung, *Signposts for the Future,* Doubleday, 1978.

_____. *The Church,* Sheed & Ward, 1967.

Juan Luis Segundo, *The Community Called Church,* Orbis, 1973.

PART THREE

A CONTEMPORARY
PASTORAL LOOK

In an industrial and technological society, the word "pastoral" seems something of an anachronism. It is a word left over from a bygone age when families owned their own herds. The animals had to be cared for if the family was to survive. Tending them was a serious business of the highest self-interest, self-preservation. Were it not for the New Testament story of the Good Shepherd (John 10: 1-21) we might never have adopted the analogy of the shepherd as the model for priesthood. Consider, that shepherds always ended up fleecing and slaughtering their flocks, a strange image, indeed, through which to view the Christian priesthood. It is helpful, only if we agree to overlook the fact that the shepherd cares for the sheep *for his own interests,* and concentrate on the loving care he gives them regardless of his reason for doing so. There is a Good Shepherd story in the Old Testament that forms the context and background for the gospel parable, and it might be well for us to recall it here. We read in Ezechiel 34:1-16:

Son of man, prophesy against the shepherds of Israel. Thus says the Lord Yahweh: Woe to you shepherds of Israel who have been pasturing yourselves. Should not shepherds, rather, pasture their sheep? You have fed off their milk, worn their wool, and slaughtered the fatlings, but the sheep you have not pastured. You did not strengthen the weak or heal the sick, nor bind up the injured. You did not bring back the strayed, nor seek the lost, but you lorded it over them harshly and brutally. So they were scattered for lack of a shepherd, and became food for wild beasts. Therefore, shepherds, hear the word of the Lord Yahweh: As I live...I swear I am coming against such shepherds. I will claim back my sheep from them...I will save my sheep...I myself will look after them...I myself will pasture my sheep; I myself will give them rest...shepherding them rightly.

Jesus is called the "Good Shepherd" because he represents the fulfillment of the Lord Yahweh's oath to come himself to shepherd his people. The oath mentioned in Ezechiel finds its fulfillment in the Lord Jesus, who henceforth will "shepherd the people rightly." Unfortunately, those who shepherd in Jesus' name have not always "shepherded rightly," and so we have always had those who, like the shepherds of ancient Israel, have "lorded it over the people harshly and brutally."

Most Catholics have run into both kinds. Indeed, whenever Catholics gather, they are bound to end up swapping "pastor stories," in much the same way as soldiers trade "sergeant stories." Such stories are an integral part of the lore of any local church. It is the "pastor" who exercises ecclesiastical authority at the parish level, where we cannot help but have contact with him in our everyday dealings with the church. The power of his office has touched our lives for good or ill. Consequently, some of our pastor stories are edifying and wonderfully touching, while others of them are horror stories of the first magnitude, all of which shows that being "pastor" does not insure that one will "shepherd rightly" or be "truly pastoral."

With apologies to all those priests and pastors whose devotion and care have been exemplary, I want to pursue just a bit further this matter of pastors who are not pastoral. Though things are changing, my experience is that "nonpastoral" pastors are still in the majority. Such men are not malicious, so how are we to account for their situation and our predicament?

Over a hundred years ago, Soren Kierkegaard came up with an answer when evaluating the situation of his day, an evaluation that sounds strangely contemporary. He wrote in his *Journals* (Hong & Hong ed. 3187) on May 17, 1855:

> What is a pastor? Pastors are those unhappy creatures who in the days of their youth got a wrong perspective on Christianity and as adults do not have the strength to tear themselves out of the error into which they have come, and now do the greatest harm in the name of Christianity. More and more men are becoming increasingly doubtful of the pastor, that what he says is not his own conviction but is something official, with the result that the pastor is more and more in the habit of putting up a bold front. So it is my opinion that a pastor is the unhappiest of persons.

Evidently, the first requirement to be "pastoral" is that as a youth one not get a wrong perspective on Christianity, but if one does, then the person as an adult has to have the courage and strength to give it up. This seems to apply not only to pastors but to each of us as well, and should show the wrongheadedness of those Catholics still trying desperately to hold on to their pre-Vatican II church. It is really impossible to be pastorally present to another person if I have a mistaken notion of the Christian agenda. For as will become clear, being pastoral is not solely a function of any ecclesiastical office or special ministry, but is rather the Christian's way of being present to other people in a caring and loving way. In the past, our erroneous notion of what the Yahweh-God was about and our rigid dogmatic and moral stands made it practically impossible for the ordained and the nonordained alike to be present to others in a truly pastoral way.

Once I am freed from my erroneous understandings of the faith, it becomes easier for me to fulfill the second and major requirement for being a pastoral person: *that I know, love, and believe in people, and that I allow them to know, love, and believe in me.* Though I have elsewhere called this "redemptive intimacy," in the present context let us refer to this second requirement for being pastoral as the human connection. Being pastoral is a way of relating to other people out of Christian faith, properly understood. We have already seen that means having a proper understanding of the unconditional love and forgiveness of God, of the ancient dream of Yahweh incarnated in the Lord Jesus, of the liberating and redeeming presence of God within all of humankind, and finally of the authentic role of the institutional church in the whole process.

In April 1978 I had the opportunity to make a presentation before members of the U.S. Bishops' Committee on the Laity, and on that occasion I tried to indicate that the human connection was the central point in the ministry of priests.

> I know this will be painful, but I feel obliged to say it. Our current understanding of priesthood is bad news because it is divisive of church. It separates priests from the rest of us because they are the ones with the power, the power to forgive sins, and consecrate bread and wine. (I speak only of sacramental power although administrative power could be used as well, whereby priests sometimes tend to dominate their people.) To look at the priest as the "man with the power" is a most unfortunate view of ordained priests. It is unfortunate because it divides them off from the rest of us as persons with special powers, and that can hardly be termed good news—for them or for us. But that was surely bound to happen once priestly powers, which are secondary and peripheral at best, are made out to be the essence of priesthood. I don't for a moment deny such powers, but I don't think they are the essence of priesthood.

> Ordained priesthood is or ought to be unbelievably good news for each of us because in any age it is the priest who is called upon to *incarnate for his people the Lord's own faith in them.* The priest ministers to his people not primarily by leading them (leadership may well be a charism located elsewhere in the community) but primarily by *incarnating God's incredible love of and belief in them.* Whenever that has occurred, you never have anti-clericalism (because you don't have clericalism) or hear anyone talking about the divisions between priest and lay people—for they have become the Lord—together.

What I was trying to say was that it is not because priests have power that they are thereby empowered to be pastoral. No. The reverse is true. Being pastoral is what confers on the priest his power and authority with his people.

Consider the Lord. Jesus, the Nazarene carpenter, burst upon the religious scene of his day with an authority the likes of which the world had never seen. Yet he gave no orders, exacted no obediences, meted out no punishments. All of which goes against the accepted view of authority as the right and power to command obedience, a view, so Scripture tells us, that Jesus explicitly rejected (Matthew 20:25-28). Jesus, the Good Shepherd, shared a vision of new life and invited others to live it, trusting that they were capable of doing so. He healed others of the obstacles that stood in the way of that new life. He confronted the structures in his society that crushed his people and forestalled the coming of the Kingdom. In short, he was pastoral. As a result, people were fascinated with him and he had great authority with them. To have authority is to have the people hear the deepest aspirations of their own hearts when you speak. It was that way with Jesus, and so it is, or is supposed to be, with us. Those who, operating out of a wrong perspective on Christianity, "lord it over us harshly and brutally," may hold ecclasiastical offices but they lack authority since they are unwilling or unable to speak to us "in the name of the Lord." But thanks be to God, there are others, ordained and nonordained, who continue in our day to accept the Lord's invitation to be truly pastoral persons in his name.

The chapters of Part Three take a contemporary "pastoral" look at matters of some importance to the adult faith community. Chapter 7 addresses itself to two widespread misunderstandings that skewer efforts at being pastoral with ourselves or with others, such as the absolutely erroneous accounts we continue to hear bandied about regarding devils, hell, and the meaning of salvation. These are the very sorts of misunderstandings that Kierkegaard told us we acquire in our youth and that cause us, as adults, to do the greatest harm in the name of Christianity.

Chapter 8 tries to get clear on the requirements and characteristics of being a pastoral person, and to present a pastoral view of morality along with some contemporary theological accounts of sin.

Chapter 9 is devoted to taking a contemporary pastoral view of human sexuality and marriage. Chapter 10 does the same thing for the most troublesome sexual issues facing the adult faith community these days. Chapter 11 takes a contemporary pastoral look at the highly volatile life and death issues: abortion and euthanasia. In Chapter 12 we are concerned to treat the "justice" issue, an area in which the moral rules are most widely violated in our culture. The book concludes with some pastoral considerations of reconciliation, the theme of Chapter 13.

CHAPTER SEVEN

Hell, Devils, and All That

I have often asked myself why it is that I so often find myself at odds with the traditional wisdom of the church. If one is honest with oneself at moments in which questions like that arise, she cannot help but wonder whether it is merely pride or self-aggrandizement that motivates her. After all, why would I think that I am called to take up the cudgels against the whole Christian tradition? Down through the ages people with far greater faith, intelligence, and sanctity than I possess seem to have been at peace with the tradition. Isn't going against such people just a bit too pompous to be authentic? Possibly. Yet, as the dedication of this book claims, that same tradition has done an awful lot of harm as well. Were that not the case, I suppose I could be at peace about being silent. But in the light of the tremendous amount of ontic evil unnecessarily inflicted on women and men down through the ages by the tradition, even someone like myself feels compelled to speak out. There is no area where this seems more urgent, I would think, than regarding hell, devils, and all the horror stories that have arisen around those themes.

The Pastoral Use of Fear

Consider the following. In the 1913 edition of the *Dictionnaire de Theologie Catholique,* in the article "Hell" (Vol. V, col. 118-119) we read:

> From a pastoral point of view, one must ask whether it is useful to preach on hell in our day, and human wisdom tends to respond, no. True traditional wisdom has thought otherwise. Certainly, it is always better to come to Jesus because of love, but fear is capable of leading to love, even fear of hell. It is necessary to temper that fear with love, but it is also necessary to engender love of God through fear of his chastisements, and to avoid sin by the thought of the divine sanction, i.e. hell. Now that fear is just as necessary today as it was of old, because human nature is always basically the same.

It is bad enough that one would recommend the engendering of fear (even for so noble a motive as the subsequent engendering of love), but to do so in the name of being "pastoral" is really more than one can be expected to swallow. I, for one, cannot. We were able, in Part Two of this book, to present the essentials of Christian faith without even once alluding to "hell" or "devils." Not only is it possible to do so, it is recommended that it be so done. More than that, in my judgment if one wants to be "truly pastoral," it is positively required.

If there is any message that comes through loud and clear in the Judaeo-Christian Scriptures, it is that we are to "be not afraid"! Over and over, we are told to set aside our foolish fears because the Lord God is with us. Now while it might make sense psychologically to speak of making the journey to love through the intermediate stage of fear, pastorally it is counterproductive. It is counterproductive precisely because whatever you say about "hell" and "devils" is really something said about God. We have already seen that much of what we Christians say about God turns out to be slander and defamation of character, and this is nowhere more true than in our discussions of hell and devils. (This is why I am so wary about even attempting to write this chapter.)

With the best intentions in the world, around the turn of the century the liturgical rubrics of the Roman Catholic Church stipulated that the Prayer to St. Michael was to be said after all low Masses. So it was that in my youth every time we went to Mass (if it wasn't a high or sung Mass) we prayed together:

St. Michael the Archangel, defend us in battle. Be our protection against the wiles and snares of the devil. Restrain him, O God, we humbly beseech thee. And do thou, O Prince of the Heavenly Host, by the power of God, cast into hell Satan and all the other evil spirits who prowl about the world seeking the destruction of souls. Amen.

Certainly if the situation is as it is described in that prayer, no one could fault the church for requiring its people to pray it. Indeed, if the world is invaded by Satan and his minions of evil spirits, who in hellish hordes go about their devilish business sight unseen, then humankind desperately needs help against such unseen foes, and what better strategy than to invoke the help of our unseen benefactors?

Such a view of the world is an unacceptable vestige of the ancient dualism against which Israel constantly battled and which remains so prevalent in fundamentalist Christian circles. In its ancient version, there were two supreme beings—one, the God of Light and the other, the God of Darkness. Human beings were the pawns each used in its struggle with the other. Now ancient Israel knew full well that there was no God but Yahweh, and so the Persian god of evil was demoted from its divine status and became a creature who had become evil by revolting against Yahweh. That way the absolute supremacy of Yahweh was protected. But at a price. To be an evil adversary of God and still remain a creature meant that God became implicated in evil, at least to the degree that he allows the creature free reign of humankind. That became a problem as the book of Job attests, but evidently it was thought to be worth it, if only God's supremacy was unquestioned. To this day, those who talk so knowingly of "devils" and "hell" cannot help but implicate God in inflicting evil on humankind, whether they mean to or not.

It is always better to leave such subjects unaddressed, not only because it is pastorally destructive to engender fear, not only because you end up inadvertently implicating God in the infliction of evil on humankind; but primarily because the truth is that when we speak about "devils" and such, we don't know what we are talking about! That is why I am somewhat amazed to find myself writing a chapter on this subject. As will become clear, the reason I thought I would never do such a thing is because *I don't know anything about either devils or hell.* I don't mean that I don't know what most Catholics know about those things; after all, I have been reared with those stories just like many others. And like others, I believed them for a good portion of my life. But then something happened, one of those revelatory experiences, after which things are never quite the same. Since then, whenever I have been asked about devils or hell in public, I have told the questioner to go talk to someone else who knows about such things, because I honestly do not. To many, I am sure, that seemed like a ploy I used to get off the hook, and to avoid having to make an embarrassing public denial. But that was not the case. I really do not know. And what is more, neither does anyone else, be she pope or pastor. By sharing a revelatory experience that had such a profound effect on my life, I shall explain why.

"What About Hell, Daddy?"

Like so many of the wise insights I have been gifted with during my life, this one occurred in the bosom of my family. Families are like that. They are seedbeds of wisdom if only we be alert to that fact. In any case, it happened one weekend when I was left alone with my children, a salutary experience for any father, and one that makes him all the more appreciative of his wife. The four college-age boys were in school but living at home, and our two daughters were in the early grades. It was a Friday, and so it fell to me to fix dinner for the family, something at which I was barely adequate and by no means expert. I could have used some help, but the boys, as is often true of college students, were living busy lives of their own and were involved in studying or so they said, and were cloistered in their second-story rooms. They were too busy to help, but they always came running at the sound of the dinner bell.

My youngest daughter must have sensed my plight, for she came over to ask me if she could help. As I tended the large six-burner stove as if it were an intricate machine requiring constant attention, I set my daughter about the task of setting the table. After a while, I realized I could not hear the usual noises that come from shuffling plates and silverware. I glanced over at the kitchen table, and there Ruth was, her head in her hands, tears streaming down her face. "Ruth Ann, what's wrong?" I asked. She replied, "Oh Daddy, I'm scared." Totally unstrung by the suddenness of it all, I remember saying to myself, "Oh God, she's having her period. Where's her mother when you really need her?" A bizarre thought, I admit, since Ruth was in the third grade at the time.

I shut down the stove, bringing dinner preparation to a full stop. I called up to the boys, not without some satisfaction: "Dinner will be late!" (Served them right for not helping!) Then I took Ruth in my arms, carried her into the living room, and with all the paternal tenderness I could muster, asked, "Now, Ruth, what are you so scared about?" Sobbing, she managed to get it out through her tears, "Daddy, I'm scared I'm going to hell!" Under other circumstances I would have been tempted to laugh out loud. But one look at Ruth told me she was dead serious, and I was filled with consternation. How could this very conscientious, loving and faith-filled little girl have come to such an horrendous conclusion?

Well, it turned out that that day in class, the sister had been talking about heaven, hell, and purgatory. Ruth had gotten upset at school and began asking the sister (who is a personal friend of mine, by the way) very difficult questions about it all. Finally, wishing to get on with the class, she said, "Ruth, why don't you go home tonight and ask your father!" Docile as always, that's exactly what she had done. And now the ball was in my court. Perhaps it was possible to handle it deftly and quickly and not make too much of a big thing of it. Well, it was worth trying.

"Ruth, do you remember the words of your favorite song?"

"I think so, Daddy. Let's see. They go: Do not be afraid for I am with you, I have called you by your name and you are mine." "And do you believe that, Ruth? I mean, do you *really* believe those words?" "Oh yes, Daddy, I *really* do believe them." "Well then, don't you see that you have nothing to be afraid of? He has called you by your name, and you are his." With that she brightened considerably and I was able to put her down. I excused myself to return to my scullery and my dinner preparations. As I walked back to the kitchen, I was congratulating myself. "Well now, that wasn't too hard was it? I think you did a marvelous job, if I do say so myself." And then it happened. As I was about to turn into the kitchen out of Ruth's sight, she asked, "Daddy! Daddy! Then, what about hell?"

I knew in that instant why sister had sent her home! I stopped in my tracks and with my back still to her I remember praying, "Lord, this is not the question of a student in class. Nor of someone attending a public lecture. Lord, this is my own flesh and blood, this is my youngest child, this is my daughter. What do I say to her? I don't know what I think about hell, Lord. Please help me. And don't let me hurt the little one."

With that, I turned to face Ruth. She was standing with her legs apart and her hands on her hips, and you could feel the defiance in her. She was not stupid. If God made her, and if God called each by name and holds each in the palm of his hand, then what about hell? It made no sense. My daughter was questioning not only me, but the whole of the Christian tradition. Where were all those teachers and theologians now? That weighty matter was going to be definitively settled, for good or ill, in my own living room. *I* was going to have to do it. And I didn't have the vaguest idea what to say to my daughter.

She was about twenty feet away from me, but I moved only very slowly toward her stalling for time. I was well aware that I didn't know what to say. Nonetheless, as I passed the ten-foot mark, I noticed that I was talking and that I was answering her question. I was fascinated by the whole thing, and thought to myself, "I'd better pay attention to what this guy is saying, because I don't know the answer." And, of course, the "guy" was me. I don't know where it came from, but this is what came out of my mouth on that Friday evening a decade ago:

Ruth Ann, do you know the three hardest words for a teacher to say? Well, I'll tell you. The words are *"I don't know!"* I don't know what it is with teachers, but they find it difficult to admit that they don't know. And the church is no different. The Lord invites us to walk with him, and he tells us that if we do we shall have life as we have never known it before, and that we need never be afraid. And if we try to bargain with him and ask, "But what will happen if I don't walk with you?" the Lord remains silent. He merely repeats his invitation to "Come walk with me." And that's how the Lord did it, Ruth.

Now the church realized that there was no answer to the question, "What happens if we don't walk with you?" but it wasn't happy with that situation. It wanted an answer to that question. It is a teacher after all, so it didn't like having to say, "I don't know what will happen if you don't walk with the Lord." So it invented a story it could use to frighten people into walking with the Lord. That story has been told so often now down through the ages that people have forgotten that the real answer to the question is, I don't know!

And Ruth Ann, when I tell you that *I* don't know about hell and all that stuff, I mean it. But what is more *no one else does either*. No matter what they tell you—they don't know either. The Lord calls us in faith to walk with him, and tells us that if we do, we need never be afraid. For those who want to bargain or haggle with him, and ask what will happen if they don't—there is no answer. No one knows. All we have is that made up story. But the truth is we really don't know.

Ruth seemed considerably consoled by what I had said. Her fear and her defiance had melted away, and she seemed to be at peace. Next morning, as I later learned, she went to school, walked up to the sister in question and said with authority, "My Daddy says that hell is a story *you* made up!" Well, that's not *exactly* what I said. But that's not bad for a third grader.

As for myself, the incident has had a profound effect on me. For one thing, I learned that sometimes our prayers are answered immediately. I prayed not to harm my own child. Not only did it not harm her, it benefited me as I came to understand what I did not previously know. Though the normal way to learn something is from experience over a long period, the Lord can facilitate the whole process by revealing something to you in the blink of an eye. When that happens, you are profoundly aware of his presence.

Secondly, from the moment that I spoke those words to my daughter, I never doubted that they were true. It now seems to me to be so true that I cannot understand why it was that I had to come to that understanding so late in the game.

Thirdly, the incident has raised in my mind the question of just how many other areas of Christian doctrine and morals there are in which the appropriate answer to the central question is, "I don't know," and we have been traditionally afraid to admit it. I wondered about that a lot of the time and promised myself that I would eventually look into it. Alas, I still have not had the time to do it, but it remains an important item on my agenda.

And finally, if ever I had to learn that the engendering of fear was a pastoral mistake and psychologically counterproductive, I learned it that day. Ever since, whenever I have been asked about devils or hell in public, I have simply said that I don't know. If questioners are serious about getting answers to those sorts of questions, I tell them to talk to people who claim to know about such things. (Sometimes I have added that I do not think those people really know anything about those matters either, but more often than not I have, until now, kept that to myself.)

We Really Don't Know

Of course, there are many Christians who really believe that they do most certainly "know" about hell, devils, and all that. Goodly numbers of those people think that such knowledge is integral to the Christian story and hence essential for salvation. To those in the latter group, not much can be said, because to tamper with their understanding of devils and hell is to temper with their faith. It is to be expected that they simply refuse to change their minds on so important an issue. My remarks are therefore addressed to the former group—those who think they know something about devils and hell, but are open to being convinced otherwise. I would remind such persons that the main reason we think we know something about devils and what lies in store for those who don't walk with the Lord is because Scripture is filled with stories that "seem" to give us that kind of information. But do they?

Since I have already given a "pastoral" account of Scripture elsewhere (see *Redemptive Intimacy*, pp. 35-45), there is no need to repeat it here. I would merely add that it is by no means obligatory to take the accounts of Satan, devils, and demons that occur in the Bible as literal accounts. They are, to some people, to be taken as "evidence" that such things actually exist. That is the crassest kind of fundamentalism, which we have already seen leads us into trouble on many other fronts as well. I would grant that to take Scripture literally requires one to accept the existence of Satan and other evil spirits, but it also gives rise to the Monster-God, that cruel caricature of the God of faith. As we have seen, people of faith need not go that route. Indeed they cannot. But to have said all that still does not tell us what we are to make of the "devil stories" in Scripture. (Those interested in a detailed answer to that question are referred to two helpful books by Richard Woods. See his *The Occult Revolution,* Herder & Herder, 1971, pp. 121-130; and *The Devil,* Thomas More, 1973.)

If we recall that the Old and New Testaments are the faith accounts of God's presence and his marvelous works first among the Jewish people, and next in the first Christian communities, then we have a context for understanding all those infernal "devil stories." The Good News in both the Old and New Testaments is that God loves us, that he dwells with us, and that his salvific presence transforms not only human hearts, but our world as well. As was their custom, the ancient writers personified whatever opposed and contradicted the ancient dream of Yahweh. That personified entity became known as "The Adversary," which is more of a title than a name. "Satan" comes from the Hebrew which means "to oppose," to be against"; it names a stance, a lifestyle, a situation, and is not a proper name. Just as "Santa Claus" embodies the "spirit of Christmas," so "Satan" embodies the "spirit of hatred for the human and opposition to the Kingdom." With the poetic license so characteristic of ancient peoples, this evil spirit was personified, and has come to be seen as the source of all counter-Kingdom evils.

We know that Santa Claus does not actually exist, but the spirit of Christmas most certainly does. So the story of Santa Claus is not without meaning or reality to us, even though he doesn't exist. So it is with Satan. It is precisely because the spirit of evil and of opposition to the Kingdom exists in our world that the story of Satan still remains meaningful and real for us even today. This remains true even if we deny that devils exist and prowl the world seeking our destruction. It is just that the meaningfulness of the story of Satan is not a function of his actually existing. What then is the significance, for faith, of Satan?

As we have seen in earlier chapters, *all moral evil without exception originates with us.* If anything is clear from the Genesis story, it is that sin entered the world by means of human agency. But there is something peculiar about moral evil. It acts like a gas when it is released from a small pressured cylinder; it expands to fill all available speace. What started out small and compact, easily controlled, suddenly assumes proportions that put it beyond our control. The moral evil we introduce into our world does not always remain small and insignificant, merely the evil of one lone individual. It can join with the residue of evil from preceding generations; it can mix with the evil of others and take on the power of an atomic reaction, far exceeding the powers of its originating causes. This is especially true when the moral evil of individuals becomes institutionized, and the taken-for-granted way things are done. Before we know it, if we're not careful, it has moved beyond our control by quantum leaps. This common human experience with uncontrollable evil led ancient peoples to attribute it to a superior and malevolent agent, the devil. Soon the situation gets completely out of hand, and we would lose hope were it not for our belief in the salvific acts of God.

The truth is that we have no incontrovertible evidence of the existence of super-malevolent agents. *We are the only sources of moral evil there are in the world!* It is common knowledge that when people hear of a case of demonic obsession or possession, the number of such cases increases dramatically. The power of suggestion in this area is so great that the church has prudently suggested that exorcisms be very private affairs, so as not to trigger mass hysteria. There is no absolute evidence that such possessions are not of psychological origin. After all, when the ancients spoke of "evil spirits," they were talking about what they took to be the causes of physical and mental disorders in humans. We cannot be sure that any of the alleged cases of possession were in fact such. There are in every such case elements of uncertainty and ambiguity. The fact is, we really don't know, and it is pastorally irresponsible to act and speak as if we did.

It is no different with "hell." We have already seen that the Kingdom is not primarily a place but a state of being, so it should come as no surprise to find that hell isn't a geographical location either. Just as "Satan" is a symbol of the state of alienation, division, the lack of solidarity that has marked human existence from the beginning, and will continue to mark it until the Kingdom fully comes, so the "fires of hell" take their origin from the "fires of Gehenna," which had special meaning for every believing Jew.

South and west of the ancient city of Jerusalem (Jebus) there was a place called the Valley of Ben Hinnom, and it was for the Jews of old what places like Dachau and Auschwitz are for my generation. For it was in the Valley of Hinnom that humans (most likely, children) were sacrificed to the pagan god Molech in the days of Jeremiah and Isaiah. The usual method of immolation was by consuming the sacrificial offering by fire. In time, when Israel ruled the territory and Jerusalem was the capital, the Hinnom Valley, known as Gehenna, became the city garbage dump where Jewish garbage was burned as an insult to the old pagan cult and god. And as with such dumps, the fires constantly smoldered, emitting stench and smoke into the air, and at night you could see the glow, and from time to time there were flashes and flare-ups of flames. Lepers and those with communicable diseases were forced out of the city for health reasons, and they took up life in Gehenna, foraging for food amid the garbage. Life there was so utterly awful that Gehenna became the symbol of life apart from the community, separated from God's people outside the coming Kingdom. As such, it became the symbol of the ultimate in punishments. A suitable place, all Jews would agree, for the enemies of Yahweh. The union of the Satan and Gehenna stories was so logical as to be inevitable. If Satin the Adversary represented the counter-Kingdom spirit, and if Gehenna was the place that in Jewish experience best incarnated that same spirit, how logical to have Satan dwell in Gehenna/hell. Of course, over the centuries the rabbis and Christian thinkers have embellished the ancient stories until we have today the devil and hell stories with which we are all so familiar. But however helpful those stories are as symbolic and poetic expressions of our deepest fears and aspirations, they do not really give us one iota of hard information about what is to happen to us if we choose to reject the Lord's invitation to be his Kingdom-people. After all the stories, after all is said and done, to the question: "What about hell and devils?" the most truthful answer remains: *We honestly don't know.*

Salvation, Liberation, and Eternal Life

"Yes," you may say, "that may be so, but surely we know about heaven, don't we?" I'm afraid not. After all the stories about heaven have been told, the bottom line is still best captured by St. Paul paraphrasing Isaiah: "Eye has not seen, nor ear heard, nor has it entered into the mind of man to conceive what God has prepared for those that love him" (I Corinthians 2:9).

We have become so accustomed to thinking that somehow the Judaeo-Christian tradition has privileged knowledge about the afterlife that the suggestion that this is not the case probably strikes us as absurd. We will need more time to digest the suggestion that our descriptions of both heaven and hell are anthropomorphisms, that is, stories we have created to answer our needs and not revelations from God as to exactly how it is going to be with us after death. As John Shea has told us (*What a Modern Catholic Believes About Heaven and Hell,* Thomas More, 1972, pp. 91-92):

> All descriptions of the afterlife...share in the same fundamental human dynamic. They are not literal descriptions of what happens beyond the grave but symbolic extensions of man's hope and fear. ... The law of language about the future life is that it is in-

curably anthropomorphic. It is a mistake to smile at the "great fish fry in the sky" of *Green Pastures* as the product of black fantasy and think rapt contemplation of the three divine persons is the real thing. Both conceptions spring from the same imaginative technique. ... The truth of the symbolic representations of heaven and hell lies in their ability to express and make real the true nature of man's hopes and fears. As for that death which all move toward hesitantly, perhaps the most useful virtue man can take with him is a capacity for surprise.

In typical Shea fashion, he speaks of the ability to be surprised, which is a classier way of saying that when it comes to the future life, we simply don't know.

In addition to being a bootless task, when the Christian centers her concern on the future life, she adopts an obviously "religious" perspective, thus verifying the Marxist dictum that religion is an opiate that deadens concern for the problems of this life. The truth is that Scripture has very little to say about the future life; it speaks rather of "life," "abundant life," and "eternal life." Too often it is simply assumed that eternal life *is* future life, but that cannot be so. Eternal life as "eternal" cannot begin at some time in the future. It must be a never-ending, ongoing life of some sort. But that would mean that if it were available to us we could live it now. In faith, we know that such a life has always been available to humankind from the very first moment of its existence. Were it not so, such a life could hardly qualify as "eternal."

In the minds of most Catholics, eternal life is not even a possibility in the present; it is rather the reward God will give in the future to those who have lived good lives. In his epistles and gospel John speaks often of "eternal life," but he speaks of it in this future sense only once (I John 2:25). On every other occasion when he uses the term, he speaks of the present graced life of Christians, living in faith, believing in Christ, and living the Kingdom values. Eternal life is our living now the life of the age to come when the Kingdom will be fully realized among us (see John 17:3; I John 5:11). Despite all that, eternal life remains in the popular religious mind a future reward, not a present gift to and possibility for humankind.

A similar fate befalls the notion of "salvation," which can be given a religious or a faith interpretation. Religiously speaking, salvation, like eternal life, is a future reality we shall only achieve after we die. For we shall know for sure whether we have been saved from sin or not only at death. If we have, we shall receive the rewards of eternal life, which is what most mean by "salvation." But the faith perspective sees salvation in a different light, one that brings salvation down to the present moment and makes of it not only an event in the life of an individual, but of a people, indeed all people as well.

We have already seen that sin is a disorder in creation, a lack of solidarity between us human beings with one another and with our God. To be saved from sin means precisely to be freed and liberated from that alienation and division, which means entering the Kingdom, becoming a Kingdom-person. But that is something that can and does occur every day. The Kingdom-persons we know in our lives attest to that. Still we are tempted to think of salvation in purely individualistic terms. But if salvation is deliverance from sin, and if sin is a function of disordered relationships throughout creation but especially throughout the human race, then salvation is a communal enterprise that can only be fully achieved with the coming of the Kingdom. Put another way, salvation is an equilibrium or right ordering of all the elements in creation. So the achievement of that right order is a progressive affair, inscribed in human history, and cannot be merely the successful journey of individual persons. Salvation means that all humankind is freed and liberated from sin. Obviously, that process takes more than a single lifetime, and involves the great-time—God's time—history.

What that comes down to is this. I, alone, cannot be saved. For however good and loving, however sinless I may be, I cannot, myself, bring about the right order between myself and others. For that, they too must enter the picture. Salvation means all of us coming together in solidarity and freedom, relating aright to one another, to our environment, and to our God. When we so personalize salvation that my only concern is my own "getting to heaven," we adopt a religious perspective and overlook the primary objective of faith—the coming of the Kingdom.

A Final Caution

Soren Kierkegaard spoke of how a wrong perspective on Christianity acquired in childhood does not go away, but remains to skewer our adult faith and leads us to do great harm in the name of Christianity. We must have or acquire the courage and strength to "tear ourselves out of the error" if we want to avoid those consequences. It seems to me that there are two such errors currently plaguing the adult faith community in our day, making it difficult, if not impossible, for us to be truly pastoral with one another. We must somehow find the strength to tear ourselves away from thinking and talking about hell, devils, and all that. It is unnecessary and is positively harmful to boot. And we must resist the temptation to give credence to the resurgent stories of the fundamentalists on those issues. We only engender fear and a misunderstanding of God and his ways when we talk that way.

Secondly, it is long past the time for North American Catholics to understand the real meaning and dimension of salvation and of our accepting Jesus as Lord and savior. Faith is not an insurance policy for heaven taken out on individual lives and having individual persons as beneficiaries. Salvation is just another name for that ancient dream of Yahweh, the God of Exodus and freedom, who calls us to transform not only our own individual lives but our world as well.

Once we have torn ourselves away from the misunderstandings of childhood on such issues, we can then address ourselves with profit to the problems of adult morality. To those issues we now turn.

SUGGESTED READING

Ruth Nande Ausben, *The Reality of the Devil: Evil in Man,* Harper & Row, 1972.

John Shea, *What A Modern Catholic Believes About Heaven and Hell,* Thomas More, 1972.

Richard Woods, *The Occult Revolution,* Herder & Herder, 1971, pp. 121-130.

_____. *The Devil,* Thomas More, 1973.

_____. "The Devil, Evil and Christian Experience," *Listening,* Vol. XII, No. 2 (Spring 1977), pp. 21-42.

CHAPTER EIGHT

Traditional Morality and Sin

Each one of us has done something in our lifetime for which we are not very proud. It is something we wish now we hadn't done, and even at the time of our doing it, we had a sense of ambiguity about the whole thing. Or maybe it isn't something in our past at all. Perhaps we're presently involved in something we know is not in accord with either Kingdom (moral) rules or Kingdom ideals, but despite the ambiguity this introduces into our lives as Christians, we have not yet arrived at the point where we can give it up. In other words, we're *human* and we're *sinners,* and what is more, we know that for a fact. We don't talk about that fact much in public; after all, we want others to view us in the light of our highest aspirations and dreams. Unfortunately, given the human condition, that is not always realistic or possible. The question is, at those difficult times when it is not, what would be the most "pastoral" way for someone to relate to us? Were we to answer that question, we probably would come up with a pretty accurate description of what it means to be "truly pastoral," or "to shepherd rightly." The best way to find out who's really pastoral in your parish is to talk to the more obvious sinners. They'll always know!

I suppose what we would want most in the situation where *we* are the obvious sinner is that the pastoral person be understanding. Which means what? That she be patient with us, not condemn us, not issue dire warnings of the consequences, and that she remain open and caring in our regard despite the mess into which we've gotten ourselves. Of course, by relating to us in that way, the "pastoral person" incarnates the dream from which we have deviated and calls us forth out of darkness just by being present as that kind of person. That is a pretty tall order. We want the pastoral people in our lives to be *not* like us! Obviously, there aren't nearly enough such persons around. In the preceding chapter, we saw some of the things that prevent otherwise loving Christians from being "pastoral" in the sense just described. Now let us look at some of the things that help Christians like you and me, sinners though we are, become the pastoral persons we'd like to encounter when we're bogged down in sin.

The Human Connection

When, as sinners, we say we want the pastoral person in our lives to be understanding, we speak better than we know. As incarnate spirits endowed with self-consciousness, we aspire to become what we think. If I am a teacher, I am drawn to become what I think a good teacher ought to be. If I am a lawyer, I have an image of what a lawyer should be like, and I invariably try to move in that direction. If I am a member of a street gang, I have a notion of what a street gang member should be like, and I have an attraction toward becoming that way. It is no different with being Christian and pastoral. We first have an understanding of what it means to be those things, which is why one's theology is so important. My theology of sin and of being pastoral will determine how I am present to others, especially when they are obviously struggling with sin.

The pastoral person sincerely *believes* in the nobility and goodness of human beings. Why? First of all, because she finds that goodness within herself. Since she is not unique in that regard, she supposes that her fellow humans do also. This must mean that sin did not totally obliterate the likeness to God (*imago Dei*) with which we were created. Original sin there may be in us, but there is also an original righteousness we experience even in the depths of degradation. That can only be because in our depths we remain disposed to goodness. Having discovered that fact about herself, the pastoral person recognizes it in others, in *all* others, regardless of what they may be doing with their lives at present.

Secondly, she believes in human goodness, because she knows by faith that human freedom is not a pure arbitrariness, attracted equally to good and evil. No, the human will is not neutral, but hungers for the good, and is predisposed to it. That is why William James observed, "The nobler thing just tastes better to us, and that's all that can be said about it." The call to goodness is the voice of our human nature. The moral life is not based on any imperative coming to us from without; it is the response of our very being to reality. To not answer that call, to be temporarily involved in rejecting it, is tantamount to spiritual suicide. Thus, there is no need to threaten. One must merely call the other forth to be her own best self and live. When a sinner hears that from another, she hears the invitation of her own deepest nature.

The pastoral person is *sensitive* to the great burdens we carry, for no other reason than that we are human. That sensitivity is born of her own coping with the Existential Dilemma, the Ontological Paradox, and the Moral Predicament. It is not easy to be human, much less to be most authentically so. She experiences that struggle within herself, and so is compassionate when facing someone whose coping mechanisms are inadequate or sinful. Instead of focusing exclusively on the evil unjustly inflicted on others by the sinner, she recognizes the fact that the sinner must live with the realization that she has wounded and hurt other people, and that she is not the sort of person she thought she was or ought to be. Moral evil is destructive not only of others, but of the sinner's own self-esteem and self-worth. To heal the latter is to correct the former, so the pastoral persons begin there.

The pastoral person *recognizes* that human life is a journey with many stages, and that because we are deeply involved in sin at one stage of our development does not mean that we always shall be. More than that, she knows that there can be backsliding as well as growth in human development, and she works toward the goals of having the journey as a whole turn out all right. It is always too early to condemn, for as the English colloquialism has it, "One swallow does not a summer make." And to have a stormy and sinful adolescence, young adulthood, or mid-life passage does not necessarily make for a wasted or evil life. Often people simply grow up, move out of their sin and get beyond it. Not without the grace of God, of course. But knowing this, the pastoral person can see the sinner's present predicament in the context of that person's life as a whole. She knows that "one's life as a whole" is far more important in the long run than any single individual act, be it sinful or virtuous. All the votes are not yet in, so there is always reason to hope.

This understanding of the human condition that the pastoral person has makes her less judgmental and more caring of others. She exhibits a willingness to become involved in another's groping for what is right. Aware that growth toward being fully and authentically human can only be facilitated, and not caused, by another, she makes herself available to the other as "gift" rather than as authority figure or disciplinarian.

In keeping with that posture, she does not attempt to give answers to the moral dilemmas of others. Caught up in the ambiguity of her own life, and fully conscious of the uniqueness of every moral situation, she is more concerned with helping others clear away the obstacles from their past, which inhibit them from seeing themselves for what they really are, and hence from being able to judge the present moral situation for what it really is.

Finally, she always manages to manifest in word and deed the ancient dream of Yahweh of the coming Kingdom, that "beyond" that transcends mere morality and was pefectly incarnated for others in the Lord. She knows that as Christians we are called not only to avoid immorality and sin, but are called to become

Kingdom-persons, that is those whose very lives witness the presence of the Lord God in all of humankind. By being such a Kingdom-person for the other, she stirs and excites the hunger for goodness deep within the sinner, engendering hope and energizing potentialities for goodness perhaps long forgotten. May each of us have such a pastoral person in our lives when we find ourselves losing sight of the dream and caught up in sin!

Traditional Catholic Moral Teaching

In every age of the church there have always been pastoral persons such as I have just described. But in ages past, the traditional Catholic moral teaching would have been, if not a direct obstacle to be surmounted, at least the source of very little encouragement to becoming pastoral in that way. The pastoral person is just too tentative, too uncertain, too open to other possibilities to be fully compatible with morality as traditionally taught. For if anything is the hallmark of traditional Catholic moral teaching, it is the absolute certainty with which it was presented. It seemed to have clear-cut and definitive answers for practically every moral dilemma.

Although certainty is appropriate in some contexts and comforting in others, that supposes it is authentic and true. As we have seen, it does little good, and may do great harm, to be certain about hell and devils on the basis of Scripture, when it turns out Scripture offers little reason for such certainty. Actually, its mythic and storied nature requires us to be uncertain about such matters. But given the far-reaching ambiguity of the human condition, there will always be something very attractive about certainty, whether it be authentic or not. So it was in the former ages of the church. To have a church with all the answers and with absolute certainty about its moral proclamations was seen as a boon and a blessing. Even today, one hears the church praised for maintaining that posture in the face of recent developments that show it to be largely a pose—a pose to which the hierarchical church still clings, despite the evidence to the contrary presented by its moral theologians since Vatican II. Like the Emperor in the Hans Christian Andersen fairy tale, the church counts on its members not to take public notice of its nakedness. But there is always the child in each of us who can't help but blurt out the truth.

The fact is that there are growing numbers of responsible Catholic moral theologians calling for changes in the church's teaching on contraception, sterilization, divorce and remarriage, abortion, euthanasia, etc. More and more lay people are also in open disagreement with the church's public stands on these and related issues. What is more, there is not only disagreement over what is taught by the hierarchical church, but also over the methodology used to arrive at its moral stance. Rome remains reluctant even to admit that such growing disagreement is occurring, fearful of the effect on the faithful, were they to find out that she has been naked all along. But that seems a frivolous reason for resisting the truth, because in their hearts the faithful have known of the nakedness for centuries, and have loved and appreciated the church nonetheless. The truth will set us all free, free of having to sustain in public a position we all know to be a pose. It is time for the hierarchical church to give up its traditional approach to moral matters, since it was never really true, and now is no longer persuasive. That she will be forced to do so is as inevitable as the sunrise.

At the heart of that traditional approach and methodology is the familiar recourse to natural law, but natural law understood in a very restricted and specialized way. Far from wanting to abandon natural law as an element in moral discourse, contemporary moral theologians reject only a particular interpretation of natural law, the interpretation chosen by the hierarchical church. To interpret natural law differently would lead to conclusions far different from those that the hierarchical church has made normative for Catholics.

The very expression "natural law" seems to indicate something that applies to the humanity and rationality of all human persons. It sounds as if it is something all humans share in common and should therefore be something about which human beings are in agreement. That is what one would expect, and in a way, that is why the church has recourse to natural law in its thinking, because what is moral or immoral according to natural law would be so for all of humankind and not just for believers. How then are we to account for the fact that when the church proclaims that birth control, extramarital sex, abortion, euthanasia, etc. are against the natural law, we suddenly find ourselves divided from many of our sisters and brothers? It cannot be that they are unenlightened compared to Catholics, because we are talking about "natural law," something amenable to every rational adult. Because it is "natural," it takes no special revelation to know it. It must be due to the fact that the traditional Catholic understanding of natural law runs amok somewhere, and therefore no longer receives the communally-funded support of all rational, right-thinking persons. Where did it go wrong?

There seems to be agreement with the fact that natural law is unwritten; that it is not created by human beings but is rather dicovered by them; that it is not a specific code of rules but rather an innate tendency by which the morality of all human-made codes and rules are measured; that it has some basic constancy about it, not being subject to change at the whim of individual human beings. On that the Catholic tradition and the common tradition and experience of humankind seem to agree. The disagreement begins when the Catholic tradition goes on to say that it is human nature, and *human nature alone,* that determines what the person ought to do. But why is that a problem? It seems totally righteaded to say we ought to act as befits a human person. Of course it is righteaded to say that, but that is not what the traditional Catholic understanding of natural law means. If it meant only that, there would be no disagreement. What the tradition is saying is that what befits us as persons is never something we are to work out; it has already been determined by the kind of beings we are, that is, by our human nature. This, of course, is just another way of saying that we are "determined" by our natures.

Such an account would make perfect sense if we were horses, or cows, or living things without self-awareness. For, lacking self-awareness, what befits us is precisely what nature dictates. What seems to have been overlooked in the Catholic tradition on natural law is that the beings endowed with human nature are spirits, albeit incarnate spirits, who therefore happen also to be "persons." As persons endowed with self-awareness, they cannot be determined by their natures, because they are called, at least within certain limits, to fashion them in some sense. As Rabbi Heschel observed (*Who Is Man?* Stanford Univ. Press, 1973, pp. 7-8):

> Statements about man magnetize the inner space of man. We not only describe the "nature" of man, we fashion it. We become what we think of ourselves. Thus the truth of a theory about man is either creative or irrelevant, but never merely descriptive. A theory about man enters his consciousness, determines his self-understanding, and modifies his very existence. A person is in his thoughts, particularly in the way in which he knows or understands his own self. His thoughts are his situation. *His nature includes what he thinks he is.*

The fact of the matter is that the traditional Catholic understanding of natural law is not the only or even the best way to interpret it. Without malice, our tradition has focused on an understanding of natural law that undermines personal creativity and freedom, and thus ends up denigrating the human. Human nature, unlike the natures of lesser beings, is a spiritual nature, which means it is an open nature, capable of being finally determined only by the person herself. As Sirach (Ecclesiasticus) 14:15 suggests, "In the beginning, God made man, and left him in the hands of his own counsel." We are not so much subject to natural law as we are invited to creatively incarnate it. Or in Herb Hartmann's happy phrase, "Just as God *is* the eternal law, so man *is* natural law." The problem, then, is not that Catholics hold a theory of natural law, but rather that we are being asked to adopt the most crude and inadequate of such theories. That was bound to lead to serious problems when it came time to use it in fashioning moral pronouncements.

The textbook example of that, of course, is the current state of affairs regarding artificial contraception, or birth control. Any interference with the possible fruitfulness of an act of sexual intercourse is labeled "unnatural." The "natural" thing to do is to have intercourse with no artificial barriers to possible conception. That isn't natural; it is primitive. It says that because originally human beings didn't quite understand the reproductive processes, and hence were unable to control them, now that they do makes no difference in human nature, and we must proceed as if we didn't know how to control human reproduction. We are determined, as it were, by our biology. What is overlooked is the fact that with new self-awareness and new knowledge, human nature changes. As John Macquarrie put it, "The pill and the condom are now part of human nature."

What has led to all the trouble is that human nature was conceived as a closed natural system, complete in itself, rather than as personal and hence open to possibilities as limitless as the human mind. It simply will not do, then, to describe what is befitting humans as that which is in accord with their nature, seen as something fixed. Rather, what is befitting is that which, among all the possibilities, we are able to conceive as leading to the most authentic personal and human life. As we shall see in a subsequent chapter, what is troublesome for Christians about the use of contraceptives is not that they are somehow "unnatural," but rather that they can so easily become instruments of depersonalization and hence contrary to Kingdom-ideals. But we shall leave that discussion for later.

Aside from the fact that the hierarchical church adopted an inadequate version of natural law, the constant recourse to natural law theory in its moral pronouncements turned the thinking on such matters into a primarily deductive enterprise. This means that one began with a set of general moral principles and proceeded to derive conclusions about concrete cases almost exclusively in the light of those principles. This gave the appearance of stability and great certainty to its conclusions. When those natural law conclusions were subsequently promulgated with the additional weight of the church's ordinary teaching authority, the appearance of apodictic certainty was almost overwhelming. In that methodology, human experience counted for little, and historical development was ruled out, since the conclusions were timeless. However sympathetic the hierarchical church was to the ambiguities and vagaries of the everyday lives of its members, it saw itself as having its hands tied, because what was derived from natural law and promulgated with authority just could not be changed. That seems to be particularly the way it is right now with regard to birth control, euthanasia, and divorce. The experiences of faith-filled Catholics cry out for a less rigid approach to those matters, and the usual legalistic response is that nothing can be done—that's just the way it is. Were the church to change its stand on those issues, it would betray the "tradition," and fail in its mission.

Contemporary moral theologians are busy at work, proposing alternative approaches and methodologies which, while remaining faithful to the spirit of the Catholic tradition, do greater justice to the experience of believers. They seem to be calling for the hierarchical church to realize that the growing dissent among real believers on moral issues may not be due to the fact that they are being corrupted by the world, but rather to the fact that the church has claimed a kind of certainty in such matters that simply cannot be attained.

The classic example of that is the reaction of clergy and people alike to Pope Paul VI's encyclical *Humanae Vitae,* which reaffirmed the traditional Catholic stance on birth control for the traditional reasons. Theologians are now suggesting to the church that it not make such moral pronouncements in the future, but that it rather present the ideals of Christian living, leaving the judgment about what is morally right and what is morally wrong to the individual consciences of the people. This is an interesting development among Catholics, particularly at a time when we are seeing the resurgence of fundamentalist movements, which in their own Protestant way also run amok, undermining the dignity and grandeur of the human person in the name of misguided moral certainty.

Portraits of Sin

Another problem brought about by the traditional recourse to natural law is the criticism that by basing its moral teaching so completely on natural law, the church fails to present to the world a specifically "Christian" moral teaching. There doesn't seem to be anything particularly "Christian" or "faith-filled" about a natural law account of moral evil. Where does the Lord enter the picture?

Where do the demands of the Kingdom-ideals fit in? What seems called for among Catholics, who have traditionally leaned so heavily on natural law, is a more faith-filled approach, one that would speak more directly about sin as a theological or faith category, and not merely about moral evil and natural law, which are philosophical.

1. Louis Monden on Sin

A major contribution to this discussion was made about twenty years ago by the Belgian Jesuit, Louis Monden, whose *Sin, Liberty & Law* (Sheed & Ward, 1965) remains a seminal book in the "new Catholic morality" and still well worth reading after all this time. My first reading of that marvelous book was one of the most liberating experiences of my adult faith life. I still recommend it as the best way for those in mid-life to begin the study of contemporary Catholic moral theory. The sketchy account of his major contributions that follows does not do the book justice, and certainly is no substitute for reading it. Because his language is technical in places, I have to put it into more simplified language.

Monden distinguishes three distinct levels of human guilt, and he describes the "fault" that causes guilt feelings on each of these levels. Only the third level is distinctively "Christian." That means that we really encounter "sin" only on level three, and prior to that we are concerned with something else. Nonetheless, for purposes of this discussion we need not be quite so precise and technical. I have taken the liberty of referring to the three levels simply by Sin I, Sin II, and Sin III.

Sin I is a "fault" at the level of instinct. It is not exclusively human, for it can also be observed in domesticated animals. When your dog wets the carpeting, and you come upon the scene, the dog immediately runs under the couch to hide, giving all the signs of feeling "guilty." It isn't really guilt, because the dog is not a free and conscious moral agent. The dog exhibits what might better be called anticipatory anxiety, knowing full well that you will come after him with a rolled-up newspaper. The dog has no real understanding of what he has done, but from the sound of your voice ("Bad dog!") and your reactions in the past, it has an instinctive sense that all is not right. Cowering under the couch with his tail between his legs, head hung low, eyes downcast, he gives all the outward appearances of feeling "guilty."

Monden suggests that human beings can experience "guilt" in much the same way, instinctively and without full understanding. We sense we have done something wrong; we feel "guilty" and we anticipate some sort of punishment. Sin I is doing something unacceptable; it does not take into account the inner disposition of the doer. Imagine how you would feel if you were giving a dinner party and you discovered to your horror, as the guests were being seated, that in the rush you had inadvertently put all the forks on the right! Why, that is just never done! That's instinctive guilt, and that is what Sin I is.

The essential characteristic of Sin I is that it is always the breaking of a rule or law imposed on one from without. Monden suggests that there are Christians whose view of "sin" never gets beyond this instinctive level. The requirements of the moral law are never internalized, and actions are judged to be moral or immoral simply according to whether they materially transgress a rule or law imposed from without. As we saw earlier, this is the "religious" view of sin, the one that those of us in mid-life first encountered in second grade. This is "sin" in its most primitive and childish form.

Under normal circumstances, one cannot sustain that childish view of sin indefinitely, though some people try very hard to do so. If one is reflective and awake to what life teaches, she will inevitably find that at some moment in her life she will have an experience that catapults her out of her Sin I consciousness into the next level.

That experience can come at any time in life, but whenever it occurs, let us call it "turning 21," morally speaking. I suddenly see that evil/sin is not simply breaking a rule or law. I have a moment of insight when I finally catch on. The reason there are rules and laws is not because the rulemaker or the lawgiver wants to exert dominance and exact obedience. The reason for the rules or laws is because when I break them I am actually hurting myself. I am mutilating myself as person. I am making it impossible to grow. So the law is really there to protect me; conforming to it is in my best interests. Breaking the moral law or rules is truncating and hindering my own self-realization. When that fact dawns on a person, she has reached her moral majority, she has "turned 21." But those who have, have reached the level of Sin II.

Whenever I knowingly and willingly engage in actions I recognize as inhibiting my personal growth and self-realization, I commit Sin II. If Sin I is an offense against an external lawgiver, the Sin II is an offense against oneself.

I remember reading Monden and being completely convinced by what I read. For some time before that, I had been totally dissatisfied with the way I was going to confession. Here I was in adult life, still going to confession in much the same way I did in second grade. Reading Monden gave me, or so I thought, a way to break out of my childish ways. I realized that I had been going to confession as if "sin" were really Sin I. So it seemed natural that I should take the next step and move on to the Sin II level. But would the priest understand? What happened next was another growthful experience that makes quite a good story.

If I was going to "break out," I wanted to find a priest who would be likely to understand my predicament. We had just gotten a new young priest in our parish, and I remember walking over to the church one Saturday afternoon with Monden under my arm. I peeked in and found to my utter amazement that the new priest had decorated his confessional. It had little Christmas tree lights all over the outside, and in the penitent's compartments there was a single colorful spotlight illuminating the wall hangings or banners there. On the one side was a banner proclaiming in immense letters: "Jesus Christ has risen, Alleluia." And on the other side were wall hangings with the word "Yes" in different scripts and sizes all over them. When you walked in that side, it was as if someone were saying, Yes! Yes! Yes!...a hundred times or more. Well, I thought this was a godsend; it was just the kind of a priest I had been looking for. I cautiously entered the confessional, the one with all the Yes's. He was hearing another confession so I had to wait a bit.

As I waited, I tried to psyche myself up for what I was sure was going to be a precious moment. I told myself that I was definitely going to break out of my childish ways, and I cautioned myself not to begin with the usual rote formula: "Bless me, Father, for I have sinned . . . ." If this was going to be a "breakout," it had to be totally different, I told myself. I was perspiring profusely as I waited. I was scared. But I was determined that this was it!

Suddenly I heard the familiar sound as he slid the little door back. In that instant, my resolve was gone and instinctively I began, "Bless me, Father . . . ." But I caught myself in mid-sentence and continued after only the slightest pause: ". . . for I have sinned *against myself.*" I then told my tale of how I had wounded myself by my actions since my last confession. I finished, and breathlessly waited for the priest's response.

There was a pause that seemed like eternity. Then the little cloth that covered the confessional window was slowly raised so he could see me eyeball to eyeball. He said, "You are either a saint, or you are crazy!" Dumbfounded, I responded, "I'm no saint, Father." Then in panic, I took the copy of Monden I had been clutching in my hands, reached out of the confessional into the priest's compartment, and handed it to him. I said, "Read this, Father, and I'll be back next week!" I then got up and practically ran out of the church, feeling like a complete idiot and cursing myself for my continued confessional immaturity.

Next week never came. It wasn't my fault, however. Our pastor was so outraged by the flamboyant decorations of the confessional that the young priest was summarily transferred and I never saw him again. I didn't mind that so much, but he took my copy of Monden with him!

Seriously, the insight I spoke of came to me in that intervening week. No wonder the priest hadn't known what to say—there is no need for confession on Monden's Sin II level. Indeed, it makes no sense there. If Sin II is self-destructive, all that is required is to realize the fact in order to be immediately resolved not to do it again. Sin II remains a totally humanistic category, a totally private and individual affair; God never enters the picture. Reconciliation is a Christian sacrament for which there is no place on the level of Sin II. I had made a terrible blunder. If I had wanted to break out of my Sin I ways in the context of confession, it was not enough to have "turned 21." I would have to move on to the level of Sin III, for it was only there that one explicitly encounters the Lord, his church, and the dream of the Kingdom.

For the person of faith, sin is not primarily breaking the law, or inflicing a wound preventing self-realization. Sin is saying no to God's gracious invitation to loving intimacy with him. Sin is more than a "no" to the law; it is more than a "no" to self-realization. It is a "no" to Love itself, and to his call for us to witness his presence. The believer sees every refusal of that sort as sin. As such, it is a betrayal of the baptismal covenant, which, having been broken, requires recommitment in reconciliation. Sin III is saying no to God's invitation to love. That, for Monden, is the most appropriate meaning of "sin." It can never be simply doing something materially evil. In addition, it must rend the covenantal relationship with the Lord and with other Christians, and short-circuit not only human self-realization, but the process of our divinization as well.

Monden's most significant contribution to the current moral dialogue was not his distinction of the three levels of sin, but rather his distinction between *choice* and *option*. It is a logical consequence of his position regarding Sin III, but it proved to be quite revolutionary. It effectively put the discussion of sin on a whole new plane; it opened up exciting new pastoral possibilities; it cast new light on the traditional distinction between mortal and venial sin. This is reason enough to explain why the book continues to be read with profit almost twenty years later.

An astute student of the human condition, Monden knew that human beings are not always wholehearted in what they do. There is often an ambiguity and an inner dividedness in both our good and evil actions. He refers specifically to a parable found only in Matthew (21:28-30):

There was a man who had two sons. He approached the elder and said, "Son, go out and work in the vineyard today." The son replied, "I am on my way, sir" but he never went. Then the man said the same thing to his second son. This son said in reply, "No, I will not"; but afterwards he regretted and went.

Assuming that each son acted in freedom, what does their behavior reveal? Monden theorized that human freedom is exercised on two different levels, profoundly on the deepest level of the person, and less profoundly, more on the surface of our lives. The exercise of the deeper-level freedom accounts for who we really are as persons; the exercise of freedom on the less profound level accounts for what we *do*. Monden calls that profound exercise of freedom *fundamental option,* and the less profound *object-choice.*

The sons of the parable in Matthew 21 each made an initial object-choice that was not in accord with his fundamental option, but pulled himself together and subsequently made a second object-choice that was an accurate expression of his fundamental option or orientation. Monden theorized that for a human person to act in the fullness of freedom, it was necessary that her object-choice be in accord with her fundamental option. Our freest acts are those flowing from a choice that incarnates our fundamental option. While object-choices are varied and manifold and "offer an infinite number of possibilities," Monden thinks with his account of Sin III very much in mind that "the fundamental option is made between a 'yes' and a 'no' in which man, as spirit, unconditionally commits or refuses himself." He concludes then that our object-choices will have greater or lesser freedom depending on the degree they share in the freedom of the fundamental option.

This insight had profound repercussions on the traditional Catholic account of mortal sin. In the old moral theology, a "mortal sin" was grievous matter, done with sufficient reflection and full consent of the will. Put simply, it was something seriously evil, done in freedom. But Monden's account of what constitutes freedom allows Catholics to look at "mortal" sin in a whole new light. Take the example of an adolescent boy masturbating. If that is done knowingly and willingly, then it is a mortal sin by traditional standards. But Monden would say that it is not so easy to determine whether the lad committed a "mortal" sin or not. One would first have to know whether his object-choice was so profound as to alter and change his fundamental option, wherein he said yes to God and the invitation to love. Unless it changes that fundamental yes to a no, it cannot be death-dealing (mortal) sin. By definition, a mortal sin will always be one that kills the "yes" to God at my center.

What makes that so revolutionary for Catholics is the fact that it requires us to take into account a person's life as a whole as expressed in her fundamental option when judging, if not her actions, at least the effect of them on her moral status. By Monden's account, there are obviously fewer "mortal" sins than we were led to believe, according to the traditional account. Monden's account is also much more in keeping with our own experience, in which we often find ourselves involved in destructive object-choices but remain committed to our yes to God and the ancient dream. The implications of that are far-reaching, and moral theologians are still trying to come to grips with them today. They, at least, are trying, while the hierarchical church seems to be proceeding as if Monden had never happened. But happen he did, and we are all the richer for it.

2. John Shea on Sin

Lately, we have also been greatly enriched by the work of one of our theologians, John Shea, who has been called the premier Catholic theologian in the United States. One can hardly avoid being enriched by an encounter with any one of his many works. In the present context, *What A Modern Catholic Believes About Sin* (Thomas More, 1971) calls for special attention. With his consummate skill and insight, he gives a brilliant account of a post-Vatican II understanding of sin, an account that gives the average Catholic access to and a feeling for the contemporary moral perspective of the experts. Once again, this brief summary is meant to encourage the reader to read Shea, not to render that wonderfully growthful experience unnecessary.

Shea understands the predicament of the modern Catholic. With all the changes, we don't talk much about sin because we really don't know what to say. Our vocabulary is bankrupt, since what we learned in grade school is no longer adequate. It no longer suffices because there has been a shift away from seeing sin as a "breaking of commandments"; "it" is now seen as the "rupturing of relationships." Then, too, in the past we were accustomed to identifying sin with moral evil, but Shea thinks it makes no sense to talk about "sin" unless you view the action in question as having been done "before God." As we have already seen, "sin" is a faith category, not a philosophical one. So "sin" points to the faith dimension of our lives; it is a violation of the personal bond between God and his people. One can get a handle on this difference by noting that the opposite of moral evil is moral good, but the opposite of sin is grace. "Grace" is the word we Christians use for our intimate union with God, and "sin" is the word for the rupturing of that union and of our being alienated from God.

If that is so, then it is important, as Shea says, that we not allow our sense of sin to fade from our lives. We must recapture an authentic sense of sin. At its root, sin is the death of the human because it cuts us off from the very source of our humanization, God. The question of sin is always a question of whether and how we respond to God. Sin contradicts not only God's law, but God himself. It is possible, Shea thinks, to get a good picture of sin by looking at the God of faith, and identifying those human actions that contradict what God is. That is "sin."

First of all, God *is* love, and so he loves. The sinner manipulates. Our love is never quite completely other-centered. Our love is a mix of self-interest and concern for others. To the degree that we use or manipulate others for our own interests, we are unlike God and we are in sin.

Secondly, God realizes his power in intimacy and dialogue. The sinner attempts to dominate others through force. More than anything, this seems to mark our age; indeed, the twentieth century could be called the century of violence. Rejecting dialogue and intimacy, while resorting to force against my fellows—that too contradicts who God *is* and involves us in sin.

Thirdly, God is truth, and he calls us to truth. The sinner is a deceiver. God remains ever faithful to his word, while we so often do not. Sham, duplicity, and artifice mark our relations with one another. When we so act, we again contradict the very being of God, with the inevitable consequence that we are in sin.

So "sin" can be described, according to Shea, as dominating, manipulative deceit in our relationship with God and with one another. An examination of our conscience will reveal that in our every effort to love there are vestiges of manipulation. In all our attempts at dialogue and intimacy there is the shadow of domination. We need the truth if we would ever be set free, yet we give in to deceit, especially its most pervasive form—self-deceit. Fortunately, our God is love, and knowing us as he does, he does not demand immediate purity of action in all these areas, but rather issues a call for us to recognize the vestiges of sin in our lives and to constantly struggle against them. For when we cease to struggle against our inclinations to manipulation, domination, and deceit, then we are solidly in sin. Once that happens, the logic of sin is such that we then grow deaf to the call of God, become frozen in our proud and sinful lifestyle, and hence more and more dehumanized. Should sin ever become completely victorious in our lives, then we would no longer be human, no longer persons; we would have become reduced to the status of things.

Shea then goes on to talk of the "power" of sin. The real power of sin is not found in the individual sinner, but in the society and culture. Sin becomes established in a culture; it gains a reputation and can even become the traditional way of doing things. When that happens, it is all the more difficult for individuals to choose rightly. The sinner may be blind because of his sin, but sin itself is not blind. Hardly. It embodies a definite set of values, proceeds toward definite goals, moves in a definite direction. The direction of sin is threefold: inward, backward, and deathward.

The momentum of sin is *inward,* that is, away from concern for others and toward making oneself supreme. The momentum of sin is *backward,* that is, away from the future and the coming Kingdom, and back toward a time when the presence of God in humankind was even more obscured than it is now. And finally, the momentum of sin is *deathward,* which is to say, away from the newness of abundant life that the Lord came to insure for each of us. If the truth be told, the world left to itself seems to move irrevocably in a sinful direction, that is inward, backward, and deathward. We have not been left to ourselves, however, as we know full well in faith. God is gracefully present to all of humankind, counteracting the momentum of sin, helping to give to human life the momentum of grace, which will one day culminate in the Kingdom.

So it is that "church" is a people who struggle to give human life the direction Jesus gave it, that is, outward, forward, and toward resurrection. As a community, church attempts to form a countersituation to the situation of sin, namely, the situation of grace, of union with God. The task of the church is to "situate humankind in grace," to provide the environment where true human possibilities can be realized. The battle imagery so prevalent in the past, along with its stories of devils, is being replaced by one of evolution toward freedom and the Kingdom—that is, toward the future that humankind finds modeled in the life of Jesus.

That, in outline, is John Shea's contemporary portrait of "sin." My rendering hardly captures the literary artistry with which John Shea always writes. For that, the reader is directed to the book itself. It is a classy and classic account of "sin" from the contemporary perspective.

3. Leo Mahon on Sin

A final protrait of sin comes from the most pastoral person I know, Leo Mahon. He is pastor at St. Victor's parish in Chicago, and prefers to proclaim Good News rather than write it. He is a preacher of special talent, so I am unable to refer to a book. But I have been fortunate enough to be present with a tape recorder when Leo Mahon was doing his thing. I am, therefore, in a position to share his thoughts on sin with you.

Since Leo Mahon is a great storyteller, I'd like to share a story he told, and then add some interpretive remarks he made about it. First the story.

> Once upon a time, a long time ago, a child was born, a brawling male child, a large infant. And that infant grew up and passed through its awkward stages but never got over its awkwardness. He became a man, a very strong, big man, who turned out to be awkward, almost graceless. He could vary from fits of towering rage to a kind of strange meekness. At times, he'd exhibit qualities of genius, and at

other times he was incredibly stupid. At times he would be sensitive, at other times completely insensitive. He had enormous strength, but was very torn, a very anguished person. Then into that man's life came a woman. Very small, very supple, very loving. And she began to teach him things. How to value his past. How to have hope for the future. How to be patient with himself and his own condition. How to celebrate life a little bit. But the encounter between them wasn't always peaceful. At times they wouldn't even talk at all. At times they shouted at one another instead of dialoguing, but sometimes they got together. And there is no way to tell you how this story came out between the man and the woman, because that encounter is still going on. Because that man is humankind. And the woman? Well, the woman is the church, the People of God.

A marvelous story, which Leo further explained as follows. The man in the story (humankind) is a big, strong being, awkward, very ambiguous, and seriously wounded. He is wounded by his own lusts; for money, for sex, and for power. In other words, the man indulged in loves that demeaned him and made him less than he really ought to be. The worship of these three lusts put together is what we generally call "paganism." Paganism so understood is the condition of humankind. I don't want to say that the man is irredeemable, because he isn't. There is great, great good in him: genius, generosity at times, even purity at times, but it is all mixed up.

And the woman? The woman is God's own plan, an alternative to the man's paganism. God started it all with Abraham. He said, "We must present an alternative lifestyle to the paganism of humankind." So God called Abraham out of his own land, and from there built a people through Moses and culminating in Christ Jesus. That people is powerless when compared to humankind, not nearly as intelligent, not nearly so strong, not nearly so shrewd, but far more loving, and far more focused.

So the dialogue between them began. It was not always successful, and sometimes the woman became worse than the man. But there were times, the times of the great men and women of faith, when there was a real dialogue between them, and a real alternative lifestyle was presented to the man (humankind). And the man learned something from the woman (that is, from the people who were a sign of God's presence), namely, that there is another way toward greatness, toward goodness, toward real happiness, indeed toward life itself.

Jesus incarnated that alternative lifestyle. Disciples gathered around him two thousand years ago, and we're still doing it today. We're trying to walk with the Lord and so we say, "Lord, we want to live your style, not just for ourselves, but we believe that we're the only salvation for the world, in the sense that we've got to give the world an option. There must be another way besides the killing of self and of others, besides the debasing and manipulation that goes on." It ought to disturb us as we wonder whether we are any different from the rest of the world. If not, then we are no longer the woman, we are no longer church. We are called to present an antidote, a counterculture to the paganism still rampant in our world today.

Mahon's point, of course, is that Christian morality is more a matter of lifestyle than doing individually good acts. He sees Christians as called to greatness in the drama of the world's salvation, not merely to some sort of personal goodness. And it is in the light of that position that he went on, on another occasion, to give the following account of "sin."

While visiting my class in the Pastoral Institute of Loyola University one summer day, one of the students asked him to comment on "sin." Leo Mahon gave a most provocative and helpful response, as I have found he always does.

It is becoming more and more clear that true sin is always in the singular. We have two levels of sin to be concerned with. One is "sins" (in the plural) and this is where most people get stuck. We conducted confession for hundreds of years never getting beyond "sins," never getting to the "sin" underneath the "sins." "Sin" (in the singular) is not only *not* choosing the good, but it is actually denying it. "Sin" is bitterness; that is the essential sin, and it is a rejection of life. If you reject life, you reject God who is the author and very substance of life. If you are mad at life, then you are mad at God. God is not a person off some place; God is *person, is life,* is *love.* So if you are out of love, then you don't love God. "Sin" is bitterness, resentment, personal alienation, and it causes all kinds of things on the level of "sins." So the point is to start by getting down to the real thing—"sin"—then the "sins" will take care of themselves.

We all know very good, religious people, and we don't want to make fun of them, who have a very hard time finding any "sins" in their lives, but who are full of "sin," that is, bitterness. Let us not judge them. We also know people who are called "sinners," people who are full of "sins," but there isn't an ounce of "sin" in them. They are delightful people. The Lord told us that remarkable story of the Prodigal Son (Luke 15:11-32). The younger boy was full of "sins," and the older boy was full of "sin," but had none of the former. It is very clear from the parable who the real troublemaker was, the older boy.

What should we do about that? First of all, we must recognize sin for what it is. The difference between "sin" and "sins" is so important that someone should have told us about it. It takes years to discover that on your own. We spend so much time working on "sins" that we overlook something far more detrimental right down in the heart of us. Bitterness. We have to get rid of "sin" just out of legitimate self-defense. Being bitter is like swallowing acid; it will eventually tear you apart and eat right through you. There is no way to remain bitter, and live! Bitterness is always more destructive of you than of the person or things you are bitter about. It is sheer suicide to allow that to remain inside you.

If you have someone bitter in your family, or among your friends, what should you do? Speak to them in the name of the Lord. Identify it as "sin"; perhaps they're not aware of that. Use the strongest language possible: "Get rid of it! Get rid of it before it eats right through you!" If you had a friend who swallowed acid, what would you do? You would rush him to a hospital to get his stomach pumped. You would not stand idly by and do nothing. It is the same with bitterness. There are people who are living with bitterness who wouldn't think of committing a sin of lust, which is far less dangerous. If we stand for the fact that life is good, that history is gracious, that God is love, then we must call them forth out of their bitterness before it is too late. As for ouselves, we must be like the Lord. They can nail us to a cross, but we're not going to become bitter with life, bitter with God. All the better, if in the process we can also clear out the "sins" in our lives as well.

All of us know several people who desperately need to hear Mahon's message. We can't be signs of the presence of God and his Kingdom if we're bitter. And that's the way it is. No matter how good a Christian I think I am, if I am bitter about my children not calling or because they don't live up to my expectations, if I am bitter with the institutional church, if I am bitter about anything, I am a countersign to the Kingdom and am brimming over with sin, even if I don't have many sins.

A Postscript

If one takes but a superficial look at what has been said in this chapter, it is possible that she might conclude that the new morality is really no morality at all, and that being pastoral is just a euphemism for being "soft." I am somewhat at a loss to know what to say to that. Living up to the demanding ideal of love and becoming a Kingdom-person is not child's play. It requires more maturity and courage than most of us can muster on a consistent basis. There is nothing soft about it. But if by "soft" one means that threats and fear are no longer appropriate; if by "soft" one means that we have dispensed with devils and hell for the more truthful "I don't know"; if by "soft" one means that we have slain the Monster-god in favor of the God of faith who loves and forgives us unconditionally, then I guess we *are* getting "soft." If so, I am proud of that fact, and make no apologies whatsoever for what I have been trying to do in this book. For until we become that "soft," we shall be unable to really witness the presence of the Yahweh-God in all of humankind, nor shall we be sources of hope for our sisters and brothers who can see the coming Kingdom emerging, even if ever so slightly, in us. The price for not becoming "soft" is that we shall cease to be church.

The appearance of "softness" is illusory anyway. It stems from the fact that traditional Catholic moral teaching was so rigid that any change would have the appearance of being "soft" and of being a retreat in the face of the onslaught of the world's paganism. That rigidity, as I hope I have shown, is really the result of misunderstanding and a misplaced emphasis. Therefore, I believe it is possible to become less rigid and still remain faithful to what in our tradition bespeaks the Lord and his Kingdom. But if we have a preconceived notion of what must remain, we shall be prejudiced in advance and hence unable to really seize the opportunity for the growthful change that has come to us in our days. If we still expect the kind of absolute certainty that characterized Catholic moral teaching in the past, we are doomed to be disappointed. With open minds and faith-filled hearts we must now push on to address the urgent moral dilemmas that currently face the faith community. High on that list, due to the misplaced emphasis, are the sexual issues that are not nearly as important as we were originally taught. Because they have become so important in the minds of Catholics, however, we shall begin there. Let us take a contemporary pastoral look, then, at the sexual issues.

SUGGESTED READING

Charles Curran and Richard McCormick, *Reading in Moral Theology No. 1: Moral Norms and Catholic Tradition,* Paulist Press, 1979.

_____. *Readings in Moral Theology No. 2: The Distinctiveness of Christian Ethics,* Paulist Press, 1980.

_____. *Readings in Moral Theology No. 3: The Magisterium and Morality,* Paulist Press, 1982.

Richard M. Gula, *What Are They Saying About Moral Norms?* Paulist Press, 1982.

Louis Monden, *Sin, Liberty & Law,* Sheed & Ward, 1965.

Juan Luis Segundo, *Evolution and Guilt,* Orbis, 1974.

John Shea, *What a Modern Catholic Believes About Sin,* Thomas More, 1971.

CHAPTER NINE

Human Sexuality
and Marriage

Getting Our Heads Together

I got the notion to write this book on morality precisely because of a sexual issue—one I found to be currently causing great pain and fragmentation in the adult faith community. Everywhere I turned, I found the devastating effects, and people were asking me for advice and for help in understanding what had happened. If you are in mid-life and have children in their twenties, then you probably have had the experience I am talking about. One or more of them is, or has been, "living together" with someone. Practically every Catholic family with adult children seems to have had that experience by now. Some have even had to face the situation in which the adult child returns home for the holidays with her or his lover, and expects to occupy, if not the master bedroom, at least the same bedroom. What should Catholic parents say, and do, in that situation?

My experience has been that far too many of us immediately go into our famous imitations of the "Monster-god," with the inevitable result that people are deeply hurt, families are divided, and there is no peace in the land. When I asked myself why otherwise loving parents acted that way, it seemed clear that it was because they thought they were supposed to. After all, the church had taught them that such premarital relationships were gravely immoral. What can one do when public immorality, even in the person of one's own children, invades the sanctity of one's home, other than resist it with a vengeance? (If you did not begin the book here, you will know by now the direction my answer to this question will take, indeed, must take. It comes, however, in the next chapter.)

Without going into the details of an answer at this point, let me share with you the story of a Catholic mother who seemed to know instinctively what to do. She is a giant in my eyes, though I am sure she would protest that she was merely being a mother. What a mother! It seems that her daughter had decided to live with a young man and she knew that breaking that news to her father would present problems. So she decided to tell her mother first, hoping to enlist her aid with father. As it was reported to me, the young couple arrived at the house nervous and filled with anxiety. After some initial chitchat, the young woman could stand the suspense no longer. She decided to blurt it out in one quick burst, just to get it over with. "Mother, we've got some good news and some bad news. Steve and I are going to get married in a year—and we're going to live together until then!" As if exhausted by the prodigious effort, the young woman sank back in her chair in silent apprehension at what her mother might say. But there was no long, shock-induced pause at all. Looking tenderly at the daughter whom she knew and loved, the mother's response was as instantaneous as it was gentle and understanding: "And what's the bad news?"

If you want to know what God is really like, if you want to know how a Kingdom-person should act, if you want to know what it means to witness the presence of the Yahweh-God in a human situation, then I know of no better example than that mother. Unfortunately, most of us did not act so graciously when we got that news from our children. We became angry and bitter. Need I repeat what Leo Mahon has told us about bitterness? It is like swallowing acid, and it will eat right through us. Of course, we didn't need him to tell us that. We've swallowed the acid of bitterness both with regard to our children's attitude toward church-going as well as with regard to their "live-in" lovers. It is time for us to spit it all out! But that isn't going to be easy for people like us who were reared with traditional Catholic moral teaching. Our heads are so freighted with "religious" ideas, attitudes and preconceptions, especially when it comes to sex, that we are really no longer able to trust our instincts or interpret our experience with our children anew in the light of faith. The path to inner peace, in all such matters, requires that we first get our own heads together. Only then shall we be able to relate to our own children in some sort of loving solidarity as befits Christian parents.

The casualties down through the centuries from the church's moral teaching on sex are legion, and they continue to pile up in our day. More people have been driven from the church over sexual matters than from any other single cause. The church is praised for its consistency, but the truth is that, in some cases, it has been consistently *wrong!* I say that without rancor or bitterness. It is just that if one lives long enough and gives heed to her life, she comes to realize that fact. On sexual matters, the Catholic Church, obviously well-intentioned, is simply wrong! Let me immediately add that our culture is even more wrong regarding sex than is the church, and its views are much too self-serving to be deemed well-intentioned. If one were forced to choose between the prevailing cultural view of sex, and that of the Catholic Church, it would be no contest; the church is closer to the truth than is our prevailing culture. Still, the official teaching of the church is further from the truth than is the communally-funded experience of its faith-filled members. That is why disagreement over sexual morality exists not only between the church and the culture, but also between the "official" church and its own members. In what follows, I shall attempt to give some sort of reasoned justification for the position of those dissenting members, of which, of course, I am one.

Where the Church Went Wrong

As is so often the case, the church's official stand is more a function of errors, which it historically had to combat, than of its positive mission to witness the coming Kingdom. Nowhere has this proved more unfortunate than in the area of its stand on human sexuality. The dispute was an early one, occurring in the first centuries of the church, but the effects are still being felt in our day.

The Catholic tradition seems to have a hang-up with "procreation." Why? We all recall the covenant the Yahweh-God made with Abraham, and the promise that his descendants would be as numerous as the stars of the heavens and the sands of the seashore (see Genesis 15:5, 26:4; 22:17). When you couple this with the fact that in that ancient Semitic culture women were not considered equal to men and still aren't in the church, you can see why marriage and procreation came to be viewed as synonymous in the Old Testament. Polygamy was allowed to insure the fruitfulness of the marriage bed and being barren was the greatest tradegy that could befall a Jewish woman. Yet, despite the centrality of procreation in the Jewish scheme of things, there is not one single prohibition in Jewish law against contraception. Not one. Amazing.

Nor did the prohibition against contraception begin with the Lord. The truth is that the New Testament, like the Jewish law before it, is absolutely silent on the topic of contraception. What the New Testament writers did do in thinking about marriage was to replace procreation at center stage with Christian love, and proposed the hitherto unimaginable ideal of celibacy or virginity for the sake of the Kingdom. But if celibacy and virginity are such goods, what are we to say about marriage and the genital relationship between spouses?

Certain Christians, called Gnostics, were so impressed with the New Testament endorsement of celibacy and virginity that they began teaching that marriage and sexual intercourse were forbidden to true Christians. An outrageous error, which the church had to combat. In combatting it, it moved itself into a posture that has led to most of its mistakes with regard to human sexuality. In its fight with the Gnostics, the church knew it would not do to merely quote the New Testament to the effect that marriage was good, because the New Testament did not say why it was good. Besides, to have simply quoted Scripture to the Gnostics on the nobility of marriage would have gotten nowhere, because they would have simply quoted back the texts on celibacy. If any real progress was going to be made in the dispute, the church would have to come up with an answer to that question: Why was marriage good?

Since Scripture doesn't really answer that question, it should not surprise us to find that the early Christian communities turned to the philosophers for a possible answer. When you pose a philosophical question like that, it is natural to seek a philosophical answer. In any event, the early Christians found the philosophical answer they were seeking in the Stoic philosophy of the day, which was a spin-off of Platonism.

Stoic philosophy was characterized by the downplay of human emotion as beneath the dignity of reasonable males. A man was to control his emotions, and Seneca, a great Stoic, is quoted as having said, "A wise man ought to love his wife with judgment, not affection. Let him control his impulses." Obviously, human sexuality was a real problem for the Stoics. As the most explosive of human emotions, it could not be good in itself, for a thing is good only to the degree that it fulfills its purpose. A good axe is one that is sharp and cuts wood properly. A good meal is one that satisfies one's hunger and the nutritional needs of the body. Similarly, a good sexuality is one that fulfills its purpose, procreation. For human beings to engage in sexual intercourse for any reason other than procreation makes them even less than the beasts of the earth who never do that. Marriage and procreation could be called good then, according to the Stoics, only if they were aimed at procreation.

Why would the second-century Christians adopt this stoic position? Mainly for two reasons. It gave them a way to respond to the Gnostics who had said that sexuality and marriage were never good and should be shunned by genuine Christians. Second, it allowed them to speak in favor of sexuality without adopting the secular attitude of their day, which seemed to be, as it still does in our day, an unbridled search for pleasure. It short, it was simultaneously an argument for sexuality and against promiscuity. That remains an essential ingredient in any valid Christian account of sexuality. Christians must always argue for sexuality and against promiscuity. The church has certainly been right about that.

Adopting this philosophical justification for sexual intercourse was not an unmixed blessing. It may have helped them answer the Gnostics, but it raised a goodly number of practical problems. If intercourse was good only to achieve its natural goal of procreation, what about the sexual relations between spouses when the woman was known to be sterile, or was already pregnant? What about the sexual relations between spouses who were beyond childbearing years? According to Stoic teaching, such sexual relations could never be good. With consummate good sense, the early church, while accepting the overall Stoic view, rejected their judgment on the practical cases. It seemed to violate common sense. (Too bad it wasn't noticed that the overall view does, too. We could have been spared so much pain.)

Adopting the Stoic position posed another difficulty for Christians. The two most famous New Testament texts on marriage are contained in letters of St. Paul, I Corinthians 7 and Ephesians 5. The Stoic doctrine was perfectly compatible with the Corinthians text, but is strangely discordant with Ephesians 5. I suppose the reason this did not seem important to the early Christians was because they lived at a time and in a culture when women were treated as the possessions of men, first of their fathers and then of their husbands. It was not likely that a people raised in such a culture could even begin to understand the beauty and inspiration of St. Paul's remarks to the Ephesians. So the early tradition on marriage was centered on procreation without benefit of light from that Ephesians text, which is unique in all of Scripture and says most perfectly what Christian marriage ought to be.

It was a costly move for which Catholics are still paying, for it laid the foundation for what we called earlier in this book the church's rather crude and primitive understandings of natural law. What is so ironic about the whole thing is that although it has become the "Catholic tradition," in reality it isn't "Christian," but

Platonic and Stoic in origin. We have seen earlier that such a Platonic interpretation of the human condition invariably ends in some sort of spiritualism, a context in which sex was bound to be misunderstood. Thus sex and procreation became inextricably linked in the Christian mind. If, in order to be "good," sex had to be procreative or at least open to that possibility, one logical consequence was that sex be limited to marriage because infants required a home and a stable family life to survive and thrive. Because extramarital sex undermined that obvious natural requirement, it could never be considered acceptable. Having arrived at those conclusions by logical deduction from Platonic and Stoic origins, the church then went on to add the weight of its ecclesiastical authority to the position, branding all violations of the ideal arrangement as "immoral," even when there was no unjustified infliction of ontic evil involved. As every Catholic knows, that is pretty much how the situation stands to this day.

Having begun by viewing sex as something of a hindrance to the spiritual life, and limiting its good use to situations legitimately open to procreation, it was only natural that the church would find little else positive to say about it. Although not wanting to accept the conclusion of the Gnostics, namely, that sex and marriage were things not to be engaged in by "authentic" Christians, the church was always sympathetic to their premise that celibacy and virginity were a higher way. To accept that premise, though, was in a way to accept the Gnostic conclusion in practice, as people began to look on the priests and religious who chose the celibate and virginal way of life as "super" Christians. One cannot help but feel that in the long run the Gnostics have won out. The dissension in the post-Vatican II church over sexual morality is merely the latest battle in the war with the ancient Gnostic position.

Just as the early church was outraged at the position of the original Gnostics, so in the twentieth century more and more Catholics have become outraged with the teaching of the hierarchical church, and for the same reason. The teaching does not do justice to communally-funded human experience. Indeed, if the church can be so off base regarding sex, one wonders whether it is not at least equally off base regarding celebacy. My opinion is that the church has been so concerned with extolling celibacy and virginity that it ended up devaluing sex. The current dissension in the Catholic Church on those matters is merely the latest attempt in the long struggle on the part of Catholics to remedy once and for all the situation precipitated by the early Gnostics.

Where the Culture Goes Wrong

There will be those who think that our culture has gone wrong in proclaiming, "Whatever is done sexuallly between two consenting adults, if it does not hurt anyone, cannot be immoral." But strangely enough, that is one thing about which the culture is correct. We should remember this is merely saying that when an act inflicts no ontic evil it cannot be a moral evil. It could still be a "sin" in the eyes of the Christian if what is done involves saying no to God's invitation to love, or if it contradicts Kingdom-ideals. It should be clear by now that, although every immoral act is a sin, not every sin is an immoral act. The culture has it right in this instance. The culture is also rightheaded when it insists that when there is no question of moral evil, adults should be left to exercise their freedom unimpeded. As Christians, we can accept that too, because we know that the Kingdom cannot be brought about by force. The culture is right, at least in those instances, but it is wrong if it thinks that this is all there need be said on the subject.

More specifically, the culture runs amok when it suggests that sex is merely a matter of pleasure, and when it encourages the "worship of sex," which is a principal ingredient of paganism, as we have seen. All attempts to make that case are dead wrong and whenever they have occurred, the church had no choice but to try to present a viable alternative. Christians simply cannot agree with humanist professor, Robert Tyler, when he said in 1970:

> Marriage in all its many forms has clamped some kind of social control on sex to make fun and games serve such stuffy values as child rearing, the inheritance of wealth, or the transmission of social status and tradition. From the beginning, Americans frowned on all those

extramarital sports discovered by older and wiser cultures. But sex has finally burst the boundaries.

We believers simply cannot concur with the reduction of sex to "fun and games." It is much too important for that.

We would be much more comfortable with the account of the Whiteheads (Evelyn and James Whitehead, *Marrying Well,* Doubleday, 1981, p. 393) that does greater justice to our experience:

> The "simple casual affair" is not easy to sustain. Genital love is seldom innocent of complications. That in fact is part of its fascination. Sex goes somewhere. . . . Sex is fun but we know that it is not to be treated lightly. Sex is a powerful experience in our lives, with intellectual and emotional ramifications that often extend beyond our immediate control.

Sexual activity is not only wildly exciting and fun, it has not only a natural function, that is, procreation for us humans, it also has a meaning and a significance. Very early in this book we encountered the notion that we humans cannot simply live, or simply copulate, or simply do anything. We are not animals, after all. We are spirits, albeit incarnate ones; whether we like it or not, want to or not, we take a stand in freedom, and have a relation to all the things of our lives. That is another way of saying that in our sex lives we hunger not only for pleasure but also for meaning.

When he tells her, "You turn me on," or "I'm hot for you," or "I find you desirable and irresistible," and "I want you," why is she still so hesitant? (Don't accuse me of being sexist here. I am aware that the situation just as easily goes the other way these days. And the response would still be the same, for it is a human, not a male or female, response.) Isn't his affirmation enough for her to say yes? No, not really. So she says, "I know. But do you love me? Will you respect me in the morning?" She is seeking clarification about the significance of going to bed with him. She is asking about how he as spirit views, and participates in, the lovemaking he proposes. She wants to know how he relates to it, and to her as person.

The culture would have us overlook all that, and would, as Professor Tyler did, see it as an attempt "to control sex and make fun and games serve some stuffy purpose." But separating sex from its human significance is no longer to speak about human sexuality at all. Of course, many of us don't come to understand that until we have succumbed to the siren call of the culture at some time in our lives, be it in adolescence, in early adulthood, or later. Then we discover that the culture is right about one thing: sex can be wildly exciting and fun, even addicting. What the culture didn't tell us was how difficult it is to keep it on a merely hedonistic level. There seems to be an inner dynamic that keeps pushing us toward relationship. My sexual partner unexpectedly comes to be important to me as a person. I become concerned for her or him. I find that I can't go on treating our sexual activity casually as fun and games anymore. When I try to, I feel more and more dissatisfied, less and less human. The culture said it was just "fun and games," but experience reveals that sex is not that carefree. (In both senses of the word, not free of anxiety and misgivings, nor of thoughtfulness and consideration.)

I recall about ten or twelve years ago I conceived a project that failed because of the unwillingness of Catholic adults to share what they had learned about sex from their own experience. At the time, my sons were in their adolescence and I was into giving them sex talks from time to time. It seemed that the only people talking about the meaning of sex were either the hedonists, or the celibate priests who conducted high school and college courses on marriage. The hedonists mercilessly ridiculed marriage and fidelity in magazines, novels, plays, TV talk shows, and especially in the lyrics of rock songs. It seemed to be a concerted effort to inculcate the "fun and games" philosophy of sex, and to interpret any sense of modesty, any desire to hold oneself precious and apart from overt and public eroticism, and any attempt at fidelity, to be the result of enslaving Victorian fears. To free us from such "misguided superstition," they undertook a media campaign to fill our every waking moment with erotica, a campaign that seems to have intensified in the 80s. I worried about the effect of that media blitz on my sons and on all young people.

On the other side, there were those giving marriage courses in the Catholic schools who attempted to present an alternative understanding, but who often came off as too theoretical and idealistic. Their effectiveness was further curtailed by the fact that they were presenting the "traditional Catholic moral teaching" on sex, which, as we have seen, has problems of its own. It occurred to me that a significant voice was missing from the dialogue, and hence from the input my sons were receiving: the voices of nonfundamentalist, faith-filled people who were practitioners of genital sex within Christian marriages. So I conceived of a book in which I would ask such people to write accounts of what they had learned in bed about the meaning of sex. It seemed to me such a book was sorely needed. (It may well still be.)

To my amazement, I found that faith-filled people are very reluctant to talk about their own intimate sexual experiences, even when protected by anonymity. No one wanted to do it, so the project had to be abandoned. To this day, I regret that. If hedonists alone have the audacity to promote their own sexual experiences, and those with contrary experiences are silent for lack of courage, what does this say to our young people? Still, I understand the reluctance of people to write about such things. But until the people engaged in sexual relations within Christian marriages reveal exactly what they do and what they have learned about the meaning of what they do, we won't know what the Lord reveals to faith-filled people in moments of sexual intimacy. We can only guess or judge from our own individual experiences, which may be idiosyncratic and not communally funded. From what I have said, my guess is that the revelation is not fully compatible with what the Catholic Church has traditionally said on the matter.

Too often, sex education is reduced merely to an "organ recital" or a course in the human reproductive mechanism and the techniques of sexual plumbing. Its only goal seems to be to cut down on the number of teenage pregnancies. A laudable objective, without doubt, but it hardly satisfies the hunger young people have to understand the meaning of the sexuality. If, as we have seen, human life is lived out against a backdrop of ambiguity and contradiction, it is nowhere more powerfully focused than in human sexuality. Young people have a right to expect the adult community to address that problem and to share with them their best insights into the significance of that sexuality. If sex education means anything, it means responding to that need, a need not just of the young and inexperienced among us, but of each of us as well.

The culture has succumbed so completely to the mystique of sex that it can no longer see its inherent ambiguity. It is enough for the culture that sexual activity be pleasurable. But the body is not only the source of pleasure for human beings, it is also the constant reminder of our finitude and of our inevitable decline, death, and corruption. Were we not bodies, we would not have the pleasure of sex, but we would not have to grow old and die either. Indeed, what makes sex so ambiguous for us humans is that it is precisely *because* we are endowed with sexual genitalia that we die. That is no over-statement; it is a matter of scientific fact.

Unicellular organisms that reproduce by cell division rather than by procreation, are theoretically indestructible. Barring some sort of natural accident, such organisms do not experience death. As we move up the evolutionary scale, though, organisms endowed with genitalia are expected to pay their debt to nature by pro-creating, after which they are completely dispensable. With sexuali-ty, death enters the picture. The capacity to parent is a sure sign of one's inevitable demise. Thankfully, our twenty-year-olds are blissfully unaware of that, but it is a truth everyone must face sooner or later. For most of us, that realization comes in mid-life. Thus, to seek the meaning of sex, is, knowingly or not, to seek the meaning of life and of death, since all three are inextricably inter-wined. That is why Ernest Becker observed, "Sex is a disappointing answer to life's riddle, and if we pretend that it is an adequate one, we are lying both to ourselves and to our children" (*The Denial of Death*, Free Press, 1975, p. 164). Far from answering the riddle, human sexuality is its primary manifestation.

My sexuality is not only a reminder of my mortality and future death, I also experience it as an affront to my freedom, to my con-trol of my life. The sex drive seems to have a mind of its own; it is, after all, about nature's business, but that makes me feel used and determined. This affront to personal freedom is another dimension of sexuality the culture conveniently ignores. No respecter of per-sons, the sex drive can come at just the wrong time, upsetting personal projects and goals. It can drive us to actions not really representative of who we are. It can become so obsessive that we lose our very selves in the process. There is, after all, nothing particularly "human" about copulating and procreating; all the higher animals do it. This is one more reason to see it as a threat to personal uniqueness.

In any event, it seems obvious with just a little reflection, and without even alluding to Christian faith and the dream of the Kingdom, that the culture has adopted too shallow a view of human sexuality to be taken seriously. Whatever else may be said about human sexuality, it is not simply a matter of fun and games.

The Meanings of Human Sexuality

In our discussion of the Ontological Paradox in Part One, we saw that unlike the animals our sense of self-worth is neither innate nor instinctive. We must earn it. We do this by investing the things of our lives with symbolic meaning. Things take on a new significance as they are taken up into the world of human meanings; they become more than they are; they become "signs" of something else. To really understand and get along in the "human" world, a world of facts having an overlay or aura of meanings, we must learn from our experience not only the effect things have on us, or how they function in the world, but also the spectrum of "human meanings" they do and are able to sustain. Things don't naturally "have" meaning; they are endowed with meaning, invested with meaning, by human beings.

It takes some reflection to understand that, because we naturally think that meaning is a quality or characteristic that things possess, like their size or shape. Meaning is out there; all we do is discover it. Actually, what is out there is meaningless, unless and until a symbolic self or spirit invests it with meaning. Christians should not be in too much of a hurry to conclude that the things of life have been given a fixed meaning by their creator. He created them such that they are capable of sustaining many different, even contradictory meanings. The meanings of things that come to be communally funded are always the result of human decision and choice. Since meanings are the result of the way a symbolic self freely chooses to relate to the facts or things of her world, they are a function of human freedom and can never be forced upon people. People must choose to adopt them and commit themselves to them. Every totalitarian regime, every religious cult, every fundamentalist religion comes face to face with the reality of that sooner or later.

It is no different with regard to sexuality. Meaningless in itself, it is open to being invested with a wide spectrum of sometimes contradictory meanings, but it is only when it is endowed with meaning that we can speak of human sexuality at all.

Some have interpreted the fact that sexuality can be endowed with many different meanings as evidence that sexuality itself is multilayered, like an onion. On that account, we choose how to value and give meaning to sexuality by how deeply we penetrate its reality, how close we come to its core or center. I have no real quarrel with talking that way, but I don't think sexuality is like an onion, so much as we are. Were sexuality like an onion, then its meanings would be merely discovered and not created or freely chosen by persons. Because we are incarnate spirits, we are multilayered and hence capable of investing sexuality with a wide variety of different human meanings. The question is not so much what meanings sexuality has. Rather, the questions are: What meanings do we human beings choose to give to our sexuality? and Which are the ones that our experience teaches us offer the best chance at greater freedom, greater hope, and greater humanness?

The point is that no matter what "nature" or "nature's God" may have built into human sexuality, each human participant in sexual intercourse confers on the act meanings that are quite personal. Which of them are "immoral" is not a function of whether they are in accord with nature's goal of preservation of the species, but of whether they inflict ontic evil unjustly and unnecessarily. Which of them are also "sins" for believers will be a function of whether they embody a "no" to God's call to love and to the Kingdom-ideals.

If we recall how plagued we all are with the ambiguities arising from the Existential Dilemma and the Ontological Paradox, it should not surprise us to find that, as a general rule, we humans confer meanings on our sexuality that help us cope better with these basic ambiguities. If the sexuality in question is human, we would expect it to take on significance in that context. It would seem that "nature" and "nature's God" understood that, and so constituted human sexuality not primarily for procreative reasons. Were that the case, we would expect humans to have periodic times of arousal corresponding to the periodic times of fertility. That is not the case. In human sexuality, the primary sex organ is the brain/mind, which not only makes humans more active sexually than other mammals, but indicates that the meanings we consciously endow sexuality with, thus making it human, are far more important than its procreative function. The church's understanding, borrowed from the Stoics, of what makes sex "good," and its desire to value celibacy and virginity prevented it from doing justice to this human dimension of our sexuality.

We can hardly blame the church, when we consider some of the truly immoral and really dehumanizing "meanings" we have historically given to our sexual activity. One need not even argue for the obvious immorality of rape, incest, sexual assaults (especially on children), sexual enslavement, and cruelty of any sort in the sexual context. These things all inflict unjustified ontic evil and hence are patently immoral. One cannot think of a situation, even the most bizarre, where such things could be labeled as "moral." From the start, the church championed the cause of girls and women who seem to be the chief victims of such patently immoral sex. (How ironic that in our day, the church shuns that role when it comes to the rights of women in the church. Such ecclesiastical reluctance is a clear break with one of the church's most ancient and venerable traditions: respect for the role and rights of women. How sad, because that is one of the traditional stands in which the church got it absolutely right from the start.)

Experience teaches us that sex is able to be symbolically meaningful for humans in a variety of ways that are not at all, or are at least not necessarily, immoral. On the assumption that sexual activity is always self-serving, to some degree we might make the following division:

A. Taking Sex Non-Relationally

Level 1. Self-Serving and Necessarily Immoral—where the sexual activity answers to individual personal desires, but obviously inflicts ontic evil (rape, incest, assault, bondage, cruelty).

Level 2. Self-Serving and Possibly Immoral, Depending on Circumstances—where sexual activity answers an individual need or desire, but the self-centeredness may or may not inflict ontic evil (seeking one's own pleasure, assuaging one's own loneliness, affirming one's own ego, relieving sexual tension and quieting the sex drive in order to get on with a less distracted life, etc.).

B. Taking Sex Relationally

Level 3. Self-Serving and Self-Giving—where sexual activity is sought because it answers a personal need, but also as a means of "gifting" the other (falling in love, the beginnings of intimacy, making the human connection, affirming myself and the other, choosing to conceive new life, etc).

Level 4. Self-Giving and Self-Serving—where sexual activity primarily "gifts" the other and only secondarily serves one's own interests that have become identified with the other's (genuine, mature, and redemptive intimacy; commitment; fidelity; the two have really become one).

Level 5. Sex as Sacraments and Sign of the Kingdom—when the relationship bespeaks the presence of the Yahweh-God and his fidelity, and incarnates the Kingdom-ideals. (This still remains self-serving, at least in the sense that it is always one's truest and deepest self-interest to walk with the Lord and witness his Kingdom.)

The Catholic tradition tells us that to engage in sexual activity on levels other than 4 and 5 is immoral and prohibited because it does not embody the highest of human ideals and does not incarnate the highest meaning sustainable by human sexuality. Experience and common sense teach us otherwise. Just because something is not the best does not necessarily mean that it may not be good, although a lesser one.

Take a Level 3 example, seen more and more these days, of mature women experiencing baby hunger, wanting a family but not wanting a marriage. They choose to get pregnant, often through a casual sexual experience, and intend to raise the child as their own with love and commitment. Not ideal, granted, but is it not a truly human event? May it not be called good if for no other reason than the willingness to parent with all the selflessness this commitment demands? What sense does it make for the church to label that situation "immoral"? Where is the ontic evil? Certainly, before the fact, any pastoral person would hold up higher ideals, but once the deed is done and the child is born, it would seem that what is required of believers is that they stop alluding to the rejection of higher ideals and affirm the true human good they discern to be present. That is what the Lord would do! (See John 4:4-42.)

As we saw in Part Two, human life is to be lived relationally as a gift, in solidarity with humankind. That was the order the Yahweh-God intended. So it is true that were one to attempt to live her sexual life on Level 2, it would be disordered, but it would only be immoral if the result of the disorder were that ontic evil was intentionally and unjustly inflicted. Level 2 sexuality impedes the coming Kingdom and is intrinsically disordered from the Christian perspective, but does making this statement to someone help to bring her to that realization? For in addition to being relational, human life is also processive, which means that it is not static but unfolds in stages. Given that fact, we can see in the various levels of meaning for human sexuality the possibility for growth and progression. Indeed, sex is so powerful and important a dimension of human life that it is not surprising that people prefer to learn the truth about it for themselves from experience, and not from the doctrines or teachings of others. In fact, I can't help but think it should be put even more strongly than that. Apart from Level 1 sexuality, which involves obvious and certain immorality, do people not have a right to learn for themselves which meanings they give to their sexual lives are the most life-giving and hence humanly the most satifying? In the end, is there really any other way?

Put in a faith context, my question is this: Do we or do we not believe that God is present in human life and relationships, calling people to an intimacy that is truly redemptive? If we do, do we believe that he is capable of touching the hearts of people, revealing the poverty and inadequacy of their chosen sexual lifestyles? Finally, do we believe that when they do err, he loves them and forgives them unconditionally? My point, then, is this: Haven't we really made far too much of sexual issues, at least of those that don't involve the intentional and unjustified infliction of ontic evil? Is God as worried about who is in bed with whom, as we have been taught he is? Are sexual inadequacies as destructive of the Kingdom as, say, injustices? The answers seem obvious. Yes. No. No.

Why is genital sexuality the only area of life where we are expected to be perfect before we start? In the past, it was perhaps understandable that we were wary of the consequences, because whatever meaning we gave to genital sexuality could also result in life. Now we are in possession of the technology to prevent conception and unwanted children. We have at our disposal the means of freeing humankind from irresponsible pregnancies. Still, the Catholic Church officially continues to hold out against any kind of direct contraception. Evidently, we are not be be allowed to use genital sexuality as a learning experience, a way to learn the lessons of life, of love, of commitment, and of finitude and death. Marry first—then learn! But, learn first—then marry, sounds so much more righteaded, does it not? As a matter of fact, that is the way most people do it. It is just that they are subjected to a guilt trip about their premarital sex by the church turned moral policeman. Earlier, we called for the church to get out of the "morality business." As a direct consequence of that, we must now sound the equally urgent call for the church to get out of the "marriage business"—before it is too late.

Marriage and the Church

Marriage is an area where the Catholic Church has made a real botch of things. Its vast juridical system of marriage tribunals, from the Sacred Rota in Rome down to the smallest diocese; its intricate system of prohibitory and nullifying impediments; its presumption to judge and grant annulments and impose penalties—all seem as out of place as a missile launcher in the sanctuary. As a result of its commitment to be "moral policeman" in matters of sex and marriage, it has inflicted unnecessary evil on its people; it has regularly failed to witness the presence of the Yahweh-God who forgives and forgets; it has not shepherded but scattered the sheep, and it has become, itself, a countersign to the Kingdom. In addition, the extreme "legalism" into which it has consequently fallen, and the fact that the system, in practice, tends to favor the privileged and wealthy, has made the church an object of ridicule, no longer to be taken seriously. I call for the hierarchical church to get out of the "matrimony business," not primarily to make things easier for people, though that would be a welcome side effect, but rather in order that the institutional church might fulfill its mission and become the sign and sacrament it was meant to be. Whatever juridical dimensions marriage must have because of its and our own social natures, all that should be left to the state. *That is not the task of church!* The task of the church is to offer as gift an alternative lifestyle to the paganism of the world, not force that lifestyle on people.

The Old Testament contains two remarkable stories of how the Yahweh-God acted when he was confronted with a similar situation. He acted in a way not particularly characteristic of the "religiously" interpreted God of Israel. In the first case (1 Samuel 8:7-8), the people wanted a king. They asked Samuel, who was aged and nearing death, to make that request of Yahweh. Samuel was upset that the people should make such a request, for he well knew that the Yahweh-God himself was their king. He angrily told the Lord Yahweh of the people's insulting request. Yahweh's compassion is evident in his response. He was concerned about Samuel becoming so distraught in his old age, and taking the request so personally.

> Samuel, it is not you they reject; they are rejecting me as their king.
> As they have treated me constantly from the day I brought them up
> from Egypt to this day, deserting me and worshipping strange gods,
> so do they treat you too.

Yahweh then told Samuel to tell the people what would happen if they had a human king. Their sons would be pressed into military service and the liberated people of Exodus would become indentured spear carriers behind the chariot of a king. The king would take their daughters for his concubines. The people persisted in their desire for a king, thinking it well worthwhile if only they could be like other nations and have a visible king. Yahweh's response was simply, "Give the people what they want!" He knew they would learn the bitter truth from experience and come to regret what they had done.

Nor was that the only time the Yahweh-God was so insulted by his people. Just as every great nation had a king, so every great nation had a temple wherein to worship its gods. After centuries of not having a temple, King David suggests that he build one—after he had already built himself a palace, of course. Yahweh's response was again characteristic. He sends the prophet Nathan to King David with this message (2 Samuel 7:5-11):

> Should you build me a house to dwell in? I have not dwelt in a house from the day on which I led the Israelites out of Egypt to the present. I have led a wanderer's life. . . .I have been with you wherever you went. . . Yahweh will make *you* great. Yahweh will make *you* a House. (The House of David!)

A temple indeed! Don't they understand that I dwell in them? You mean that after all this time they still don't understand that? Well, if they want a temple, let them have it. But someday they'll understand. And one day we did, well—some of us, anyway (see John 4:19-24).

The God of Exodus is the God of human liberation and freedom, and he is not in the business of forcing people into the Kingdom; they must want it. When they don't want what is necessary for the Kingdom, he does not force them or threaten them, but reminds them of the dream and then lets them learn from their own experience. However gracious and Yahweh-like the church is in other areas, when it comes to sex and marriage, it has gotten into the bad habit of threatening rather than simply mounting the dream of the Lord's alternative lifestyle. What is worse, it has played a role historically in forcing Kingdom ideals on nonbelievers. It has been instrumental in forging secular laws against divorce and contraception, making those things illegal even for those who know not the Lord. No wonder people see the church as meddling in their private lives, even the lives of those who do not share the Christian faith.

In our day, as more and more nations see the inappropriateness of that, the Catholic Church still lobbies hard to prevent the repeal of such laws. This is not to suggest that the church stay out of politics and secular law issues altogether, for it should be active in those areas when it is a matter of the Kingdom (moral) rules. How ironic that until very recently it seems to have been much more concerned with sex and marriage issues that don't inflict ontic evil than with matters of social justice that obviously do.

The fact is that marriage as an institution existed long before the Christian church came on the scene, and it was the subject of reflection by sages and philosophers for centuries. They had identified the appropriate characteristics that marriage ought to have in order to meet its natural and social objectives. It was to be an exclusive union between opposite sexes, of relatively long and stable duration, formally constituted by public contract or covenant. Marriage was geared to the establishment of a family, and procreation demands the union of female and male. The union would have to be relatively stable in order to meet the needs of rearing the children of the union to their majority. It should be an exclusive union so that parenthood of the children would be known and not subject to doubt. Finally, for the order of society, it seemed wise to make the commitment and union public and formal, again to insure certain knowledge of who begets whom.

In view of the ancient dream of the Kingdom, the church added to this list the characteristics *monogamous* and *indissoluble,* as well as the view that all sexual activity outside the confines of such a monogamous, exclusive, permanent, indissoluble, and formally constituted union of female and male was immoral—a position that went far beyond the views of the wisest of the secular sages. Common sense said that wife and husband should stay together "for the good of the children," at least until they reached their majority. But once they have, if the union is otherwise unsatisfactory, it seemed reasonable to say that at that point the parties could separate. The marriage union, obviously, had to be fifteen to twenty years in duration when children were involved, but why permanent? And why, if there were no children?

The answer the church gave was that it is in the very nature of marriage that it is indissoluble. Even if that were true, one must admit it is by no means obvious. In fact, experience teaches us that marriages are all too fragile and quite obviously dissoluble.

If someone were to tell you that a piece of glass were unbreakable, how would you determine the truth of that assertion? You might try to break it, and if you succeeded, you would find it strange should the one making the original assertion continue to maintain it on the grounds that you had not really broken the glass because while it seemed to be broken, it really was not. Such an approach would be unacceptable in other areas of human life, yet we have allowed such a tactic to work with regard to our matrimonial theology.

The marriage bond is supposed to be indissoluble, and whenever women and men have tested the truth of this assertion by actually breaking it, the reply has been that they have only seemed to break it, but in reality it remains intact, and all subsequent attempts at marriage are not only illicit and invalid, they are virtually impossible. And with no little temerity, the proponents of that position use Scripture to back up their claims. They cite Matthew and Mark to the effect that: "What God has joined together, let not man put asunder!" (19:6 and 10:9). Contemporary moral theologians are almost unanimous in seeing this question as an "ideal," not a "rule." An ideal is something to be striven for and, it is hoped, achieved. A rule sets down an obligation to be followed. That response may help the practical situation, but I would like to add a supplementary note to that interpretation of the texts, an interpretation with which I fully agree.

A little reflection makes it obvious that those gospel statements would make no sense at all if the marriage bond really were indissoluble. If that were the case, then no attempt to dissolve it could ever be successful and a commandment in the regard would be superfluous. I submit that we have this whole thing backwards. Far from establishing indissolubility, those texts do just the opposite. It is precisely because the marriage bond can be dissolved by human agency that the Lord's invitation not to do so has real significance for Christians.

How is it that human beings can do something they can't undo? If marriage is, for natural and societal reasons, a contract, why can it not be broken? Everyone knows that a contract can always be voided by mutual consent of the parties. How does it happen then that a marriage contract is in a class by itself? This is a serious question for traditional thought.

One can leave religious life and the priesthood, but one cannot leave a marriage. Why? Because it is a sacrament. Yes, but what about priests? That too is a sacrament! Well, they can't really leave, either. They are priests forever; they are merely dispensed from the exercise of their priesthood, but they shall remain priests until the day they die. It's just that way with sacraments. Fine. Then let me be dispensed from the exercise of my marriage, and you can think what you like about whether I'm married until the day I die! No, you don't understand; you can't be dispensed from the exercise of your marriage obligations. You must fulfill your marriage vows, come what may. If you don't, you're in sin. You can never be dispensed.

And so it goes, one silliness after another. No wonder the church experiences credibility problems with respect to its stand on marriage. All because it has insisted that marriage between Christians *is* a sacrament, rather than that it can *become* a sacrament.

Marriage as Sacrament

We have seen that the "religious" understanding of Christianity depicts the human condition as one of warfare between the forces of good (God) and the forces of evil (the devil). In that struggle, the sacraments are essential weapons since they are the channels of God's grace that help keep us alive in the Lord, able to resist temptation, and die in the state of grace. Obviously, given the church's stand on sex, some prodigious divine help was necessary to keep us from falling into immorality, and so it was natural to understand matrimony as a sacrament that helped spouses live their conjugal commitment "purely" and "chastely."

Obviously, the Catholic Church incarnated itself in the world the way it did, putting a parish in every neighborhood, because of its understanding of the human condition and the role of sacraments in human salvation. That understanding was an open invitation for the church to adopt the role of "moral policeman," and to cause it to adopt a juridical and legalistic approach to marriage. When we speak about changing our understanding of sacraments, we should be aware that we are really talking about changing the way our church is to be present to the world as well. The church of our old age will not be visible or operative in the world the way the church of our youth and mid-years has been.

In that church, which is gradually passing from the scene, the sacraments were considered necessary to achieve eternal life; they were its most important work. The priorities of that church are obviously mirrored in the tradtional parish structure, seeking to put a spiritual filling station in every neighborhood so people would have convenient access to a dispensary of essential sacramental grace. Thus, for the priests of a parish, life is one continuous round of baptizing, saying Mass, hearing confessions, distributing communion, anointing the sick, witnessing weddings (thereby validating their sacramental character), and burying the dead. It is a dizzying life of endless liturgical activity to keep the channels of grace open and gushing with the graces people need to resist evil and save their souls. It was thought to be God's own way of combating the situation so graphically depicted in that prayer to St. Michael, which it was customary, in many parishes, to say after Mass. But that is to see sacraments as unrelated to the coming Kingdom—which they are not. Whatever the meaning and value of the sacraments for human life, they must be, and be understood, in relation to that ancient dream.

A moment's reflection should convince us that we have badly misunderstood the role of sacraments in the Christian life. Let us say the sacraments originated in some way with Christ, but God's saving grace has been consistently lavished on humankind from the beginning, and continues to be lavished on humankind in our day, even on those of our sisters and brothers who do not know the Lord. *Sacraments are not so much sources of grace for believers as*

the celebration by believers of graces freely and already given to all.
It is not the sacraments that cause grace; it is the grace given to all
that cause the Kingdom more fully to come, thus giving Christians
something to celebrate sacramentally.

Sacraments are intimately related to God's concerns in the
world, within the human race at large, and also within the community of Christians. To participate authentically in the sacramental life of the church is to celebrate the progress of the dream in the
world as well as to signify one's own commitment as a Christian to
mount that dream in the place where one is. We shall have reason
to return to this notion of "sacrament" in our final chapter with
regard to reconciliation. At present, let us see what that understanding of sacrament reveals about marriage as a sacrament.

There is a certain ambiguity in the traditional Catholic position on marriage. It is not really clear whether a Christian marriage
is indissoluble because that is the nature of marriage (in that case,
all marriages, Christian and non-Christian, are indissoluble), or
whether it is indissoluble because it is a sacrament. One gets both
arguments. It seems clear that the nature of marriage is such that it
requires a high degree of stability and permanence for the sake of
the children, but not that marriage is in itself indissoluble. It seems
that if one is going to argue for the indissolubility of Christian marriage, it is better to do it on the basis of its being sacrament.

What is a sacramental marriage? According to the tradition,
any marriage between two baptized persons entered into freely and
witnessed by a duly authorized representative of the church, once
consummated automatically becomes sacramental and hence a
marriage characterized by indissolubility. So defined, "sacramental marriage" is a juridical label having no direct relation to the
Lord's dream of the coming Kingdom. That alone should give us
real reason to pause and rethink the whole thing.

But another indication that not all is well with our theory in
this matter is the fact that in every diocese of this country young
people who have been baptized are getting married in church before
a priest, and are doing so for purely social and familial reasons,
with no real commitment to the faith or the dream. In the eyes of

the church, such marriages are "sacramental" once they have been consummated.

There is certainly something wrong with that position. The young people in question have often been alienated from the church for years; they have no understanding of the Christian agenda, they have little or no knowledge of the Lord's dream of the coming Kingdom, and they have usually not even stepped inside a church for years. They want a church wedding because they like it aesthetically, or because they know that it would "just kill grandma" if they were not married in church. Everyone in the congregation at the wedding knows that, and we are asking priests every week to stand up there and witness what amounts to a lie. Then we want to say that because these young people fulfilled the juridical requirements for a sacramental marriage, they will not be free to marry again, should it not work out. More and more priests, fortunately, are refusing to witness such marriages, much to the chagrin of the families involved. The whole thing is a mess that cries out for clarification.

One final indication that something is wrong is that one can enter a so-called Christian marriage with little or no preparation. We insist on a long period of formation and faith development before we accept anyone into religious life or the priesthood, but young people can get married with little or no preparation. Obviously, we are thereby saying to the world that priesthood and religious life take long preparation and commitment, but a marriage in the Lord does not. Nothing could be further from the truth. It is not uncommon to be told by a couple married in their twenties that they didn't "really commit themselves to the marriage" until they were in their late thirties and forties. They grew into it once they came to understand from experience its true significance. Our teaching and our pastoral strategy should mirror, and be supportive of, this communally-funded human experience.

First, we must make a real effort to distinguish "marriage" from a "Christian sacramental marriage." A marriage in the Lord that has become a sign of God's presence and of his Kingdom is a "sacramental" marriage, and *by its very nature indissoluble.* Not every marriage "in the Lord" achieves that goal of being truly sacramental, and those that do, do so only many, many years after the wedding. Before that, the marriage is not sacramental and hence not indissoluble in principle. It is, as it were, on the way of becoming sacramental. If that is our initial premise, then how might we describe the whole process?

A young couple decides to be married and they aspire to have a truly "sacramental Christian marriage" eventually. The come up to the parish and are married in church before the community and pledge themselves not only to each other, but to work toward the day when their marriage will be truly a sign of the Kingdom and of Yahweh's fidelity to his people. They ask the Christian community to help them work toward that goal, and commit themselves to enter a process of ongoing adult Christian formation as their first steps toward that goal. Thus they not only marry on that day, but enter a process of growth in faith and in the Lord. The priest, in the name of the whole church and the community, blesses the couple, thus initiating a "marriage in the Lord." At some time in the future, if all goes well, the community will come to see in their marriage a true sign of the Kingdom. At that point, the local Christian community judges the marriage to have become a real sign of the coming Kingdom, and hence sacramental, thereby identifying the marriage as one that has achieved indissolubility.

Such a strategy has the advantage of distinguishing three types of marriage: 1) marriage, 2) marriage in the Lord, and 3) sacramental and indissoluble marriage. With these steps we acknowledge the developing dimension of love and intimacy, which is more in tune with the actual rhythm of married life that people experience. In this way we also avoid the difficulty of having priests witness falsely. They would be much more pastorally sensitive.

When I call for the church to get out of the "marriage business," I mean it should get involved only in "marriages in the Lord" and in promoting, identifying, affirming, and celebrating sacramental marriages when they occur. Such a pastoral strategy would allow the church to give up its role of "enforcer," and allow itself to mount an ideal for its people. Of course, what stands in the way of the church's adopting such a pastoral strategy is its continued and present insistence that there is only one kind of marriage for Christians (and even for non-Christians), that all sexual activity outside of marriage is immoral, and that human sexuality is inextricably bound to procreation. So long as it continues to hold those positions, it cannot help but be "moral policeman" and continue to meddle heavy-handedly in people's lives.

Imagine the exhilaration and liberation (to say nothing of the shock) people would experience were the Catholic Church to change its ways and proclaim:

> We know that people marry in many different ways, that they divorce, remarry and try again, or marry several people at the same time, but we don't think that it is up to us or any of our business to say that such arrangements are not "marriage." People are free to engage in sexual activity and to get married anyway *they* want, so long as they don't inflict unjustified ontic evil on others. But we cannot rejoice in or celebrate any kind of sexual and marital arrangements.
>
> For we also know that many of those arrangements are ultimately dissatisfying and oftentimes dehumanizing. So once you have discovered that for yourself, and you don't know where to turn or what to do next, we open our arms to you and long to share the Lord's own dream with you.
>
> Yes, we have a dream, an ancient dream, going all the way back to Abraham. Later it was incarnated in the Lord and its cornerstone is God's faithful presence to you in your deepest self. You have heard him calling you to a more noble and more significant lifestyle. If you are through with running from that call, and if you want your sexual activity and your marriage to be at last in accord with it, then we want you to join us in an effort to understand that call better. We invite you and your spouse to "marry in the Lord" and to begin the process of becoming together a sign to the nations and a light to the world in order to become Kingdom-persons.
>
> Should you not be quite ready for that and turn away, there is something we want you to know. God loves you. He waits for you to turn from a lifestyle that is really beneath you. We love you too. And like our God, we shall be here when you are ready. For we all know that there must be a better, nobler, more life-giving, and life-fulfilling way.

A Hopeful Afterthought

Some will feel that the position I have taken in this chapter on sex and marriage is more libertine than a Christian should espouse. My only response is that a position like the one I have presented does better justice to our experience. We are accustomed to say "experience is the best teacher." As people of faith, we also know why that is true. God himself teaches us in our experiences. If life is the best teacher, we must remember that God is life. The hierarchical church has always come closer to the truth when it has taken the experiences of its people seriously. I have no doubt whatsoever about the rightheadedness of what has been said here. As for the truth of it, that can only be verified by the communally-funded assent of faith-filled Christians whose experiences have revealed it to them.

We have recently seen a development among non-Christians that should give us reason to hope. Several of the gurus of the new sexual morality of the 60s are now calling upon their followers in the 80s to take a second look at monogamous marriage as the most satisfying expression of human sexuality. It seems we have come full circle. How did they come to that conclusion? From their experiences, of course. Life has a way of teaching us its most valuable lessons, whether we want to learn them or not. I am convinced that when it comes to sex and marriage, life ultimately teaches us the truth of what the Catholic tradition has always said about marriage.

If I have been critical of the institutional church, it was not because I believed that the ideals it presented on marriage were not the correct ones. It was rather because it presented them not as *ideals* but as *rules,* and as much too dependent on procreation. In calling for change in that respect, it should be clear that I was not calling for the church to lessen its ideals or scrap them. I have merely called for the church to present them in a way that better befits their nobility and dignity, and better respects the basic truth that the Christian life can be genuinely lived only in freedom.

Having set forth a theology of the Kingdom as central to a Christian assessment of human sexuality and marriage, we are in a position to apply that pastoral morality to some of the more pressing sexual issues much discussed these days. We now turn to that task.

SUGGESTED READING

James Burtchaell, *A Curious Tradition: Marriage Among Christians,* Ava Maria Press, 1977.

Bernard Cooke, *Sacraments & Sacramentality,* Twenty-Third Publications, 1983.

Donald Goergen, *The Sexual Celibate,* Seabury Press, 1975.

Andre Guindon, *The Sexual Language,* Univ. of Ottawa Press, 1977.

James Hanigan, *What Are They Saying About Sexual Morality?* Paulist Press, 1982.

Philip Keane, *Sexual Morality: A Catholic Perspective,* Paulist Press, 1982.

Anthony Kosnick, *et. al., Human Sexuality: New Directions in American Catholic Thought,* Paulist Press, 1977 commissioned by The Catholic Theological Society of America.

Evelyn and James Whitehead, *Marrying Well: Possibilities in Christian Marriage Today,* Doubleday, 1981.

CHAPTER TEN

Other Sexual Issues

I almost want to laugh at the thought of it now. It seems so completely foreign to what I have come to know about God and how he works in the world that I find it difficult to believe I actually lived in such mortal fear of him. But I did. So did most other adolescent boys with whom I went to high school. One could hardly avoid being scared to death at what might happen if he indulged in or enjoyed, ever so slightly, an erotic pleasure! Since we were students in all-male Jesuit high school and were not married, to indulge in *any* erotic (in those days called "venereal") pleasure meant we had sinned mortally. If we died after such an episode before we got to confession or made a perfect act of contrition, it was curtains for us. I still have an oft-quoted scriptural text in my head from those supposedly "carefree" days of youth: "But God said to him, 'You fool! This very night your life shall be required of you'" (Luke 12:20). I suppose that is why non-Catholic adolescent boys always derived more pleasure from their erotic episodes than their Catholic counterparts. Our pleasure was always marred by the thought that we were playing Russian roulette with our very lives. If the church wanted to make erotic pleasures less pleasurable, it succeeded. But only temporarily, because adolescent boys have a way of growing up and rejecting what was accepted naively and uncritically, due to inexperience. The image of God that emerges from that sort of view is of someone who doesn't really care what you may have done with your life as a whole, but is terribly concerned that you not violate the sixth and ninth commandments even once. When you think of it, that is a rather strange picture, not only of God, but of any intelligent person. As any parent can tell you, you are much more concerned with the overall lifestyle of your daughters and sons than you are about individual acts of drunkenness or erotic indulgence. Indeed, when those sorts of actions occur, you are most interested in knowing how they fit into the total life of your child and whether they are an indication of a change in overall direction. This is standard fare for those involved in parenting. Why wouldn't that be the same with God who revealed that he is going to "shepherd us rightly" and that he is our father?

Individual Sexual Acts vs. One's Life as a Whole

Traditional Catholic moral teaching has always been primarily concerned with individual acts, looking at them and judging them in isolation from the person's life as a whole. Contemporary Catholic moralists are much more inclined to consider acts in relation to the totality of the person, the unity that is that person's temporal existence. In that view, what is of primary interest is the continuing fundamental option (recall Monden's distinction between *object-choice* and *fundamental option*), by which a human person as spirit unconditionally commits or refuses herself. An individual act takes its full significance from the human person in her *enduring choice* with respect to the totality of existence, its meaning and its direction.

That is not to say that my object-choices are insignificant and all that matters is to keep my fundamental option straight. As we all know, when those two things are not compatible, we experience inner disgust and guilt because we have not made an object-choice that expresses our truest selves as embodied in our fundamental option. We have become a house divided; we have freely and intentionally introduced an ambiguity into our lives; we have become fragmented and are in disarray.

One of two things can be done. Either I change my fundamental option to be in accord with my object-choice; or I retain my original fundamental option or orientation and disown the object-choice as either immoral, if it unjustly inflicts ontic evil, or as a violation of my deepest personal ideals. Those are the only two things that can be done to remedy the situation.

There is a third alternative, however, and it is that I choose to do nothing and continue on in self-imposed ambiguity. Pressure builds, and it is not likely that incarnate spirits like ourselves can long endure such a state of inner disunity. We were meant to be whole, and to be at peace; we can only do the latter if we first achieve the former. Then, too, if I choose the third alternative, it will over a length of time turn into the first alternative, changing who I am, changing my fundamental option.

So we see that to lay stress in sexual matters on my life as a whole and my fundamental option does not mean that I am at liberty to do anything I please when it comes to sexual object-choices. Only certain sexual object-choices are compatible with a given fundamental option. If I am to answer the call to wholeness I find deep within myself, I shall have to take care that my object-choices consistently, if not in each and every instance, mirror what I am at my center. Failure to do that will result in a change at my center, or condemn me to ambiguity, a state in which I am unable to become who I am supposed to be.

If the faith really means something to me, if I have internalized its values and committed myself to the ancient dream incarnated in the Lord, then I have made a particularly Christian fundamental option, and only certain sorts of sexual object-choices will be capable of expressing what I am at my center, or at least not contradict it. On that much both the tradition and contemporary thinkers agree. The disagreement begins when we ask specifically what sorts of sexual activity inherently contradict one's faith commitment.

Leaving aside the major sexual offenses, for example, rape, incest, cruelty, about which there is unanimous agreement, the tradition holds that *all* sexual activity between the unmarried, and any sexual activity between spouses that intentionally frustrates the procreative function of sex are immoral and a violation of natural law, an offense against God, and an affront to faith. In this view, even oral sex and anal sex between spouses are permitted so long as male orgasm does not occur, which would frustrate the procreative meaning of sex. From that starting point, the tradition had no difficulty in reaching very clear decisions on such issues as autoeroticism, contraception, homosexual activity, premarital and extramarital sex, living together, and adultery. Such things were never really problematic; they, by definition, "contradict natural law," are objectively evil and are sins against God. Very neat, very tidy. Just a bit too neat!

That neatness is due to the totally verifiable and observable nature of the twofold norm invoked by the church in sexual matters. Are the two people married? If they are, did the male semen enter the woman's body, lodging unobstructed in her womb? If they are the criteria, then clear and decisive answers can always be given about individual acts. But the first norm is purely juridical or legal, and the second one is biological, physical, or if you will, athletic. Where is the Lord? Where is the dream? At best, those specifically Christian values or norms can enter only obliquely. Whether there is love, whether there is tenderness and sensitivity, whether there is intimacy between the spouses—we'll talk about all that later—just get the sperm in the vagina. That is what makes sex "good," and those other things only make sex better on the condition that it is first good. That is not only a crude, physical account of Christian sexuality, it is a crude account of human genital sexuality, period. Yet, saying that procreation is the primary end of human sexuality and marriage and that all other values are secondary comes down to just that.

With sensitivity, Vatican II avoided talking in terms of primary and secondary goals, and recognized the personal dimension of human sexuality as being of no less importance than procreation. Since then, it has become customary to speak of two equally fundamental aspects of sex and marriage, namely, the *unitive* and the *procreative*. That is reason enough to say that all pre-Vatican II manuals on morality and marriage are obsolete and would have to be rewritten if they are to continue to be taken seriously. But by maintaining the inseparable link between the unitive and procreative dimensions of human sexuality, Vatican II determined that the hierarchical church's answers to questions regarding sexual morality would be exactly the same as they had always been, although they would be spoken in a different language and in a more compassionate tone than before.

The only way to break out of the straitjacket of rigid physicalism in judging sexual matters is to face up to the fact that it is the unitive human dimension that is primary, and then see what consequences follow from that for Christians. (We have already seen some of them in the preceding chapter.)

So long as the unitive and procreative dimensions of human sexuality are said to be naturally linked, any actions that separate them must continue to be judged "unnatural" and therefore immoral or sinful, and marriage the only appropriate locus of sexual activity. But that is precisely what is being questioned; that is precisely what is at issue. Vatican II was not ready to strike out on a creative new path in that regard, though it made the move of raising the unitive dimension to equal status with the procreative. (See *The Church in the Modern World*, 48-52.) That is a positive development in the sense that it is going to make it easier for succeeding generations of Catholics to finally make the crucial move of making the unitive dimension more important. When that occurs, we shall be able to develop a Catholic teaching on sexuality that, for the first time since the days of the early church, is in accord with communally-funded human experience.

Returning to the ancient question, "What makes sex good?" the answer is: "Nothing; it just is." The question is a nonquestion. It arises only if one insists on taking a spiritualist approach to the human condition. The legitimate question to be asked is: "What differentiates human sexuality from that of the animals?" Clearly, the answer cannot be procreation. What is the answer then? Obviously, it is relationship, intimacy, or the human connection. Whether sexual activity is befitting human persons or not is a function of the quality and kind of relationship it both expresses and creates.

It was difficult to clearly discern that truth so long as humankind had not gained mastery over the procreative effects of sexuality, for until we were able to understand and control human fertility, the unitive and procreative dimensions of our sexuality were inseparable in practice. Their practical inseparability led some Christians to hold for their natural and theoretical inseparability as well. However, the pill and the condom have made that stand erroneous, and, as already stated, those and other contraceptive devices and techniques have now become integral parts of our human nature.

To separate human sexuality from procreation is at the same time to separate it from marriage. This is a frightening thought for Christians, and indeed, for all of humankind as well. The Council Fathers of Vatican II thought that looked too much like paganism, so they were unable and unwilling to make that move. But paganism is not characterized by the fact that its sex is extramarital, but rather by the fact that its sex is worshipped in itself, which means it is nonrelational, inflicts ontic evil, and becomes obsessive and hense destructive of human liberty.

When it comes to sex, paganism makes the very same mistake the Catholic Church made—physicalism. Indeed, it made the mistake first! Only instead of putting biological procreation in the top spot as the church did, paganism puts physical pleasure there. Physicalism in sexual matters, by any name ("Christian" or "pagan"), is equally subhuman.

Extramarital sex need not be "pagan" in any of those senses, and that is why it can be, depending on the quality and kind of relation involved as well as on other circumstances, truly human and truly good. That is not to say that it does not fall short of higher ideals, but it is to say that it need not be immoral, and may even not be sinful either. Whether it is sinful for the Christian will depend on whether it negates and contradicts one's fundamental option of commitment to God and to his dream of the Kingdom.

Of course, another reason for the church's reluctance to give up its physicalist ways completely is the awareness that to do so would make judging and evaluating human sex acts not nearly so cut and dried, not nearly so easy. The criteria for judging would be relational and qualitative, not physical and quantitative. It would mean that the church would have to give up its role as "moral policeman" in sexual matters and content itself with mounting the dream of the Kingdom and promoting the relational ideals for human life and sexuality that that requires. That looks too much like a comedown to the hierarchical church, but its faith-filled members realize it would be a step up for a church that was led astray by the Stoics early in its life. Evidently, what Kierkegaard said about pastors applied equally well to the church as a whole. Unless it has the courage to repudiate misunderstandings acquired in its youth, it will be unable to "shepherd rightly" and will continue to do great harm to the human family in the name of Christianity.

Contraception, or Birth Control

According to the tradition, contraceptive lovemaking is always immoral and sinful. The church has to say that because of what it has taken the conditions for "good" sex to be. That position, however, has led to some rather bizarre conclusions. For example, if two people are not married and they engage in genital sex, that is obviously immoral because they are not married. Now even though they are not married and therefore cannot offer any possible offspring a stable family relationship, *there is an additional moral evil,* according to the tradition, *if the unmarried couple engage in contraceptive lovemaking.* Faith-filled Catholic parents would much prefer that their children not become sexually active until they marry, in keeping with the ideals of their tradition. But if their children insist on being sexually active, those same parents would counsel them to at least practice contraceptive lovemaking until they are ready to marry. According to traditional Catholic teaching, they are obviously counseling their children to sin. The wrongheadedness of that posture alone would be reason enough to question the traditional view, even if there weren't many other reasons to do so, as we have seen there are. The Lord may well call us to be fools in the eyes of the world for his sake, but he never asks us to be stupid. That is something only others ask of us in his name. Generally, thank God, people have rejected such suggestions and have resorted to common sense to guide their actions, even though they are made to feel guilty about it.

The fact is that artificial birth control is rarely, if ever, immoral, but it can quite often be sinful. If a particular act of contraceptive lovemaking is immoral, that will never be simply because it is contraceptive, but rather because of other circumstances that cause the act to inflict unjustified ontic evil on oneself or another. An example of this evil would be if a husband were to deceive his wife by having a vasectomy without her knowledge. It is the deceit of the vasectomy that inflicts the ontic evil, not the contraceptive nature of their lovemaking. There are moral theologians who teach that contraception inflicts ontic evil on the act of intercourse itself, and therefore would be immoral if such contraceptive lovemaking were not justified for other reasons. (See Philip Keane, *Sexual Morality: A Catholic Perspective,* Paulist Press, 1977.) I have rejected that approach from the start, defining ontic evil as evil inflicted on beings capable of experiencing pain, death, and loss, which includes animals, but applies most especially to persons. Therefore, to be consistent, I must say that contraception is *never* immoral in itself, that is, because it is contraceptive, but that it may become so due to the circumstances in which it occurs, circumstances that unjustly inflict ontic evil on others.

If it is rare that contraception is immoral, it is much more frequently sinful. It will be sinful for believers when it involves saying no to God's invitation to love, or is the rejection of one's fundamental option to become a Kingdom-person. Contraception is sinful for the believer, then, when it is done out of an unwillingness to be selfless enough to witness the Kingdom. It is sinful when it creates an obvious ambiguity within me, between my fundamental faith commitment and my object-choice (contraceptive lovemaking).

The enemy of Christian marriage is not contraception, but selfishness, indifference, and all those things in ourselves that prevent us from living up to the high ideal St. Paul placed before the Ephesians (Chapter 5):

Be imitators of God as his dear children. Follow the way of love, even as Christ loved you. As for lewd conduct or promiscuousness or lust of any sort, let them not even be mentioned among you. ... There was a time when you were darkness, but now you are as children of light. Light produces every kind of goodness and justice and truth. *Be correct in your judgment of what pleases the Lord.* Wake up sleeper . . . and Christ will give you light. *Do not continue in ignorance, but try to discern the will of the Lord.*

Husbands, love your wives as Christ loved the church. . . . For this reason "a man shall leave his father and mother, and shall cling to his wife, and the two shall be made into one." This is a great foreshadowing: I mean that it refers to Christ and the church. In any case, each one should love his wife as he loves himself, the wife for her part showing respect for her husband.

Central to that ideal is the realization that there are no cut-and-dried answers that apply to every Christian couple. Each couple is to "discern for themselves the will of the Lord" and make an honest attempt to "be correct in their judgment of what pleases the Lord." Of course, in that process, it is important that husbands and wives seek the advice and counsel of the faith community in forming their consciences. But in the end St. Paul tells them that the decision is in their hands. When, how, and if their lovemaking could become contraceptive without violating the call of the Lord and his dream is a decision each couple must make for itself.

Pope Pius XII captured the spirit of this central fact of the Christian life when, in a radio broadcast of March 23, 1952, he said:

Conscience is the innermost secret nucleus in man. It is there that he takes refuge with his spiritual faculties in absolute solitude alone with himself and his God. Conscience is a sanctuary *on the threshhold of which all must halt,* even in the case of a child, his father and mother. . . .

And Piet Fransen, a Jesuit thelogian, thinks this applies even to Mother Church ("Grace and Freedom" in *Freedom and Man,* P.J. Kenedy, 1965, p. 51).

Nothing is so sacred and final as the human conscience. . . . No authority, not even the authority of the church, can take from me this burden, this duty before God or can excuse me from this personal and free decision of my own conscience.

Of course, if I think that following my own conscience is merely doing what *I* want, then I have badly misunderstood the situation. I am not alone in my conscience. Pius XII expressly said I am there with my God, and Karl Jaspers with great insight has said, "The voice of God lies in the self-awareness that dawns in the individual when he is open to everything that comes to him from his tradition and his environment." God speaks to us, then, not only through our Catholic tradition but also through our experiences. We have seen that his voice is always there, calling us to do what love requires, to be more generous and caring than we were yesterday, to remain open to the future and growing toward the freedom of Christ and the Kingdom. No one else may know if I reject that invitation, but *I* will know, and if I am trying seriously to walk with the Lord, I shall be suffering inwardly from having said no to him. I will be unable to find that peace the Lord promised; it can only be ours when we say yes to him, and to the coming Kingdom.

If a husband and wife find that the call to love, as seen in one another and in those children to whom they must already minister, requires them to take steps to avoid additional pregnancies, and if, realizing the impropriety of abstinence and the uncertainty of rhythm, they undertake contraception not out of selfishness but in accord with the call to love, then they should realize that they are in fact saying yes to the Lord; they should be at peace in their Father's presence. They should not feel like outcasts, nor be reluctant to participate fully in the sacramental life of the church. To think or act otherwise shows a lack of trust in God who is our Father and who calls us to be at peace.

Premarital Sex and Living Together

I noted at the beginning of the preceding chapter that Catholic parents are finding that their young adult children are more and more engaging in premarital sexual activity, and goodly numbers of them are deciding to have "live in" lovers either as a prelude to marriage or simply as a temporary living arrangement. This has caused a lot of heartache, and I lauded the mother who was able under the stress of that situation to witness what real love is when her daughter announced her intention to live with a young man for a period of time before they got married. The time has come to analyze why that mother's instincts were correct, and to consider what we should be saying in faith to our young people about premarital sex and "live in" situations.

One of the things we should be careful about is not transferring our notion about "impurity" and "defilement" to them. That is very difficult to avoid. We learned that such things were gravely sinful, and our image of those who engage in such activity is of people defiling themselves, making themselves dirty and in need of cleansing and purification. That is what we learned about such things. Remember the "marks" on the soul? Young people now in their twenties didn't receive that sort of introduction to moral evil and sin, and so they are not freighted with the same emotional abhorrence we feel about the so-called sins of the flesh.

Given the highly emotional overtones with which we invest such situations, I suppose it is to be expected that when our children come to us with their story, we are visibly shaken, not a little impassioned, and simply shocked. When we open our mouths, we probably say things to make the children feel guilty and less worthy in our eyes. Perhaps there is no way to avoid that. But some parents also manage to realize how really good and loving their children are; they decide to trust them in this matter. This is really not great if you think about it. What other choice do they have? Yes, I almost forgot their imitations of the Monster-god, but when you are dealing with twenty-year-olds, that act is somewhat hackneyed and almost certainly ineffective. Reflective parents know that. So they accept the news as graciously as they can, love and trust their children, and then never get a peaceful night's rest—until they marry!

Even after the children marry, parents are relieved but not at peace, because they still think that what they did was morally wrong, gravely sinful, and the sort of thing that "nice people" simply do not do. If we are to make peace with ourselves on this issue, we are going to have to change the way we think about it. The thing most helpful to us in that effort to change our thinking is the very experience we have with our children. But do we learn from it?

Does it teach us anything? What is the Lord trying to reveal to us in that experience about premarital sex and living together?

It all depends on the child and how she or he do it. After all, there are several different ways to engage in premarital sex. There is promiscuity, casual sex with lots of different partners just for the fun of it, and the living together just for the convenience of having sex *(nonrelational)*. Then there is the premarital sex between two people who care about each other, but have no intention of marrying. The prospect of learning and practicing the mysteries of intimacy is such a growthful experience and so attractive that both parties feel that it is an experience they do not want to pass up *(relational but noncommitted)*. There is also the premarital sex between two people who intend to marry at some time in the future but are not quite ready, for whatever reason, but can't stand the thought of waiting and not getting on with deepening their relationship *(relational and committed)*.

Before evaluating the three types of premarital sex in the light of faith and the dream of the Kingdom, it should be quickly noted that things don't always turn out as they appear destined to at first, or as we originally intend. This is especially true when it comes to love, sex, and intimacy. They seem to have a dynamic of their own, and we are always subject to being surprised. What starts out as fun and games and merely casual sex may end up in a committed marriage. The couple who intend to live together until they can marry may find that the rigors of intimacy are too much for them or that they are not suited to each other. At that point they may separate, or they may move to a "relational but noncommitted" arrangement. So it seems that the intention to marry, while consoling to parents, perhaps is not indicative of what is going on, after all. Even when it is sincere, it is subject to change, because reality is hard on dreams!

What did we and our children learn from those experiences?

First of all, even if our children adopt the nonrelational style of premarital sex, we find out that the world does not come to an end as we at first thought it would. Life goes on. Second, we find that the experience does not radically change our children. They pretty much remain the sorts of persons they were before engaging in premarital sex. If they are loving and giving, they bring that lifestyle into the relationship. If they are self-serving and insensitive, that is the way they enter into the experience, though we hope they emerged from it less selfish and more sensitive. They remain loving sons and daughters on the whole, if we don't do anything to drive them away.

Third, they discover, and we rediscover, where the truth and wisdom of the Catholic position on sex really lies. It is not easy to sustain a premarital sexual relationship; it brings with it not only the pleasurable opportunities for intimacy, but also the inherent challenge in all such intimate relationships that we be open enough to grow toward a better, more fulfilling kind of love, one involving honest commitment. In that sense, premarital sex always contains a strong element of dissatisfaction. It is, after all, not quite the way things should be among us. On that, our tradition and human experience fully agree.

Fourth, we become more than ever convinced of the irresponsibility of engaging in premarital sexual relations without taking adequate precautions against an untimely pregnancy.

Fifth, it soon becomes evident that premarital sex, like all relational experiences, contains a great potential for more evil and for sin. Thus, we are brought once again face to face with the human condition, and the absolute need for strategies of reconciliation, not only between the lovers, but between the lovers and their respective families.

In short, the experience is very instructive for all involved. It reveals better than any words or theories the relational and unitive dimensions of human sexuality. Granting there is no wisdom without tears, we can still question whether there is any better way to learn that truth. Isn't that the way most people learn it? Studies show that ninety percent of young people marrying today have had sexual intercourse with their partners before marriage. Up to ninety-four percent have engaged in genital stimulation to the point of orgasm. This makes premarital sex practically customary in this culture. The question remains, however: Can it be good and responsible? If so, what are the criteria to be used in making that judgment. What do we say in faith about it?

Nonrelational sex, whether premarital, marital, or extramarital, is contradictory to the unitive/communicative nature of
human sexuality, and is rightly frowned upon both by human experience and Christian faith. We are not animals, after all. Such
genital sexuality is dehumanizing and a violation of Kingdom-
ideals. Our children cannot ask us to say otherwise. We may have
to accept them and love them, even though they are in situations
where they are practicing nonrelational sex, but we never agree that
such sexuality is in accord with our ideals either as human beings or
as Christians. Whether such nonrelational sex is also a moral evil
will depend on whether it unjustly inflicts ontic evil on the participants or on others. That such sexual relations are sinful (in the
sense of contradicting Kingdom-ideals) cannot be doubted; they are
always a countersign to the Kingdom. If I aspire to become a
Kingdom-person, I will have to avoid nonrelational sex, or sincerely repent it, give it up, and repudiate it as not having any real place
in our contribution to the coming Kingdom.

That much is easy. It is much more ambiguous when we turn
to *relational but noncommitted* premarital sex. If your daughter or
son chose that kind of premarital sex, then you know what I mean.
It was at best an ambiguous experience. It had its pluses and
minuses. However it adds up, experience reveals that the pluses
were all due to the care and love expressed in the relationship and
the growth in selflessness that it effected. Experience also shows
that the minuses all arose from saying no to such growth and to the
commitment to which it beckoned both parties. Having to really
open oneself up to the needs and desires of another, to have to
break out of the natural self-centeredness we all experience within
ourselves, is good and a great learning or formational experience.

The dynamic of this sort of sexuality is always toward commitment, and to the degree that I resist that challenge and call I am
refusing to follow the dynamic of my love to its natural goal. That
"no" will always be a countersign to the Kingdom, but to the
degree that I am also learning to love and to give myself to another,
I shall be acting in accord with Kingdom ideals. So this type of
premarital sex is simultaneously saying yes and no to the Kingdom.
A "yes" to the unitive dimension of human life, and a "no" to the

commitment necessary to achieve full union. That sort of ambiguity cannot be sustained for a long period of time, for I will either ultimately say no to the Kingdom, or I will finally, more fully and completely, say yes. As a moment in the overall journey, this type of premarital sex could be judged as a normal stage of my development as a human being and as a Christian.

How individual cases will be judged will depend on the inner dispositions of the participants. If the "no" becomes paramount and the "yes" becomes lessened, the likelihood of both sin and resulting moral evil increases. If the "yes" is paramount and the "no" is merely a temporary reluctance out of which I am willing to grow, then it seems that faith would see it as a stage in growing toward maturity in the Lord and would judge it to be basically good, though not perfectly so.

By all accounts, those of human experience and those of faith, *relational and committed* sex, especially between engaged parties, is accepted as being realistic and in accord with the demands of our human nature and the Kingdom. We are assuming here that the commitment is sincere and real, of course. Indeed, it is the communally-funded wisdom in this matter that it is precisely *because* of the commitment that the sexual relations are good. Indeed, it has been suggested that couples in this situation are really married, since their mutual commitment alone is sufficient to accomplish that. The marriage has not been formalized either by church or state, but if the commitment is real, it is wrongheaded to think of those people as living in sin; rather, they are really "privately" married. In that situation, even an unexpected pregnancy is not a disaster. It usually merely hastens the formalizing of the marriage. But even in those circumstances, it is more responsible to avoid pregnancy until one is ready to make the commitment public.

It is, perhaps, not out of place to recall here something said earlier. The only reason we can talk this way about premarital sex is because we have taken the position to separate sex from marriage. To have done that means that our evaluations of premarital sex will be radically different from those offered in the past. We do *not* believe that sex and marriage are necessarily conjoined. What we *do* believe is that marriage and the kind of commitment it requires is the natural and ultimate fruition of human sexuality. But because human beings progress by stages, it is wrongheaded to suggest that they begin with fruition; that is not the normal way to proceed. Experience has long known that, and it is high time that the hierarchical church recognize it too.

One final thought. Relational premarital sex is such that its natural dynamic is toward commitment (marriage, even if it be nonformalized), and when that is not possible, toward separation. Love is like that. Once we recognize that fact, we must come up with some faith-filled strategies for celebrating such moments of pain and growth in the new directions, thus enabling people to cope with them. Why not a liturgy of reconciliation and separation? Why can't the faith community gather to mark such moments in the lives of its people? We must be much more creative in our approach to both life and to sex. It is not enough that we simply stop condemning people. We must celebrate the "mysteries" of their lives, for even when premarital sex ends in separation, to the degree that there was love in it, it remains an experience in which one encounters the God of faith and his call to intimacy and the Kingdom. To let that pass unnoticed by the faith community is regrettably a lost opportunity.

Adultery, or Extramarital Sex

Because old thought patterns die hard, and because we have a way of reverting to the meanings we learned as children, it might be wise as a footnote to our discussion of premarital sex, and as an introduction to our discussion of extramarital sex, to state once again, but we hope with greater clarity, what we mean when we say something is a sin.

We have taken great pains throughout this book to avoid simply identifying sin with moral evil. Moral evil is the intentional and unjustified infliction of ontic evil on oneself or another. As such, all moral evils violate human solidarity and cannot but be countersigns of the Kingdom, which is what I mean by "sin." But there are sins which, while contradicting Kingdom values, do not inflict ontic evil on others, for example, casual, nonrelational sex between consenting adults. Such things remain "sins" in my terminology because they cannot publicly witness the Kingdom. This is not to make a judgment of guilt or moral turpitude about the participants in such sins, but rather it is a judgment in the light of faith about the effect of their conduct in the public forum. To call an act "sinful" is to identify the act as incapable of witnessing to others the presence of the Yahweh-God and his ancient dream. It makes no claims about, nor is judgmental of, the sinner. There may be all sorts of circumstances that lessen her responsibility. Nonetheless, the act in its sign-value remains contradictory of the Kingdom. To call something a "sin" is to speak of its inherent message to others and to make a statement about its negative "public relations" value in proclaiming the Kingdom.

I am well aware of the current debate raging among moral theologians about whether any act can be judged immoral in itself—that is, whether acts are intrinsically good or evil, independent of circumstances. Nothing said in this book should be taken to suggest that I am not in complete agreement with the revisionist theologians who make a very strong case against the possibility of acts being intrinsically evil or good in themselves. (See the articles by Knauer, Janssens, Fuchs and Schuller in Curran and McCormick's *Readings in Moral Theology, No. 1,* Paulist Press, 1979.) Acts considered in themselves, abstracting from the concrete circumstances in which they occur, are not yet "moral" but "premoral." I have no intention of denying that stand when I call something in itself a "sin." It only appears that I am disagreeing with them if one ignores my definition of "sin" and insists on giving the word its traditional meaning.

In that spirit, then, I think it should be clear what I mean when I say that extramarital sex (adultery) is *always* a sin. Further, it would be a rare and unusual situation indeed in which that act would not also inflict ontic evil on one's spouse, which if unjustified would make the act also immoral. Extramarital sex is always a sin for believers because it violates a relationship, breaks a covenant, perpetrates a deceit, and witnesses to infidelity rather than fidelity. It does all that whether or not it is done with one's spouse's consent or inflicts any other ontic evil. In many ways, divorce is more honest. To put it otherwise, contrary to the prevalent opinion among Catholics, divorce is not nearly so affronting to the Kingdom as is adultery. In the concrete situation, that may account in some measure for a preference among believers for divorce and remarriage over ongoing extramarital sex.

Having said that, we should note that extramarital sex may be divided into the same three categories as premarital sex: *nonrelational; relational but noncommitted; relational and committed.* The married status of one or both of the participants in extramarital sex insures that each of the three types of extramarital sex cannot publicly give witness of and bespeak the Kingdom. In addition to all of the ambiguities present in premarital sex due to the dynamic of love and sex, there will be the additional ambiguities brought into the picture because of a previous commitment. If one is sincere in her desire to remain a believer and to continue to become a Kingdom-person ever more fully, the pressures become intolerable. Something has to give. Unlike premarital sex, extramarital sex as an object-choice is much more of a threat to destroy one's fundamental Kingdom option.

Nonrelational extramarital sex is a real enigma. We are assuming that the married person engaging in such activity has had relational sex with her or his spouse and has learned the lesson that sex is relational. If that is the case, then nonrelational sex will have to be truly dissatisfying. Young people starting to be sexually active may still have to learn that lesson, and so they may choose to learn it the hard way through premarital sex. An adult married woman or man who has already learned that lesson would normally eschew nonrelational sexual encounters. They may have the feeling that by keeping the extramarital sex nonrelational, they are still being "faithful" to their spouses because they do not really "care" for their extramarital sex partner. If that is the case, as we have already seen, they will soon learn that it is very difficult to sustain sex on a casual basis. Its dynamic is toward relationship and commitment, and it is fully satisfying only when it is engaged in on its own terms, as it were. So while nonrelational extramarital sex may be less threatening to the marriage, it is not really the sort of thing a believer will find compatible with faith, nor is it personally satisfying. It is, therefore, the most easily repented of the three kinds of extramarital sex.

Relational but noncommitted extramarital sex is, from all reports, the most common. It is estimated that only nineteen percent of the extramarital "affairs" end in divorce and in the marriage of the extramarital sex partners. That means that over eighty percent either end in the ultimate breaking off of the relationship, or are sustained in a debilitating ambiguity that adversely affects both the marriage and the extramarital relationship. Love cries out for commitment, but in this situation it cannot find fulfillment in either direction. What makes this such a painful human situation is the fact that there is real care, real intimacy, and the beginnings of real love between the extramarital partners, all of which are doomed to frustration. The toll on the marriage is inestimable, and so both the partners and their spouses are in severe pain and completely frustrated.

This is hardly a situation that can bespeak the Kingdom. Ontic evil abounds as well. No wonder many extramarital affairs are finally abandoned as hopeless—a wise alternative if divorce and remarriage aren't seen as the natural and obvious consequence of whatever love the new relationship holds.

Still, to the degree that there is real caring, real intimacy, and real love involved, valuable lessons can be learned. The need for unconditional commitment between a woman and a man is made painfully obvious. The extramarital affair can bring back to mind lessons long since forgotten by revealing the importance of intimacy and caring in sexual relationships. The experience of falling in love again after years of marriage can motivate one to try to recapture what was lost along the way in one's marriage due to neglect or habit. It can reveal that love is at the center of things, and spark the attempt to put love back into the marital relationship.

It can do all that, but it can also bring one to the realization that the marriage she is in is really no longer what a marriage ought to be, and move her toward divorce and remarriage with her new lover. In the midst of all that pain and misery, the God of love does not abandon us but continues to call us to the dream. But now the path to regaining that direction to our lives is so much more difficult, so much more painful than before we got involved in extramarital sex, for to get on track, I shall either have to break out of my marriage, or give up my lover. The Lord leaves it up to me to decide, but decide I must if I am serious about the Kingdom.

Relational and committed extramarital sex is usually a stage one reaches after spending some time in the preceding stage. Love and sex call for commitment, and once extramarital sex partners commit themselves to one another, the only logical step to take is to abandon their previous marriages and get on with their life together. But there is always an ambiguity at the heart of extramarital sexual relations once they reach this juncture in their development. For how can either partner take the word of the other about commitment when one or both of them are about to go back on a commitment previously made to their spouses? What value does their word have? Once unfaithful, always unfaithful, as the adage has it. Perhaps, but there is certainly no necessity of that. In any case, it is better to leave the discussion of that until the next section on divorce and remarriage.

Finally, it should be clear that extramarital sex, like premarital sex, is irresponsible in the extreme if precautions are not taken to avoid pregnancy. I hope I have shown there is more than enough ambiguity and frustration in the situation without factoring in an untimely pregnancy. What I have tried to do without being judgmental is to make clear the workings involved in extramarital sex. This should not be taken as an endorsement for extramarital sex. Rather, I have tried to show that believers can still respond to the call of the Kingdom even when caught up in sinful relationships. In the end, I suspect, the fundamental question is always whether we really want to walk with the Lord and be Kingdom people. That cannot be forced upon us. If we really want to, we can always find our way back out of darkness into the light, because our God is forgiving and the Lord is ever present in the darkness, ready to show us the way. As with all human growth, it will be painful and may take us a little while, but we know what must be done. As Jesus is reported to have said to the woman taken in adultery, "Has no one condemned you? Neither do I condemn you. You are free to go. But from now on, avoid this sin" (John 8:10-11).

Divorce and Remarriage

In the course of this book, I have called for the hierarchical church to give up being "moral policeman" to the world, to get out of the "marriage business" and concentrate on fostering the ideal of sacramental marriages among believers. That means that it should get out of the divorce and annulment business as well. Whatever legal and judicial regulations must be put on divorce, separations, and annulments to safeguard the common good, that is a matter for the secular authority of the state. That is no business of the church; it should stay out of such matters. Consider some of the consequences of the church having gotten involved in legal matters.

Prior to 1960, marriage cases processed by the Catholic Church's marriage tribunals could take anywhere from seven to twenty years. That is pastorally scandalous! Those were human persons who lived in uncertainty about their marital status for more than a decade. That may not be a long time in the life of the institutional church, but in a person's life it is a very long time. How could the church be so insensitive? What kind of a sign did she become to the world because of that? What does it say when the concern is more for the legal process and the marriage bond than for persons?

Then there are the sometimes bizarre results of the church's view of marriage and the indissolubility of the marriage bond. A divorced Catholic who remarries cannot avail herself of the sacraments of the church. Should she decide, however, to solve her problem by killing her spouse, and then repent it and receive absolution, she is free to marry again and be in the good graces of the Catholic Church. Evidently murder is a forgivable sin, but failing in one's marriage and trying again is not. The mind and heart boggle at such conclusions. Prior to 1966 in the United States, that "unforgivable sin" carried with it, thanks to an earlier twentieth-century decision of the American hierarchy, the additional penalty of excommunication. It would be ludicrous if such legalistic overkill weren't so devastatingly destructive of the human.

Running marriage tribunals also made the church subject to pressure from benefactors and people of prestige, power, and wealth. The process became so expensive that the average Catholic could not avail herself of this particular "service" of the church. As a result, the image of the tribunal process was marred by suspicions of its being unduly influenced by secular factors. For these and other reasons, one would have to say that the hierarchical church's entry into the judicial dimension of marriage and divorce has been something less than a spectacular success. Even if the marriage bond were naturally indissoluble, which I have tried to disprove in the preceding chapter, the practical strategy of the church in handling marriage cases was, until recent years, insensitive to the point of being disgraceful. Now, after a decade of experimenting with more sensitive procedures, there is talk of returning to former ways. Even within the tribunal system itself, it seems that the judges, advocates, and canon lawyers eager to really minister to people have always to battle the institutional church and try to beat it at its own game. What does that say about the system?

Happily, we also have instances in our tradition when individual bishops, priests, and pastors have managed to witness the Kingdom by doing the pastoral thing despite all the pressures in the other direction. Let me cite two interesting examples.

The first incident occurred in ninth-century Ireland, which was invaded by Moors who took Irish men back to Africa with them as their slaves. This left women and children without husbands and fathers. In that culture, in those harsh times, it was unlikely they could long survive, so the Irish bishops waited a respectable time, a year or two, and then simply gave those women permission to remarry *even though their first husbands were still alive.* Three cheers for those Irish bishops! Pastors all!

The second such incident occurred in Chicago in the 1920s and 1930s. The Blacks, migrating to Chicago in great numbers from the South, were eager to send their children to Catholic schools. Eventually, they themselves wanted to enter the church. This presented a problem, because many of them were involved in second and third marriages. To say the least, their marital status was "irregular." The pastors in the parishes concerned wanted to respond lovingly to those people, so they petitioned the bishops to do something about it. Faced with the problem, the Chicago bishops made the same sort of decision their Irish brothers had made a millenium earlier. They allowed such people to enter the church and arbitrarily ruled that the "marriage in possession" (the current one) would henceforth be considered the valid one. It was canonically illogical and wrong, but it was pastorally correct, witnessing compassion and understanding.

We have the mistaken notion that second marriages have always been forbidden by the church. They have never been considered ideal, nor could they be in the light of Matthew 19 and Mark 10, but the truth is that they were not banned by the Catholic Church until about the year 1000, and from the beginning, the Eastern Church has allowed them for pastoral reasons and still does. It recognizes that due to sin, ignorance, lack of faith and love, selfishness or passion, marriages dissolve. The Orthodox Church does not dissolve the marriage, but it recognizes that *it is already dissolved* and it allows both parties to enter a second marriage and remain in good standing within the church community. The second marriage, however, is not recognized as sacramental in the same sense as the first. But even there, the hope is that it may one day become so. The point I am making is that a study of the history of the church reveals that it has not been as adamant about second marriages as we have been led to believe. For half of its existence, second marriages were recognized as not the ideal, *but they were allowed.*

No more. This is a break with our more ancient tradition, and should be reconsidered. We have taken an ideal (Matthew 19 and Mark 10) and turned it into a hard and fast law, and then created all the legal and judicial trappings to cope with the mess we thus precipitated. The question to be put to the hierarchical church is this: On what grounds do we take the injunction about being peacemakers and loving our enemies found in Matthew 5 and interpret it merely as an ideal that allows us to put forth the "just war" theory, but take the injunction about divorce as an unbreakable divine command?

On whatever grounds that was done, it has proven to be a serious mistake. The indissolubility of marriage is a function of the quality of the relationship between the spouses and not a fact constituted by the marriage. We can all agree that indissolubility in marriage is the ideal that best incarnates Kingdom values and gives witness to the absolute fidelity of the Yahweh-God. It certainly does not follow, though, that all second marriages are contrary to the will of God, because concrete circumstances may be such that the second marriage becomes the best way to witness the Kingdom and hence may call for a different pastoral response from the church. We all know cases where a second marriage is more a sign of the Kingdom than was the first. That experience cannot be set aside simply because of the dogmatic pronouncements of the hierarchical church. Our dogmas must be in accord with reality as revealed by experience. And finally, it is not at all clear why the "sin" of remarriage is so unforgivable. There must be a "pastoral" way to get around the difficulty. To say otherwise is to cast aspersions on the Yahweh-God of faith as revealed to us in the Lord Jesus.

Homosexuality

I cannot end this discussion of sexual problems, which cry out for more sensitive and enlightened pastoral attention from the adult faith community, without addressing, however briefly and inadequately, the difficulty heterosexuals have in understanding and being pastoral toward homosexuals, female and male. As before, the difficulty is once again more with Christian heterosexuals and the misinformation they have in their heads than with those who are true homosexuals. That is, to be sure, of little consolation to the homosexual, since misunderstandings have actually resulted over the centuries in something very close to outright persecution.

We had trouble enough coping with the premarital sexual episodes of our children, but when it was finally revealed to us that a daughter or a son was "gay," we were devastated. We probably fell mute. But if our lips were stunned into silence, our heads were very busy rehearsing the now discredited lore about homosexuals, that long litany of insinuations, half-truths, and untruths that make up the culturally induced image heterosexuals have of homosexuals. Since the son or daughter in question probably did not embody the cultural stereotype—after all, most homosexuals do not—we found it difficult to accept the truth. Our daughter or son just didn't fit the pattern. Any hope we derived from that thought was soon dispelled as our daughter or son insisted that it was in fact true, that her or his sexual preference was for members of the same sex. At that point, our religious training came to bear on the situation as we recalled that the Bible speaks of homosexuality as an "abomination" punishable by death (Leviticus 18:22; 20:13).

Despair took told of us at the thought that this child or ours, whom we had nurtured as an infant and lovingly brought to adult life, was a pervert who, on St. Paul's account, had no place in the Kingdom and is heading for perdition (Romans 1:26-28; I Corinthians 6:10).

I recall seeing that despair in the eyes of a 55-year-old widow who told that her 32-year-old daughter was a lesbian, living in the same apartment building as she did; she described the anguish it caused her. When I questioned her about her daughter, she revealed that she was a competent nurse, much loved by her patients, admired by her associates, and respected for her competence, kindness, and generosity. A marvelous person by any account. The mother went on to reveal that as a child her daughter had twice been sexually molested by males, one of them being a family member. She felt that this probably accounted for her daughter's present sexual preference. At 32 and with that sort of past, it was unlikely that this woman was ever going to change her sexual orientation, and the mother was in despair at the thought that her lovely daughter was an abomination before God, practically assured of eternal damnation.

We do the Yahweh-God little justice when we depict him from the beginning to have been as badly misinformed on homosexuality as we have been until recently. But that is exactly what we do when we suggest that God views homosexuality either as an abomination or a perversion. Granting that our tradition, when looked at superficially or given a fundamentalist interpretation, invites us to such a posture, we know as people of faith that that doesn't sound like the Yahweh-God, the Father of Jesus. One can be a sign of the Kingdom regardless of one's sexual orientation. But before we can ever hope to see how that can be, we are going to have to exorcise those two words, "abomination" and "perversion," from the discussion of homosexuality.

Without going into all of the details (for that, see *Human Sexuality,* A. Kosnik *et. al.,* Paulist Press, 1977, pp. 188-196), it now seems clear that Scripture calls homosexuality an abomination only when it is a violation of the first commandment: I am the Lord your God, you shall not have strange gods before me. Homosexual acts were part and parcel of the worship of idols, and as such were seen as a rejection of the Lordship of Yahweh, which to any Jew *was* an abomination. We distort our tradition when we think homosexuality, taken by itself, is what Scripture is referring to. That simple misinterpretation of Scripture has been the single most important factor that has kept Christians through the centuries from being able to take an objective, much less a compassionate and pastoral, look at homosexuals.

Cultures other than Judaeo-Christian ones, that is, other than those that assume that homosexuality is an abomination in itself, seem to have been able to avoid labeling homosexuality as a willful perversion of human sexuality and a heinous evil. They accept homosexuality as a harmless deviation from the accepted norm, much as we do left-handedness in our culture. They see it as quite normal that a certain percentage of the population is left-handed and a certain percentage homosexual; this poses no threat to society and is accepted without recrimination. Not so in the societies of the Judaeo-Christian West. We have forced a small but significant part of our populations to be outlaws for something they have about as much control over as those who are naturally left-handed. We have criminalized homosexuality for the most specious of religious reasons and have tried to justify outrageous conduct by labeling it a "perversion." We take consolation in that awful label, blinding ourselves to the injustice of it all.

The fact is that all human children seem to be born with the potential of having their sexuality take either a homosexual or a heterosexual orientation. With some constancy, we find that about eight percent become true homosexuals, come what may. They didn't will it that way. They didn't plan it that way, any more than heterosexuals do; it just happens. They find that their sexual interest and erotic arousal arise from persons of their own gender. That's how they discover their sexuality and they take it to be quite normal. And for them it is.

We still don't know exactly why such an "inversion" occurs. Whether it is hereditary, due to body chemistry, or some cultural interaction in early life, or some combination of these or other factors, we simply do not know. But whatever the cause, eight percent of our young people will experience that sort of sexual inversion as natural, not having moral evil about it. It may be one of nature's ways of controlling population, and hence completely natural as a normal control group for the general population. In any case, it is simple-minded and wrong-headed to call it a perversion, as if it were something maliciously chosen by human beings. It is stupid and cruel to attempt to force such true homosexuals to see their sexuality otherwise; they simply can't. No amount of will power and no amount of spirituality can alter the fact that they are erotically aroused by members of their own gender. We must appreciate true homosexuals for what they are, help them to accept themselves as they are, despite societal prejudice and disapproval, and call them in faith to make of their homosexuality a sign of the Kingdom just as heterosexuals are to do.

Having eliminated "abomination" and "perversion" from our discussion, perhaps we can address the problem of true homosexuality in a truly pastoral way. When we do, we find not unexpectedly that the norms for judging homosexual relationships are the very ones we used in our discussion of the heterosexual. Once we accept the premise that sex and procreation were mistakenly taken to be inseparable for Platonic and Stoic reasons, and that the meaning of human sexuality is really relational and not biological, then homosexual activity, like heterosexual behaviour, must be judged by the quality of the relationship. It will be immoral if it inflicts unjustified ontic evil; it will be sinful for the believers if it contradicts Kingdom-Ideals.

As with heterosexual relationships, there will be homosexual *nonrelational* sex (one night stands, casual liaisons, fun and games sex); homosexual *relational but noncommitted* sex (relatively stable but short term live-in situations); and homosexual *relational and committed* sex (permanent commitment, the so-called homosexual marriage). What we have already said about these relationships in a heterosexual context can be directly applied to the homosexual context as well. Sex, be it homosexual or heterosexual, cries out for relationship and commitment. True homosexual adults have the right to learn that dynamic for themselves without premature criticism (so long as they inflict no unjustified ontic evil), just as we have claimed their heterosexual sisters and brothers do. The faith community pastorally must always proclaim and encourage the ideal of relational love and commitment for all sexually active people, whatever their orientation.

As with all things human, homosexuality has a special ambiguity that must be addressed before we can evaluate the meaning of the so-called homosexual marriage. That ambiguity may not touch the lives of those we have called "true" homosexuals, that eight percent of us who are clearly and irrevocably homosexual in orientation. It has been noted, however, that human children are born with a potentiality for either homosexual or heterosexual orientation. This opens up the possibility of a time in one's developmental life when that orientation is not yet definitively fixed, but remains in process. At such times, persons may find themselves ambiguous about the outcome, and so turn to both heterosexual and homosexual experiences in order to discover their proper orientation. Such ambiguous periods in a person's life should be viewed as part of the normal process of fixing one's sexual orientation, and should not be viewed as reason for moral alarm.

Should young people seek pastoral counsel at such times, care must be taken to determine whether the person is a true homosexual or whether there is a real ambiguity present. (As we saw in the case of the mother and daughter, knowledge of any significant or traumatic sexual events in childhood can often cast light on the situation.) What is to be avoided is either attempting to change a true homosexual, or failing to counsel someone whose orientation is still in flux about the advantages and wider opportunities of the heterosexual orientation. This is not because homosexuality is somehow inherently evil, but rather because its track record for being able to remain a fulfilling lifestyle for the entire duration of a person's life is just not very good. The difficulties of being homosexual are not to be underestimated.

Now to the final point in this overly brief and almost schematic discussion of homosexuality—to do it justice, one would have to write an entire book—the much disputed notion of a homosexual "marriage." There are those who steadfastly insist that a relationship can be called a marriage only if it offers the possibility of procreation. A rather narrow view, I think. On that account, even some permanent heterosexual genital relationships would not qualify, which is to say that some marriages would not be marriages.

Recalling the distinction made earlier with regard to heterosexual marriages, there seems to be no inherent reason why it cannot also be made with regard to permanent and committed homosexual unions. Those unions too might well be classified as 1) marriages; 2) marriages in the Lord; and 3) sacramental marriages. At least, let us Christians not too quickly rule out *the possibility in principle* of homosexuals achieving such satisfying human relationships, even the sacramental one.

What I am saying, quite simply, is that there is nothing at all in the requirements for a "marriage in the Lord" or a "sacramental marriage," as we defined them earlier, that would automatically disqualify homosexuals. I do not know whether any homosexual relationships have ever actually reached the level of a "marriage in the Lord." Given the misguided attitude of Christians toward true homosexuals, it seems unlikely that the Christian community would have been able, until quite recently, to recognize a homosexual union as sacramental even if it occurred right in its midst.

Blinded by the thoughts of abomination and perversion, we have simply written homosexuals out of the Kingdom, thinking them incapable of achieving the highest of Christian ideals. We had no expectations that they were capable of incarnating the ancient dream in their sexual relationships. Consequently, we did not call them forth. We did not reach out to aid, console, and assist them on their journey. Believing homosexuals are our sisters and brothers in faith; they share with us our commitment to the Lord and to the dream of the Kingdom. It is high time heterosexuals recognize that fact and treat homosexuals accordingly.

Summing Up

From the "traditional" perspective, I am sure that all that I have said in the last two chapters can only be judged shocking and contrary to Catholic moral teaching. That, of course, is not at all surprising since I have proceeded from a different set of principles. I submit that the account I have given of human sexuality is in accord with communally-funded human experience, and that it is possible for a Catholic to espouse it, if only she take a "faith," rather than a "religious," perspective. In any case, experience reveals the following elan or dynamic in human sexuality:

1. The primary end of human sexuality is relational and unitive.
2. The dynamic of relational sex is always toward love and commitment.
3. The dynamic of commitment is toward a relationship characterized by exclusivity and permanence, which is traditionally called "marriage."
4. Human procreation is fully responsible only in that context of commitment and permanence.
5. Marriage is not by nature indissoluble. Indissolubility is its highest ideal and goal, and it is achieved only as a function of the quality of the personal relationship between spouses.

In the light of this progressing nature of human relationships in general and human sexual relationships in particular, we would expect to, and we actually do, find people at every level of the progression, believers and nonbelievers alike. What does Christian faith bring to this enterprise?

I have tried to suggest that whatever contribution the faith makes, it cannot attempt to short-circuit the enterprise and make it nonprogressing. That, in effect, is what traditional Catholic moral teaching tries to do, whether intentionally or not. In addition, the church has used force to implement its views, something I judge to have been a terrible mistake. Accepting the built-in dynamic of love and sex, the church should minister to people wherever they are in the process. It should also minister to them by upholding the ideal of the Kingdom as it applies to their situation. What does it mean to "uphold" an ideal? Just that—to hold it up—and no more. It means to incarnate it so that it becomes visible in everyday life, thus revealing an alternative way of life to the one the culture may present.

To those engaged in nonrelational, fun-and-games sex, Christians should uphold the ideal of relational, caring, and concerned sex. To those engaged in relational sex but unable to commit themselves, Christians are to uphold the ideal of relational sex which is, in addition, committed. To those who have arrived at a sex life that is both relational and committed, the Christian community should uphold the ideal of openness to new life, whether through procreation or selfless service to others. And to those who already incarnate those ideals, we should uphold the highest Christian ideal, that of the special relationship that bespeaks the presence and fidelity of the Yawheh-God, and that transforms human love and intimacy into sacrament. And so, wherever people are struggling with the tremendous ambiguities of human love and intimacy, the church should be upholding the ideal appropriate to the level they are on, and to present it as gift that may be either freely accepted or rejected. The church should do all this without a word about the dire consequences of rejecting so noble and good a gift. In short, the church should be truly pastoral about it all. Threats are particularly ungracious and they transform the Christian enterprise into something akin to blackmail. This is terrible way to go about witnessing the Yahweh-God to the world!

An additional reason why threats are unnecessary is that life has a way of teaching the lessons of love and intimacy to those who frustrate the dynamic of relational love and relational sex. Failure to follow the built-in dynamic of those realities is bound to bring great suffering to oneself and to others. The appropriate Christian response to people in that predicament is not more threats or inflicting more pain, but loving compassion as the Lord would give it—graciously. That is why it is imperative for the church to get out of the "marriage tribunal business" and thus become more fully the church of Christ.

For the record, I really believe that promises ought to be kept and that fidelity is an absolutely indispensable human and Christian value. In those important sectors of human life characterized by love, intimacy, and personal relationships, we need, yearn for, and will settle for nothing less than fidelity, or at least the striving for it. And yet . . . and yet . . . reality is hard on dreams.

I also truly believe that amid the vicissitudes and ambiguities of life, the Lord meant us to be at peace. No one should be forced to stay in priesthood, religious life, or marriage unless she really wants to. Commitment is a function of freedom. Experience teaches us that there are second marriages that are both humanly and Christianly better than many a first marriage. Though virginity once lost can never be regained, it is altogether different with fidelity. No matter what has gone before, it is never too late. One can always begin again to be faithful.

If that looks as though I believe contradictory things, so be it. The ambiguity of life requires some such posture. We must never lose sight of the ideal nor fail to uphold it for our world in the Lord's name. But we must never lose sight of the fact that it is an ideal to be courageously striven for. As Christians, we are also called to deal much more compassionately with those who, for whatever reason, fail to achieve it. To do the first without doing the second makes us a countersign of, rather than a witness to, the Kingdom.

Having given an account of how to look at the major sexual issues from the point of view of the coming Kingdom, we can leave it to the reader to apply the principles illucidated here to the remaining sexual issues: pornography, auto-eroticism, masturbation, etc. It is time for us now to turn to the life and death issues that currently so divide the faith community. I am speaking of abortion and euthanasia.

SUGGESTED READING

Ernest Becker, *The Denial of Death,* Free Press, 1975. Ch. X, pp. 208-252.

John Dedek, *Contemporary Sexual Morality,* Sheed & Ward, 1975.

Dennis Doherty, *Divorce & Remarriage: Resolving a Catholic Dilemma,* St. Meinrad, 1974.

Mary Durkin and James Hitchcock, *Catholic Perspectives: Divorce,* Thomas More, 1979.

Stephen Kelleher, *Divorce & Remarriage for Catholics?*, Doubleday, 1973.

John Noonan, *Power to Dissolve: Lawyers and Marriages in the Courts of the Roman Curia,* Harvard Univ. Press, 1972.

Richard Westley, "Some Reflections on Birth Control" in *Listening,* Vol. XII, No. 2 (Spring 1977), pp. 43-61.

See also the suggested readings at the end of Ch. 9.

CHAPTER ELEVEN

Life and Death Issues

Immorality is characterized by the ontic evil it intentionally and unjustifiably inflicts on others. As we saw in the preceding chapters, the sexual matters with which we Catholics have become so obsessed are more often than not such that they do not inflict ontic evil. Therefore, those acts may well be violations of Kingdom ideals and violations of our baptismal covenant to become witnesses to the Kingdom (sins), but they are not immoral acts as such. They call into question how serious we believers are about walking with the Lord and presenting his alternative lifestyle to the world, but they do not make us immoral.

All that changes when we turn to the life and death issues. Here we are talking about acts that not only inflict ontic evil, but that inflict what we have called earlier the "supreme" ontic evil. Death deprives us not only of life, but of every other good as well. Unjustified death-dealing not only violates the ideals of the Kingdom, it is the height of immorality. We would therefore expect the church to take a very strong stand on these matters, and of course we know that it has. But to take a strong stand vis-a-vis the life/death issues does not exempt us from having to reflect critically

233

on our stand and to work to see that it is implemented in a truly pastoral way.

We saw earlier that the most basic reason for being moral arose from an experience of the preciousness and uniqueness of persons. And it was noted that in the absence of that sort of experience, morality becomes at best a matter of ultimate self-interest. Daniel Maguire (*The Moral Choice*, Doubleday, 1978, p. 72) describes the importance of this foundational moral experience as follows:

> The foundation of morality is the experience of the value of persons and their environment. This experience is *the* distinctively human and humanizing experience and the gateway to personhood. It is this experience that sets us apart from beast and barbarian. It is the seed of civilization, the root of culture, and the badge of distinctively human consciousness. Without an in-depth participation in this experience, morality would seem a meaningless intrusion on our whim and fancy, and moral language would be non-sense. If human activities, institutions, and religions do not enhance this experience, they are negligible and indeed objectionable, for they are failing at the constitutional level of human existence.

How marvelously put! Maguire's comments deserve serious reflection in an age such as ours when individual rights and freedom seem to be the major focus of discussions of morality. However sophisticated, intelligent, and technologically competent we become, we remain "barbarians" if we lack a basic sensitivity to the value and rights of others. The Catholic Church has always attempted to enhance the foundational moral experience of the intrinsic value of persons, each one precious and made in the image of the Yahweh-God. It may have made a botch of sexual and marital morality, but it has, throughout its history, stood as a bulwark against the cultural drift toward barbarism in all its forms. With regard to the life and death issues, the church has generally been on target, and its position requires only some "fine tuning" to distill off some of the obviously "religious" elements and bring it into fuller compatibility with incarnational faith. For however righteaded its position has been on the life and death issues, the religious elements of that perspective have insured that we Catholics continue to say some pretty silly things about God.

The Yahweh-God and Killing

Although it is true by definition that every morally evil act inflicts ontic evil, it certainly does not follow that every infliction of ontic evil is immoral. Those who think otherwise have mistaken ontic evil for moral evil. It is true that moral evil is never justifiable; that's what makes it immoral, but the same cannot be said for ontic evil. We seem to have no difficulty understanding that, when it comes to lesser evils than death. We condone amputating diseased limbs, removing diseased organs, engaging in various therapies with devastating side-effects, all of which are ontic evils. We even condone the taking of a human life, the supreme ontic evil for the one killed, in circumstances of self-defense, just war, and as punishment for capital crimes. In these cases, we discern that although an ontic evil is certainly inflicted, it is justified by the circumstances. So we generally have a firm grasp on the distinction between merely ontic evil and moral evil. When it comes to the taking of innocent human life, though, we sense the gravity of the situation and feel safer simply holding that *all* killing of the innocent is immoral. But then we must be prepared to say why this is so. Why is it that killing an innocent can *never* be viewed simply as a tragic ontic evil that is justified due to unfortunate and extenuating circumstances? Why is killing an innocent an intrinsic and absolute moral evil *regardless of circumstances?*

The Catholic tradition has generally given two responses to this question. First, the innocence of the victim precludes any hope of justifying the killing due to circumstances. Circumstances only justify killing in those situations in which the one killed cannot be said to be completely innocent. To kill an innocent person is beyond the realm of circumstantial justification. Second, to make the decision to kill another human being who is faultless is to appropriate a divine prerogative to oneself. God alone has dominion over life and death, and it is immoral for a creature to presume to exercise that prerogative on his own authority. Thomas Aquinas

(*Summa Theologica* II-II, 64, 5, c) uses this very argument against suicide as well as the killing of the innocent.

> To kill oneself is never allowed because life is a gift to man from God who alone has authority to kill and to give life. Hence whoever takes his own life sins against God in the same way that he who kills another's slave sins against the slave's master, and as he sins who takes on himself for judgment a matter not entrusted to him.

Circumstances cannot be extenuating in the case of killing oneself or killing an innocent, because such an act not only usurps a divine prerogative, but also inflicts ontic evil on one of God's servants, thus depriving God of that person's service. What makes killing an innocent intrinsically and absolutely morally evil, then, is the fact that in whatever circumstances it occurs, it usurps a divine prerogative and violates divine rights. End of discussion!

Not quite. For one thing, what does it mean to say that God alone has the prerogative to kill an innocent? That sounds peculiar, to say the least. Would the Yahweh-God, who is life itself, ever want to do such a thing? Most of the horror stories in the Bible are accounts of God killing or asking a human agent to kill those who violated his laws and did not walk in his ways. I have already noted the contradiction that a literal rendering of Scripture creates in those cases, due to the Yahweh-God's revelation of his unconditional love and forgiveness. If implicating God in killing the guilty can be questioned, what are we to make of the Abraham story, in which the Yahweh-God ordered Abraham to sacrifice (kill) Isaac, his only and innocent son?

The Catholic tradition on killing was profoundly affected by the fact that the Abraham story was taken to be literally true. What would *you* do if God appeared to you and ordered you to kill one of your own children? First of all, if you are a person of faith, you would know that God would never do that. If God appeared to me and asked me to kill one of my sons, I would bluntly refuse. "If you want to get someone to kill my son, then you'd better get someone else. I won't do it. After all, I am the lad's *father!* Besides, if you are so insensitive as to make that sort of demand of me, then I know you're a fraud. You're not the Lord!" If, as to this day I remain convinced, that is what Abraham should have said, if, indeed, that is what any person of authentic faith would say, why, as our father in faith, did Abraham not say it? In a way, that is the wrong question to ask. Abraham didn't have to say it, because the Yahweh-God never asked him to sacrifice Isaac! It is not a question of Abraham, but rather of the Old Testament writers and why they told his story the way they did. In those ancient times, it was normal for people to think of the king as having absolute power. Their experience showed that earthly kings exercised that kind of dominion over their subjects, having the power of life and death. If Israel looked on the Yahweh-God as their king, then it is to be expected that the oral tradition about him from which the Old Testament writers drew would be filled with stories of the kingly status of the Yahweh-God. That those stories are now seen as contradicting what God ultimately revealed of himself in the Lord Jesus is due to a more recent and better perception of who God is and how God works in the world. We are not his subjects; we are the incarnations of his presence and the living signs of his Kingdom. But that became clear only much later. The Old Testament writers told the story of Abraham in a context with which the ancient peoples would be most comfortable. It never occurred to them that they were setting up tremendous theological problems for Jews and Christians of succeeding ages.

The principal aim of the Abraham story was to show why he was our father *in faith*. To ancient peoples, this was revealed best by the willingness of Abraham to do whatever the Yahweh-God asked of him. He left his homeland, entered into the covenant, and believed in the promise that he would be the father of a great people. His trust in and commitment to Yahweh are put in stark relief in the story of his willingness to sacrifice his only-begotten son, who represented the sole hope for the realization of that ancient promise. It never occurred to the ancient writers that the story as they told it was really slander and defamation of character against the Yahweh-God. It seemed quite normal, judging from their experience, to have God act that way. But to show the difference between the Yahweh-God and earthly kings, they end the story with the Yahweh-God staying Abraham's hand and repeating the promise—a hint that "killing in the name of the Lord" is not to be done either. Evidently it was only a hint, since the Judaeo-Christian tradition continues to teach in our day that one is free from moral guilt if one kills at the command of God. That has been welcomed news to religious fanatics through the centuries. It makes no sense at all to people of faith.

In the light of the divine prerogative to kill (even the innocent) Aquinas has said, "To kill onself is never allowed because life is a gift to man from God who alone has the authority to kill and to give life." But there is a hidden contradiction contained in that statement. For if life is truly a "gift" from God, then it would be assumed that a person could dispose of it as she sees fit, and suicide and voluntary euthanasia should be permissible. But Aquinas (*Summa Theologica* II-II, 64, 5, ad 3) thinks not for the following reason:

> That a person has dominion over himself is because he is endowed with free choice. Thanks to that free choice a man is at liberty to dispose of himself with respect to those things in this life *which are subject to his freedom*. But the passage from this life to a happier one is not one of those things, for one's passage from this life is subject to the will and power of God.

Obviously, Aquinas thinks that human freedom extends "to the things of life" but not to life itself. A strange conclusion to draw if life is truly a gift from God. To give someone a gift is precisely to give them power over that gift. Now either life is a gift from God, which is truly ours and hence something over which we rightly have dominion, or we are given life the way the servants in Luke 19:11-27 were given money, which means that life is never truly ours but is only temporarily entrusted to us. It is difficult to see how the tradition can have it both ways. Either we hold our lives as stewards, and then it is out of place to call it a gift, or life is truly ours by gift, and then to speak of stewardship is out of place in this context.

We can see why the tradition is in need of some fine tuning. We have portrayed the Yahweh-God as capable of asking a father to kill his own son; we have portrayed his gifts as anything but the pure gratuities they are. If we were capable of these portrayals, perhaps we could be mistaken, too, in our assessment of mercy killing, or euthanasia. On that possibility, it might be wise to reconsider the matter.

Euthanasia, or Mercy Killing

There are only three basic positions regarding the prolongation and termination of innocent human life. I shall call these the *fundamentalist, liberal,* and *radical* views. The current "right to die" controversy is being argued within the perimeters set by these three positions.

The *fundamentalist* view is unambiguous, straightforward, and admits of no exceptions. According to this view, human life is everywhere and under every imaginable circumstance an absolute good, which as a gift from God is inviolably sacred. Everything possible must be done to prolong that life, regardless of its degree of vitality, since God alone has dominion over life and death. Our obligation is to sustain human life, without the slightest reservation, to the very end. This position, espoused by significant numbers of pro-lifers and physicians, is sometimes mistakenly taken to be the "Catholic" position.

The *liberal* view maintains that human life is good, but not absolutely. Thus, because innocent human life is inviolably sacred, one is never permitted to take direct action against it, though one is under no obligation to prolong it in any and every circumstance. What makes this view more liberal than the preceding one is the morally significant distinction between killing someone and allowing her to die. In the light of that distinction, we are allowed both to suspend hopeless treatments and refuse to undertake extraordinary ones. Those who espouse this view, which is really the "Catholic" position if such there be, maintain that once the situation becomes hopeless, extraordinary means simply prolong the dying process and we are under no moral or Christian obligation to do that. However much fundamentalist and liberal disagree on that point, they remain in total agreement that under no circumstances may direct action be taken against innocent human life.

According to the *radical* view, it is generally true that it is immoral to take direct action against innocent human life, but it is not absolutely true. There are situations and circumstances that invite and even compel us to act directly to terminate human life. The classic case cited by the radicals is the situation in which a person is in fact: a) presently incurable; b) beyond the aid of any cure or restoration that may reasonably be expected to become available within her lifetime; c) suffering intolerable and unmitigable pain; and d) of a fixed and rational desire to die or has previously certified a wish to die in the event that the first three conditions should ever come to pass. Precisely at that point the "right to die," "death by choice," and "decision to die" advocates espouse taking direct action against human life. One reason the radical view is urged so forcefully in our day in that the techniques of modern medicine have not only worked marvels for many, but have also greatly increased the number of people who find themselves in the classic situation just described.

It is widely assumed that a Christian is obliged to espouse either the fundamentalist or liberal views, and that the radical view is by its very nature contrary to Christian faith. Upon deeper reflection, I think it becomes obvious that direct mercy killing need not be either a moral evil or a sin. What is more, under certain circumstances it might even become obligatory if one is going to live up to the foundational moral experience. That is difficult for many to accept because they hold to the divine prerogative principle, which clearly states that God and God alone has dominion over life and death. But how can that be true?

We have already seen that our tradition holds that we are permitted, if not exactly encouraged, to exercise that divine prerogative in cases of self-defense, just war, and, after due process, execution for capital crimes. In those cases, at least, we seem to be able to appropriate the divine prerogative without blame. Making life and death decisions is not exactly unprecedented for human beings, not even for human beings who walk with the Lord. Still, we are told that we humans cannot assume to make life and death decisions in cases that involve killing an innocent. That, only God can do. We have also seen how truly strange that assertion is, because, the Abraham story notwithstanding, it seems inconceivable that the

God of faith would ever want to do such a thing. Evidently, we shall not be at peace with, or be able to give serious consideration to, the radical view unless and until we can show that it is morally and Christianly permissible for us to assume the divine prerogative in some situations involving killing innocents.

What are we to say then, about mercy killing, or voluntary euthanasia? Many conceptual difficulties would have been avoided if our ancestors in faith had recorded the fifth commandment differently. By giving it the form "Thou shalt not kill," they introduced an ambiguity into the matter that has haunted Jews and Christians through the ages. As we have now come to understand, the fifth commandment should have been given the form "Thou shalt do no murder." "Murder" is a complete moral notion indicating an unjustified taking of human life. Our very language does not permit us to talk about "good" murders. By definition, there are none. It is altogether otherwise with "killing." It is an open moral notion, which requires one to use the adjectives "good" and "bad" in order to make its moral significance explicit. But if from the moral point of view some killings can be labeled "good" and some "bad," then again our language does not permit us to make absolute prohibitions against "killing" the way we can against "murder." Only confusion awaits those who attempt to violate these basic canons of our language.

Why is it then that mercy killing is not murder? Because in order to be murder, there has to be an unjustified infliction of ontic evil. But given the circumstances in which mercy killing looms as a viable moral possibility, namely, that the person is in such dire straits that to kill her cannot be interpreted as doing her harm, there seems to be the possibility that death is no longer the supreme ontic evil *in that situation*. That death can become a good is evident from the fact that, in those circumstances, it can be actually desired or sought after.

Two things must be considered when judging whether a particular act of killing is morally evil or not. Is the killing against the will of the one killed? And, does it do her undeserved injury or harm? If the answer is yes to one or both of those questions, the act is murder and morally reprehensible. If the answer is no, then it is an act of killing that is not morally wrong. When a person is reduced to such a state that to kill her can no longer be interpreted as doing her harm, then the only thing preventing direct action is that person's consent. One is under no obligation to give such consent, but in cases of bonafide euthanasia both conditions are met, and so we may conclude that mercy killing is not always morally evil.

What can be said about killing an innocent from the perspective of the believer? Will it matter whether the believer takes a "religious" or a "faith" perspective? Being human, we have always found it difficult to accept the faith perspective. Our fear of life, our terror of death, and our own anxiety about the hereafter have always tempted us to mix ever greater doses of religion with our faith. As we have seen, even the writers of the Old and New Testaments can't seem to keep religion out of their faith stories. Their accounts alternate between a God in whose presence we are but dust and to whom we owe religious obedience, and a God who becomes human and reveals himself as Father, declaring the adoption of our race *to divine status*. The point, of course, is that Scripture may be read either way. Because it can, one cannot invoke those Scriptures to settle the dispute as to whether Christianity is more authentically interpreted as a "religion" or as a "faith." Believers must themselves choose whether to see the Scriptures as a call to religion or faith. Put another way, in answering the call to keep faith with the Catholic tradition, we are going to have to decide whether that means keeping faith with the religious elements in our tradition or with its faith elements.

We are constantly being told that the reason we may never take direct action against innocent human life is because life and death are under the exclusive dominion of God. So they are—*in the religious version of Christianity*. But though the story of divine dominion may be an essential ingredient in the religious account of Christianity, it is unnecessary and even foreign to incarnational faith. Incarnation means, among other things, that the divine and human are inextricably wedded to each other and that with respect to acting in the world, it is bootless to talk of divine vs. human prerogatives. Through incarnation, God has freely chosen to make his work our own, and it is in and through faith that we accept that challenge. If one still insists, in this context, on speaking of God's dominion over life and death, then thanks to incarnation, God's dominion is in some way carried out by us. We are his people, incarnating and witnessing his presence, and foretelling by our lives the coming of the Kingdom.

This is well illustrated in a little story going around these days:

> A man is sitting at a second-story window of his house as rising flood waters inundate his house. A boat goes by and the occupants urge him to come with them to safety. He responds, "No, my trust is in the Lord." The waters rise higher, driving the man to his roof. A second boat passes by. Again he refuses to leave his house saying, "My trust is in the Lord!" Finally, he is standing on his chimney, and a helicopter lowers a ladder to take him to dry ground. Again he refuses with the line, "My help is in the name of the Lord."

> Of course, the man drowned. And when he arrived at the pearly gates, he said to St. Peter, "Where's the Lord? I'm really ticked off at him." Peter directs the man to where Jesus is. The man walks up to the Lord and says angrily, "I'm really ticked off with you. How dumb can you be? I put absolute trust in you and you let me down. You let me drown! What kind of treatment is that?" To which the Lord responded "You're the dummy! *I* sent you two boats and a helicopter."

In similar fashion, we stand around at the bedside of dying people who beg to be released from their travail, and we do nothing, thinking our hands are tied and that we must wait for some special divine intervention. *We are the divine intervention!* We think we must wait on God, refraining from any direct action against innocent human life even when the circumstances seem to call for action. St. Thomas, speaking for the tradition, expressly denies the right of anyone to end either her own life or the life of another who is innocent. But in 1516, no less eminent a Catholic than St. Thomas More portrayed the "right to die" as in accord with reason and love. In Book II of his classic account of a mythical and truly humane community, Utopia (*Utopia,* ed. E. Surtz, Yale Univ. Press, 1964, pp. 108-8) he wrote:

> If a disease is not only incurable but also distressing and agonizing without any cessation, then the priests and the public officials exhort the man, since he is now unequal to all of life's duties, a burden to himself, and a trouble to others, *and is living beyond the time of his death,* to make up his mind not to foster the pest and plague any

longer nor to hesitate to die now that life is a torture to him, but relying on good hope, to free himself from this bitter life as from prison and the rack, or else voluntarily to permit others to free him. In this course he will act wisely, since by death he will put an end not to enjoyment but to torture. Because in doing so he will be obeying the counsels of the priests, who are God's interpreters, it will be a pious and holy action. Those who have been persuaded by these arguments either starve themselves to death, or being put to sleep, are set free without the sensation of dying. *But they do not make away with anyone against* his will, nor in such a case do they relax in the least their attendance upon him. They believe that death counseled by authority is honorific.

Almost three centuries separate Thomas More from Thomas Aquinas, but of the two saints it seems More got it exactly right. Thomas More is indeed "a man for all seasons"! His statement of over 450 years ago still captures the best of what so many call for today: unrelenting care and concern for the dying to the end, respect for their personhood and freedom, the need to take counsel with the community when arriving at a life and death decision, respect for the individual's decision once made, and a strong belief in the individual's "right to die."

There seems to be little doubt that the position of Thomas More is destined to one day become *the* Catholic position. It has the right fit. It feels better and it allows us to adopt a more genuinely pastoral approach to the problem. What has kept us for so long unable to see that is our stubborn insistence that to make such life and death decisions is to usurp a divine prerogative. If one cannot grasp the truth of the matter by faith, then advances in medical knowledge and technology should reveal that God has obviously put those decisions in human hands, whether we like it or not.

Those who argue so strongly against any taking of innocent human life say that the dignity and preciousness of each individual life calls for such a stand. The fact of the matter, however, is that modern medicine has made such strides in its ability to keep people alive *beyond the normally expected time of their death* that we are seeing more and more cases where health care itself becomes the source of dehumanization and the profanation of people's dignity.

In that situation, it is only natural that more and more people would ask to be terminated. The Christian community must take those requests much more seriously and not simply refuse them in principle because we do not want to "play God."

When we insist that mercy killing is immoral and sinful in principle, we should remember that we are making an implicit statement about God that implicates the Yahweh-God in the needless suffering of people. As more and more Catholic families must actually face having their elderly and loved ones in terminally-ill situations, it is going to be harder and harder to convince the families that God wants them to stand by and do nothing while waiting on his will. Experience is going to reveal to us, as it always does eventually if only we reflect on it, both the propriety of directly ending innocent human life and the conditions and circumstances in which it may be done blamelessly. For example, the state of the person is so bad that killing her cannot be interpreted as doing her harm; she really wants to be killed. The killing is done for the best interests of the one killed, not for the interests of others. God does not expect us to be infallible in making such life and death decisions, for ourselves or for others; we are to do the very best we can. However we choose to act, we must strive to be respectful of persons and act in accord with our highest Kingdom-ideals. When the situation is such that killing the person better fulfills than any other alternative the requirements for being moral and for witnessing the Kingdom, you can be sure that such killing is neither immoral nor sinful.

I do not mean to imply that mercy killing is anything less than tragic whenever it occurs, but when the conditions are such that we cannot reasonably call the act "murder," and a good case can be made for the fact that the act witnesses the Kingdom better than any alternative, then mercy killing is called for and is the best we can do under the tragic circumstances.

Nor do I mean to appear to be urging mercy killing. That choice must be left up to the person who is ill and in dire straits. But however much ambiguity that situation contains, it will be increased immeasurably to the degree that there is doubt or uncertainty about whether the person really wants to die. We all know the dangers of having others talk someone into allowing themselves to be killed. This can be a totally self-serving move without any real concern for the suffering person. It should go without saying that direct, involuntary euthanasia could never be moral, nor bespeak the Kingdom; our tradition is absolutely correct about that. Killing is an awful business at best; it becomes horrendous and murderous when it is done against a person's will. Thus I have been arguing only for the fact that truly and genuinely voluntary euthanasia is not necessarily contradictory of faith, and indeed might well be an expression of it.

What makes the abortion issue significantly different from the euthanasia issue is precisely the fact that we can never get informed consent from the fetus. It should be clear, then, that abortion is a whole other matter, to which we can now turn.

The Abortion Debate

Ten years ago I wrote a book entitled *What a Modern Catholic Believes About the Right to Life* (Thomas More, 1973) in which I tried to say that the national debate over abortion or the right to life was a fruitless enterprise that could not be brought to any satisfactory closure and would by its very nature go on endlessly in stalemate. I catalogued and criticized the ten most frequent arguments used by both sides in the debate, showing that the results were always inconclusive (Ch. II). I proposed a rational alternative to publicly debating the right to life (Ch. IV). In the concluding chapter, I adopted a faith perspective that pretty much took a view of the matter I now see was a forerunner of the approach to morality adopted in this book. Much has transpired in the intervening decade, but nothing to make me doubt my general approach nor to change the assessment of abortion I gave then (p. 98):

> I know of no act which is more out of keeping with the nature of church than abortion. By as much as a faith community opens itself up to abortion, by that much it ceases to be church. . . . Abortion is the epitome of unchurch, and is by nature incompatible with the mission of the Christian community.

I did not mean to say, of course, that each and every act of abortion was a countersign to the Kingdom, but rather that the *practice* of abortion was. Life is filled with tragic choices, and sometimes abortion is the lesser of two evils as in the life-against-life case. In such circumstances abortion need not be opposed to the Kingdom, but to have a national *policy* of abortion is obviously an anti-Kingdom stance, and part of a lifestyle to which Christians are committed to offer a viable alternative.

The abortion controversy still remains highly inflammatory and volatile after all these years, eliciting violent reactions from both sides. What accounts for the intensity of emotions? When ontic evil is opposed with the kind of passion we see in the abortion issue, it is generally because the evil is considered especially immoral because it is a particularly blatant violation of human persons. When moral evil reaches that sort of intensity and goes beyond the ordinary order of everyday immorality, people feel a profound sense of profanation and revulsion. The result is a kind of moral shock such as was experienced by those confronting the Holocaust or the Beirut massacres.

So it is with abortion. Proponents and opponents alike are operating out of a sense of outrage and profanation. Proponents are outraged at violations of women that occur in the context of sex and procreation. People have become so accustomed to these violations that they are now taken for granted as the way things should be. The efforts to keep women from aborting are seen as the last straw in a long litany of abuses perpetrated on women by a male-dominated society, medical profession, and the male-led church.

Their opponents are in turn outraged at what they take to be the calloused disregard for innocent human life brought on by the legalization of abortion. The highly profitable abortion clinics have turned destruction of innocents into a multi-million dollar industry, which has become a national scandal. Hence the outrage of the pro-life groups.

The point is, of course, that both sides are rightfully outraged. Instead of joining forces to lessen the outrage on both sides, their strong passions drive both into uncompromising positions that make fruitful dialogue virtually impossible. Each side sees itself on a crusade or holy war in which any sort of compromise is regarded as defeat. It is unlikely that either side will be able to hear what is said from a pastoral perspective. Rigidity and passion have driven each side into extreme and untenable positions.

How else to explain the claim that abortion is *always* immoral, or that it is *never* immoral because it is a fundamental right of women to abort? Those who hold the former position are confusing Christian ideals with moral rules, while those who take the latter position fail to realize that one can only *have* a right to something in situations in which that something *is* right. In the abortion controversy, that is the very point at issue. Only in those situations in which abortion *is* morally right, can one properly speak of a woman's right to abort.

1. Abortion: The Legal Issue

On January 22, 1973 the Supreme Court of the United States handed down a famous landmark decision in Roe vs. Wade (see *United States Law Week*, 1-23-73, Vol. 41, pp. 4213-4247). The result of that decision was twofold. It struck down the anti-abortion laws of the individual States, and it made abortion within the first trimester a personal medical matter between a woman and her physician with no more legal ramifications than those ordinarily governing the practice of medicine in the United States. The High Court went on to say that the state has a real interest in the health of the expectant mother and of the life she is carrying, so that to protect both, the state could impose regulatory restrictions in the second and third trimester, but these would have to be aimed at protecting the health of both mother and fetus. But, the Court observed, to have such regulations reach back into the first three months of pregnancy would be an unnecessary infringement on the rights of the woman.

Interestingly enough, that ruling met with opposition from both sides of the abortion controversy. Those who supported legalizing abortion did not rejoice in the decision, because they saw it as a halfway measure at best. It made abortion legal throughout the whole nine months of pregnancy, but the decision was not left solely up to the woman and her physician in the second and third trimesters. This was interpreted as an unacceptable limitation on the inherent right of a woman to decide what was done with her own body. So the pro-abortion/pro-choice forces began immediately to lobby for granting women fuller freedom in the matter of abortion.

On the other side, those who opposed the legalizing of abortion began to work to have the states severely limit the acceptable reasons for abortions in the second and third trimesters. The Supreme Court had granted the states the right to regulate abortions from the third month on, and this was seen by the pro-life forces as leaving open the possibility for the states to strongly curtail late abortions, if they could not ban them altogether. What seems to have been overlooked in that approach was the fact that the Supreme Court had granted the states the right to intervene, but only in order to regulate and protect the life and health of the mother and the fetus. It was inevitable that as the states began to pass laws restricting abortions, the matter would once more be put to litigation, and an astute observer of the scene could not doubt the outcome.

It came on June 15, 1983, approximately ten years and six months after the original decision. In the Akron Decision, the Supreme Court struck down state laws that attempted to restrict abortions to accredited hospitals by disallowing abortions in the second trimester that were performed in the so-called abortion clinics. This reversal of the state laws was seen as appropriate, since the abortion clinics had proven to be as safe to women aborting in the second trimester as were accredited hospitals. The evidence did not show that second trimester abortions performed in clinics posed any real threat to the well-being of women, and so the regulations banning such abortions were seen as once more an unnecessary infringement on the rights of women. Because of the possibility of complications and of delivering a viable fetus, states could still require third trimester abortions to be performed in accredited hospitals. In addition, Akron had passed an ordinance requiring abortion clinics to notify the parents of all women under 18 who came to them for abortions. The High Court struck that down again as a violation of women's rights, because the ordinance did not distinguish between teenagers who were competent and mature enough to make that decision and those that were not.

Obviously, it is the intention of the Supreme Court of the United States to give women the legal right to abort with minimal interference from government in that decision. The only thing justifying governmental interference and regulation of abortions are the issues of the health and well-being of the mother and of the fetus, if and when viable. The Akron Decision makes it abundantly clear that the anti-abortion forces in this country cannot use the right of states and municipalities to regulate abortions as a way of indirectly working their will that abortions be not allowed. Such regulatory bodies can only act on very specific grounds, and all regulations must meet those preconditions or, it seems, they in turn shall be struck down.

It is all too easy to criticize the Supreme Court for not assuming the role of "moral policeman" in this matter, but it is not really fair to do so. Its task is not to uphold the highest ideals either of morality or faith (we have seen that is the role of church), but to guarantee the rights of all citizens before the law. As the 1973 decision itself noted (Section IX of Roe vs. Wade):

> We need not resolve the difficult question of when life begins. When those trained in the respective disciplines of medicine, philosophy, and theology are unable to arrive at any consensus, the judiciary is not in a position to speculate as to the answer.

In that same place the Supreme Court noted that the official Catholic position that life begins at the moment of conception has been in the church's official teaching only since the 19th century. It also noted that this is by no means the unanimous position of other religious denominations or medical authorities. Lacking any real unanimity on the matter, the High Court really had no other alternative but to grant women the discretionary freedom to exercise their own consciences in the matter with minimal government interference.

Many believers unwilling to accept the legal facts of life, are now working for a constitutional amendment to circumvent the

Court. Such a strategy is doomed to failure pragmatically, and is a use of coercion unbecoming to people of the Kingdom. The constitutional amendment is doomed to failure on two counts. First, it would be totally unenforceable as law. Second, even if it passed, it would do so by so slim a margin that, like the prohibition amendment before it, it would soon be repealed as the opposition marshalled its forces to strike it down. All that would be accomplished is even greater division in the country, greater acrimony, which is hardly a suitable way to achieve the kind of solidarity that bespeaks the Kingdom.

This should not be taken to mean that the present abortion policy of the United States is acceptable to people of faith. In our outrage at the rampant disrespect for unborn life, we can resonate with Charles Carroll ("The Right to Life: Given or Won?" a talk by Rev. Charles Carroll, ex-Chaplain, Univ. of California at Berkeley, May 15, 1970) when he lamented:

> Life has become increasingly cheap in our time. And *in utero* and *ex utero* it is becoming ever cheaper. Man at one and the same time has abandoned faith in his Creator and become the creature of his fears. The right to life is no longer an inalienable right with which we are endowed, there is no longer a Creator to so endow us. The principle that utter helplessness demands utter protection has been discarded. As a Christian, I think it is time for us to "do" the truth rather than merely "proclaim" it. I can do no other than believe in Him who gave life its sanctity and man his dignity. A radical doctrine? Yes. As radical as "Whatsoever you have done unto the least of these my brothers, you have done unto Me." (Mt. 25:40) And "Whosoever will save his life, shall lose it. But whosoever will lose his life for My sake shall save it." (Mt. 16:25) We shall defend each one's God-given right to life *in utero* and *ex utero* or we shall surely lose our own. We shall see Christ in each and every one, and be Christ to each and every one or we shall *justly* perish from the earth. We shall embrace each other in love, or we shall embrace each other in the ashes!

The eloquence of those remarks and their appropriateness should not mislead us into thinking that the abortion issue can be settled with law. The people of the United States remain committed to the sacredness of life and demonstrate that fact by being unwilling to accept willful murder and genocide, suicide except when it can be identified as euthanasia, and "wars of interest" as opposed to genuine "wars of self-defense." In addition, capital punishment is no longer accepted as inevitably right and just. On these matters there seems to be a general consensus if not total agreement.

When it comes to abortion, however, we remain sorely divided and unable to come to any substantial agreement. That should suggest that perhaps there is something about abortion, an inherent ambiguity in its very nature, that accounts for the disagreement. In any case, it would be both wrongheaded and futile to try to legislate the inherent ambiguity out of the situation. It is to the credit, not the shame, of the Supreme Court of the United States that it has resisted the temptation to do that, and has in the face of the ambiguity left the choice as much as possible up to the woman.

2. Abortion: The Moral Issue

It is embarrassing to have to admit that for all our technology we still don't know exactly when abortion becomes a moral issue. That, more than anything else, accounts for the fact that the Supreme Court felt obliged to rule as it has. Many think that the decisions of the Supreme Court have settled the issue of the morality of abortion. Actually, the truth is otherwise. Judging itself not competent to pass on the morality of abortion when there is no consensus among religious leaders, philosophers, and theologians on the matter, the High Court left the moral decision up to the individual consciences of the women involved. The Supreme Court decisions, far from saying that all abortions are moral, implied that some are and some are not, but that it is not the task of the government to make such determinations. Further, even when a given act of abortion is immoral, that is never sufficient reason for the government to criminalize it. (Cases in which a viable fetus is aborted and then subsequently killed continue to be prosecuted, but this is not because they are acts of abortion but are rather closer to infanticide. A woman's decision to abort never involves the right to kill a viable infant outside the womb.) One may agree or disagree with the Supreme Court on that issue, but it remains true that making abortions legal in the United States left their morality or immorality unaddressed.

When one addresses that issue, the norm employed is the one we have used all along in our discussions. Does the act willfully and unjustly inflict ontic evil on another person? If it does, then it is obviously immoral. True, but what is not nearly so obvious is whether and at what stage the fetus is a person.

Anti-abortionists say *always*. From the first moment of conception we are dealing with human life, which, as such, is sacred and inviolable. What can two humans produce but human life? Attacks on the unborn at any moment in their development are violations of human persons, contradictions of the foundational moral experience, and hence immoral. It is obvious then that a human *conceptus* could be killed only for the gravest of justifying reasons, for example, to save the life of the mother. To kill it for any lesser reason is an unjustified taking of innocent human life tantamount to murder.

Pro-abortionists say *never*. Fetuses are never persons because so long as they remain fetuses they are within the mother, and that would mean that we could have "persons existing inside persons," which is impossible. To be a person is to have an independent existence. Fetuses cease to be fetuses and become persons at birth.

There is a neatness and clarity about each of the extreme positions that makes them very attractive. God knows we cope with enough ambiguity in our lives, but there is an eery inhumanity about the lack of ambiguity in each position as well, which is reason enough to suspect that neither is correct. The official teaching of the Catholic Church has become the basis for one of those extreme positions, namely, the anti-abortion position. How can that be? Why would the Catholic Church endorse an obviously extreme and erroneous view?

The Catholic Church, rightly convinced in faith that abortion is a violent and calloused breach of human solidarity and hence a countersign to the Kingdom, wanted to keep its people from such an act. In its zeal to do so, and in its role as "moral policeman," it has claimed to know when the human soul is infused into matter, that is, at the moment of conception. The truth is that to this day we still don't know exactly when that occurs, but there is a growing body of biological evidence that whenever it happens, it cannot be at the moment of conception. Fearing that upholding Kingdom-ideals would not be enough, the church has reasoned to the immorality of practically all abortions on the basis of a claim now seen to be false. Once again, the institutional church is in trouble having its credibility questioned, because it could not bring itself to say, "I don't know" and because it insists on playing "moral policeman." (The credibility of the Catholic Church on this issue would be greatly increased if only it did not maintain against common sense that all contraceptive lovemaking is immoral; if it admitted that we do not know when the human soul is infused; and if in its own dealings with people it were not so consistently exploitive and oppressive of women.)

What sort of evidence can be brought against the official Catholic teaching that the human soul is infused at the moment of conception? Two interesting arguments have emerged. The first has to do with the number of spontaneous abortions that occur in the early weeks of pregnancy. It is estimated that up to ten percent of all pregnancies end in a natural abortion in the early weeks. It seems to be nature's way of lessening the number of bad pregnancies. God is no fool, and one would think that he knew nature's ways very well. It strikes us as strangely uneconomical of him to infuse all those human souls when he knows that thousands will be lost each month. It seems much more likely that the infusion of the human soul would be more wisely delayed until after those early weeks.

The second argument goes beyond the claim of appropriateness for a later infusion of the human soul, and actually demonstrates that such must actually be the case. The basis of the argument is the phenomenon of "twinning" in which a single fertilized ovum divides into two. According to our present knowledge, "twinning" can occur as late as the second or third week. That fact presents us with an embarrassing situation if we hold that an individual human soul was infused at conception, for in that case, when "twinning" occurs we would have to hold that a unique and individual human person was somehow divided into two human persons. But a person as individual is by nature indivisible so we must either hold that an individual human soul (or souls) is infused at the moment of twinning or at some subsequent moment, or if at the moment of conception, that a human person is not so unique as to prevent its becoming two. It seems altogether bizarre and strange to hold the latter. It seems much more appropriate and more in keeping with human experience to hold that the fetus does not become individually human until some time after conception.

The phenomenon of twinning is not without its pastoral consequences. If twinning can occur up to several weeks after conception, it means that there is a period between conception and possible twinning when the fetus is not an instance of "individual" human life, and hence cannot be a person. This means that there is an interval when the fetus is developing toward individuality but has not yet achieved it. Should the fetus be killed or destroyed during that time, it would not be the infliction of ontic evil on a "person" and hence would not fulfill the requirements for an immoral killing. This would also mean that contraceptive devices that are abortifacient, such as the IUD, could not be judged to cause the expulsion of human life that was personal. It would further mean that in rape cases the woman would have two weeks or longer in which to rid herself of any *conceptus* without the fear that she was destroying a human person.

What I am suggesting is not that we know at what moment the human soul is infused, but rather that in the present state of our technical and scientific knowledge, it seems veritably certain that it cannot be at conception. Advances in our knowledge may reveal evidence in the future that might move the moment even farther along into the pregnancy than the first several weeks. This would corroborate the communally-funded experience of women that to abort early is not to destory *personal* human life.

Faced with these hard facts, many pro-lifers have fallen back to a second line of argumentation, which goes something like this. Granted that the fetus is neither individual nor personal from the moment of conception, it has the full potential to become so. It will become so if only it is not interfered with. It is a violation of the fetus' inalienable right to life and individual humanness to terminate its development prematurely. But such argumentation in the moral context seems wrongheaded (we shall see that it becomes meaningful only in the context of faith), for if the fetus is only potentially a person, then its right to life and to individual humanness are also only *potential* rights. But a potential right is actually no right. Therefore, the argument fails to accomplish what those who formed it set out to do.

In the light of all that evidence, it seems particularly unpastoral and extremely doctrinaire to insist that abortion at any time after conception is the destruction of individual and personal human life. Our commitment to the Kingdom and its ideals does not allow us to distort or misrepresent the truth when it comes to taking a moral stand on abortion. Although our faith commitment will always keep us from being advocates of abortion, it should not prevent us from an impartial and realistic look at the facts of the matter and their impact on any evaluation of abortion from the moral point of view.

As we have already noted, the Supreme Court seems to have done just that, and rendered its legal decisions in the light of the uncertainty and ambiguity permeating the abortion issue. It is time for the Catholic Church to do the same. To hold out dogmatically against the evidence shows a lack of trust both in God and in the people in whom he dwells. In addition, it further erodes the church's already damaged credibility, and prevents it from showing the sensitivity and compassion that should characterize its pastoral mission.

Since we remain uncertain as to precisely when a fetus becomes individually and personally human, what would be a good pastoral stance to take in this matter? Before answering that question, let me propose the following thought experiment. Suppose that upon becoming pregnant, a woman's abdomen became transparent so that she could better monitor the developing life within her. At what point would women of good will judge the life within them to be individual, personally human, and morally beyond tampering? My own instincts tell me that there would emerge a consensus on the issue that once the fetus looks human, it is probably individual and personal as well. Leaving aside all abstract, metaphysical discussions, it would become a rule of thumb that it is immoral to tamper with fetuses once they "look like us." (That occurs around the twelfth week—the end of the first trimester.)

That little thought experiment reveals something else as well. Realization quite often comes from really looking at something. No woman feels good about aborting, a traumatic and painful experience. The pain and trauma involved would normally be enough to reveal the truth about what one is doing if only the situation were not otherwise so desperate. It would be cruel, so the story goes, to have the woman view what was aborted; it would only further traumatize her. But what kind of logic is that? A woman cannot really know what abortion is unless she experiences it and really looks at it. But we advise her not to look; she won't like what she sees. Besides, it will be easier for her to forget what she did if only she doesn't look at it.

Our culture has a way of doing that with unpleasant realities. That is the way it is with death, disease, and old age, too. We just don't really look at those things. We get a select group (police, firefighters, health care personnel, and morticians) to have the experience and do the viewing for us. That means there is always a small group of people who face the awful truth so that the majority of us can go on in blissful ignorance. Such a strategy for coping with unpleasantness does not benefit us as incarnate spirits.

The whole abortion policy of the United States is built on such a foundation of willed ignorance. Only lack of direct experience with late abortions allows the pro-abortionists to claim that abortion is a woman's right up until the time of delivery. Only lack of direct experience with abortion allows society to ignore the desperate plight of women, driving them to abortion as their only hope. There must be a better way.

3. Abortion: The Faith Issue

Abortions have no place in the Kingdom. Indeed, when the Kingdom comes, when God reigns and his Spirit rules, all those things that now seem to make abortion necessary will have disappeared, making the abortion issue moot. Until then, however, it is the task of Kingdom-people to present an alternative not only to abortion, but to all those conditions that seemingly justify abortions. There is something hypocritical about denouncing abortions while at the same time being indifferent to the agonizing and dehumanizing situations that bring them about. If we would be authentically and genuinely pro-life, we must work to correct a social order that condemns growing numbers to poverty, exploits women, promotes lust, and rejects graciousness as a way of life. Even when it is not immoral, abortion remains a countersign to the Kingdom by not bespeaking the presence of the gracious and loving Yahweh-God, and even by positively proclaiming his absence.

Still, we must take life as it is, not as we would like it to be. This does not mean that we must accept life just as it is as the last word and that there is nothing more to be said or done about it. Rather, we accept life with all its ambiguities as the locus and starting point of our challenge, as Christians, to transform it in the name of the Lord. As we have already seen with regard to the sexual issues, that means upholding an ideal for people, not condemning them and adding to their misery. The outrage and profanation we feel over abortion must be tempered with compassion for those caught up in the harshness of life, without resources, without loving support, without faith, just trying to survive. Were we in their shoes, can we say with certainty that we would act otherwise?

It is not at all surprising that only a relatively small number of Catholics are affiliated with the right-to-life movement. Some may feel that this is because we are insensitive to the "slaying of the innocents" in this country, or that we are too comfortable and self-satisfied to get involved. That may not be the whole story. There is something about the right-to-life movement that doesn't seem quite right. Upon reflection, we immediately see that there is too much anger, too much bitterness, too much vituperative language, too much condemnation about their enterprise to allow us to say it is appropriate for Kingdom-people. Their cause may be just, but their strategies are too lacking in graciousness and compassion to bespeak the Lord. One wants to say to them, in the words of Leo Mahon, "Being bitter is like swallowing acid. It will eventually tear you apart, and eat right through you. There is no way to remain bitter and live!'' That's it. How ironic: pro-life people whose bitterness destroys life—their own.

The longer one lives and reflects upon life, the clearer it becomes that the essential Christian virtue, the primary prerequisite of the Kingdom, is *graciousness,* which seems to be the one virtue that cannot be turned into a vice. All the other virtues can be flawed if they are not exercised with gracefulness or graciousness. The Lord was always gracious in his dealings with people. Consider his attitude toward his mother Mary at the wedding feast, Zacchaeus, Mary Magdalen, Judas, Peter, the woman at the well, and the woman taken in adultery. Recall the parables the central theme of which is graciousness: The Two Debtors, The Prodigal Son, The Laborers in the Vineyard, and The Good Samaritan. And when they came to nail him to a cross, Jesus remained gracious to the end: "Father, forgive them...they don't know...they just don't understand."

What does it mean to be gracious? And why is it so important to the Christian? If there is anything that characterizes the Yahweh-God's relations with humankind, it is their absolute gratuity. We cannot merit or earn them. We are graced and gifted with them. So when it comes to moral evil and sin, the question believers ask themselves is this: If the Yahweh-God has been gracious to you and has gifted you so, how could you act otherwise to your sisters and brothers? Indeed, the ten commandments are really to be understood in just that way. For example, the fifth commandment is not so much a command as an exhortation that might read as follows:

> Since the Yahweh-God has given you life, has freed you from your
> enemies and favored you with health and well-being, if you want to
> bespeak his presence in the world—*thou shalt not kill.*

So it is with every sin and moral evil. They are countersigns to the Kingdom not only because they wound and hurt others, but because such acts are particularly ungracious in the light of God's absolute graciousness to us.

In the light of that truth I wrote ten years ago: "Abortion is the epitome of unchurch, and is by nature incompatible with the mission of the Christian community." By rejecting the gift of new life, abortion is the ultimate in gracelessness. It says that gratuity is not central to human life; it makes life itself, God's greatest gift, conditional. But that is to undermine the coming Kingdom and to abdicate one's Christian mission. Still, we must be careful that in opposing abortion in the name of the Lord we do not ourselves undermine that Kingdom by our own lack of graciousness.

SUGGESTED READING

Daniel Callahan, *Abortion: Law, Choice & Morality,* Collier-Macmillan, 1970.

John Dedek, *Human Life: Some Moral Issues,* Sheed & Ward, 1972.

Daniel Maguire, *Death by Choice,* Schocken, 1975.

William May and Richard Westley, *Catholic Perspectives: The Right to Die,* Thomas More, 1980.

John Noonan, *The Morality of Abortion,*   Harvard Univ. Press, 1972.

Bruno Schuller, "Direct Killing/Indirect Killing" in Curran and McCormick, *Readings in Moral Theology No. 1,* Paulist Press, 1979, pp. 138-157.

Richard Westley, *What a Modern Catholic Believes About the Right to Life,* Thomas More, 1973.

Jerry Wilson, *Death by Decision,* Westminster Press, 1975.

CHAPTER TWELVE

The Justice Issue

Unjust! Who Me?

They are at it again. There seems to be a concerted effort to put people like us on some sort of a guilt trip. Many people want to make us feel guilty about having achieved some sort of success in the world, of leading decent lives, and even of rearing our families well. Take Walter Wink. He was really trying to book middle class Americans on a guilt trip when he wrote ("Unmasking the Powers" in *Sojourners,* Oct. 10, 1978, pp. 13-14.):

> Greed, the oil of capitalism, inheres in the system itself. According to traditional capitalist theory, private greed was supposed to lead to public good, since competition would restrain the selfishness of each to the benefit of all. We are contending against greed reified into systemic solidity by a host of persons over a long span of time.

So far so good, but then he continues with this little bit of prose:

> The economic system is greedy *in our behalf.* We as individuals are thus free to have clear consciences, treat people politely, raise lovely families, live in nice homes, and care about humanity in general.

And John Topel (*The Way to Peace*, Orbis, 1979, p. 174, #16) puts in his oar when he answers the question of whether there can be honestly acquired luxury:

> It appears to me, however, that all luxury, superfluous wealth, can arise only because the system has defrauded someone somewhere.

I am offended when it is suggested that somehow I am personally responsible for racism, sexism, or other social evils, all of which arose long before I was born. That strikes me as grossly unfair and as the crassest kind of scapegoating. I resent attempts to put me on a guilt trip over the fact that I am White, male, and middle class. I did not have a thing to do with any of those things either. I was conceived by White middle-class parents who had a son, not a daughter, and I had absolutely no say in the matter. If anyone thinks that there is something inherently wrong with being White, male, and middle class, they can't blame me, I am sure. I can only be blamed for those acts I have done deliberately and with conscious intent. I most certainly am willing to be held responsible for those of my actions that were tinged by racism, sexism, and other prejudices, but please don't blame me for the present state of the world. I am as much a victim of that world as anyone.

And yet. . . we are not bad or malicious people. Granted, we are not sinless, but our track record over the years is one of authentic caring and service, of genuine faith and Christian love. We are the Lord's own people called to walk with him as a sign of the coming Kingdom. If the truth be told, we haven't been all that unsuccessful at all, which is clear from the fact that in our families, parishes, and neighborhoods, among our friends and acquaintances, at work and with business associates, we have been recognized as somehow wonderfully different. Time and again in those situations and circumstances, our Christian witness and service have been affirmed and re-affirmed by those who tell us that we have been gift to them, and that their encounters with us give them hope.

All that is true, but it didn't happen in a day, or a month, or even a year. We have all spent the major portion of our adult lives becoming ever more like the Lord, ever more loving, ever more giving, ever more serving. It has been a wonderful adventure, and though we have come a long way, we know we still have a long way to go. But we are determined to continue on that path to the end, even if it takes us, as we know it will, to Calvary. It is never easy. It has never been easy to give up so much of yourself for others. The pains are real, but the realization that the alternative lifestyle is even more unacceptable, keeps us faithful to the dream. We have made our choice, and continue to make it day by day as we walk with the Lord.

Leo Mahon recently spoke of that choice as follows (*Gambit,* NBC-TV, Ch. 5, Chicago, Dec. 13, 1981):

So Jesus gives us the same choice he made in his own life. It is a choice and decision he made that we have never, never forgotten. The human race tried for I don't know how many years to get rid of that memory of Jesus. It hasn't been able to. It is a very powerful thing. What he did was deliberately and gracefully and freely say: "I shall live for others, not for myself." And he was well aware of what he was doing, and what choice he was presenting to his followers. If we dedicate our lives to others, then we clean up the world, we put beauty and life and love into the world. If we live only for ourselves, we are going to foul it up even more, like fouling up a nest. That is a very important decision, and it is the first one that has to be made or remade by every Christian. Now we're not so corrupted, and we're not so dumb that we don't recognize greatness in that sort of sacrifice. There are still a lot of people around who have weaknesses, are part of the world, but who would love to be great and love to be significant. We would like to leave this world better than we found it.

Yes, that's us, weak and defective in many ways and part and parcel of our world as it is part and parcel of who we are. But despite that, we have seen the Lord, have been inspired by his dream, and in our own very personal ways we have been trying to love and to be significant. We do want to leave our world better for our having passed through it, but that is also exactly why we resent people getting on our case about social justice. It is not as if we were rapists, murderers, thieves; it is not as if we were dishonest and exploitive and filled with miserly greed; it is not as if we were pleasure-seekers who live only for ourselves. No, we have made the choice to be "for others," and it seems cruel to lay the burden of guilt for social injustice at our door. We are not the problem; the problem is those others who know not the Lord and who live only for themselves.

And yet...and yet...precisely because we have been honestly trying to live a life of love and giving, the outrage of the rampant injustice in our world does move us. We are sensitive to our sisters and brothers in pain and need, due to oppressive social circumstances, and we are filled with compassion for them and show it whenever we have the chance. Somehow, though, down deep in our hearts, we have the feeling that something is wrong; we have not been or done all that we should. We have the nagging suspicion that there may be some truth in the allegations against us. When we are being completely honest with ourselves, we must admit that there is an aura of unfinished business about our spiritual journeys. A gentle voice deep within us keeps asking urgently, "And what about justice? When will you be free enough to face that issue? It is the heart of the matter if you would truly walk with your God?" But until now we have not been able to face that issue squarely, nor quiet the voice within. Yet, each of us knows that until we do we shall not have inner peace in its fullness.

The Real Moral Evil: Injustice

Several years ago there was a popular book entitled *Whatever Became of Sin?* and it is not at all surprising that someone should have asked. Sin seems to have fallen on hard times. Even believers don't talk about it much anymore. Some take this to be an indication that in the current pagan culture, the Christian/Catholic Church is weakening and so is grudgingly giving in to laxism. Those who take that view of the matter gravitate toward fundamentalist movements and make loud noises about a return to former times when personal sin was the central concern of Christianity. Interestingly enough, those people seem to be terribly offended by "sins of the flesh" but are almost immune to the horrors of injustice, which they take to be "the good old American way."

A more plausible explanation why there seems to have been

until recently a conspiracy of silence about "sin" is because we didn't quite know what to say. As I have tried to show, the confusion between ideals and moral rules made it particularly difficult to speak coherently on the subject in the post-Vatican II church. Our silence should not be seen as condoning the rampant paganism of our time, but rather an an indication of the fact that we have rediscovered the true biblical account of sin. That rediscovery has rendered us temporarily speechless. We have the growing suspicion that sin has to do primarily not so much with personal chastity and who is in bed with whom as with social justice. That realization reveals that we are all implicated, in one way or another, in our society's injustice. A devastating thought for true believers. No wonder we fell silent for a time.

We can be silent no longer. The time has come for us to speak out of our new awareness, speak both to our world, to one another, and to our children. (Undoubtedly, our children have already had some things to say to us about the evils of the system!) But where do we begin?

We begin by giving up the notion that we are sinless because we didn't "do" anything. Scripture speaks of sin with at least two different meanings. There is the sin we commit by *doing,* and there is the sin we are involved in by *not doing.* The former is the result of action, the latter of inaction, indifference, and hardness of heart. Because we were accustomed to exclusively center on the first kind of sin, we were able to judge ourselves blameless even though we were at the time implicated in the most lethal and death-dealing (and hence "mortal") of sins of the second sort. More people have died in human history due to hunger, poverty, and social injustice than from all the wars ever waged. At this very moment, the nations of the world spend a billion dollars a day on weapons, while children starve and eight hundred million people go to bed hungry. *That's mortal sin!* It kills. It kills not only the physical life of people, but it dehumanizes them, killing their political, social, ethical, and spiritual lives as well. But since it is not done directly, because it is not consciously willed by individuals, we have failed to brand it as "sin," even though it destroys human solidarity, affronts the dignity of persons, and is destructive of the Kingdom. As we have now come to see, Scripture views the matter otherwise.

We are not accustomed to talking about this second kind of sin, "not doing"; we don't even have an adequate language to talk about it. The terminology is less fixed, more fluid. So let us agree to call the second sort of sin, what Scripture calls the "sin of the world," *social sin.* Social sin resides in the group, in the community, and in its institutions. It is not produced by deliberation and free choice. It produces evil consequences, but not guilt, because there is no single person or group of persons to whom it may rightly be attributed. Scripture tells us that this sort of sin happens because of our apathy, lethargy, and blindness. It was this sort of sin the prophets of Israel railed so forcefully against. Opposition to this sort of sin must become the paramount concern of Exodus-people in the final decades of the twentieth century.

The poor, oppressed, and exploited of the world have little or no trouble recognizing the moral evil of social sin; they are the major objects of its painful consequences. But we middle-class North Americans less readily recognize social sin because we are so well insulated from its devasting effects by education, success, and our own struggles for a fuller life. More than that, in order for us to have succeeded, the social sin of our culture had to become an integral part of our mindset. We now take social sin for granted as a legitimate way of operating, and we consider the poor and disadvantaged as an unfortunate but necessary by-product of our way of life.

We are, for all of that, still a believing, loving, and generous people. There is nothing wrong with our hearts; our heads are the problem. We carry within them the myths, symbols, and ideologies that legitimate the way things are; these blind us to the extent of our implication in the social sin of our times. Then, too, as Walter Wink observed, the present culture works to our advantage, so we naturally have little taste for changing it and are extremely critical of those who try.

A brief look at the levels of social sin identified by Gregory Baum (*Religion & Alienation,* Paulist Press, 1975, pp. 201-202) may help to explain our rigidity in this matter. The *first level* of social sin is the concrete order of everyday life, in which there are built into the institutions of collective life unjust practices and dehumanizing trends. As people go about doing their daily work fulfilling their duties, the destructive trends built into the system take their toll. As we watch colleagues unjustly treated and severely oppressed in the work place, in the office, in the university, and in the church, we are face to face with social sin at the first level.

Normally, it would be assumed that people on the scene would take up arms against such things, but usually they don't. Why? Because they are afraid the same could happen to them and because the unjust practices of the first level are protected and made to seem invisible thanks to the *second level* of social sin. This level is made up of the cultural and religious myths and symbols in the minds and imaginations of people, fostered by society and religion, that legitimate the unjust practices on the first level. The injustice goes unchecked, harming growing numbers of people. For example, the obvious injustice of denying ordination to women is legitimated by the story that if Jesus wanted women ordained he would himself have done so.

Recourse to bogus stories and symbols to legitimate injustice deepens the social sin and gives rise to the *third level*. At this level, thanks to the myths and symbols, a false consciousness is created in people that allows them collectively to condone destructive actions as if they were doing the right thing. So it was that those who hunted down runaway slaves in this country thought they were acting righteously and didn't feel the least tinge of guilt. They felt "justified," which is the zenith of social sin. Not only is injustice done but it is done in the name of justice.

Obviously, if that is the dynamic of social sin, we see how important the false cultural symbols and myths are to keeping the whole thing going, for without them injustice could not be internalized and hence would be more easily uprooted. It is precisely because our very mindset has been deformed by cultural symbols and stories that good people like us can be involved in social sin without consciously willing it, or even being aware of it.

We now know that people don't necessarily experience reality as it is. The myths and symbols that dominate our minds and imaginations make us select what we regard as the most significant aspects of life, and that is what we take to be real. For example, if my mind is formed by the story that all Blacks are lazy and shiftless, it will be impossible for me to see the high unemployment among Blacks as the result of inequities and injustice, for I shall just "know" that the reason they are not employed is because they are very poor workers. By that simple mechanism I have blinded myself to injustice.

Conversely, if through faith I allow my mind and imagination to be formed by the Exodus story and the coming Kingdom promised by Jesus, then I begin to "see" things as real and important that cannot be seen any other way. I become more sensitive to the destructive trends of the world, and more discerning of a gracious, life-giving presence at work within humankind. So the sort of world I dwell in is at least partially determined by the symbols and myths I choose to use to interpret the meaning of my experience. See how different the *Magnificat* appears to you once you view it from the perspective of Exodus-liberation and the coming of the Kingdom (Luke 1:46-55):

> My soul proclaims the greatness of the Lord and my spirit exults in God my savior; because he has looked upon his lowly handmaid. Yes, from this day forward all generations will call me blessed, for the Almighty has done great things for me, holy is his name, and his mercy reaches from age to age for those who fear him. He has shown the power of his arm, he has routed the proud of heart. He has pulled down princes from their thrones and exalted the lowly. The hungry he has filled with good things, the rich sent empty away. He has come to the help of Israel his servant, mindful of his mercy, according to the promise he made to our ancestors, of his mercy to Abraham and to his descendants for ever.

Is this a young girl's prayer of praise, or is it a powerful, prophetic reiteration of Exodus-liberation themes? Whichever you take it to be is a function of the controlling myths and symbols with which you view it. But it could be interpreted to be as radical as the Communist Manifesto. Interesting!

When it comes to sin, the controlling image and story we had allows us to see sin only as an individual phenomenon, committed with full consent and conscious reflection. That means that we have been generally unable to recognize our implication in the social evil of our times. We deplore the poverty and oppression in which so many of our sisters and brothers must live. We deplore the racism and sexism that surround us, but we simply cannot see these things as "sins" because the symbols and myths through which we view the world will not allow it. Nor are things likely to change unless we break with our present mindset, get back to the biblical roots of Christianity, and begin to look at our world through the symbols of Exodus, Jesus as Liberator/Prophet, and the Kingdom he promised.

Even if we changed our theological understanding of sin and began to view the call of Christ as a call to justice, we would still find ourselves divided and in contradiction. We would still retain in our heads all those bogus myths and symbols about free enterprise, capitalism, and the American way. As Michael Novak has written (*Ascent of the Mountain, Flight of the Dove,* Harper & Row, 1971, pp. 150-1):

> No matter how sensitive the family, idealistic the church, informative the school, someday young people enter the "real" world. What conditions the world? The necessity to work for a living. The need for money. Now we're getting down to the nitty gritty. The gut issue is the pocketbook. Money is the dirty little secret of American society. The economic system is the basic instrument of survival and well-being. But an economic system has built into its daily operations an image of man. It is a reality-constructing system. It teaches us in practice how to regard one another, whatever our beautiful theories might be. What counts is who gets what, when and how. The "real world" in which the economic system induces people to live is a world of assigned inputs, rewards, roles, strategies, attitudes and skills. Given the sense of reality, the stories, and the symbols implied by such an economic system, how could its participants be serious Christians or Jews?

That is the question we cannot help but ask ourselves when we gather with other believers and once again mount the dream of the Kingdom. That is the question that continues to haunt us as an integral part of the unfinished business of our spiritual journeys. That is the question we must somehow find the courage to face anew, putting aside all the glib and traditional answers our culture has taught us to make. Are we willing to look at the implications of our capitalistic economic system in a critical and gospel way? Are we willing to admit our contributions to the injustices in the land? Can we repent and then start a whole new phase in our walk with the Lord?

The Prophets of Israel in Perspective

If the Exodus is the controlling event in the Old Testament, we would have to say that the prophets, who called Israel to task for the injustices and enslavement that had arisen with Jew exploiting Jew, must be seen as calling the people back to the values the God of Exodus had revealed as central to his covenant relationship with them. In order to understand why it was necessary for the prophets to speak out the way they did, it will be necessary to trace briefly Israel's history after the Exodus.

Moses and Joshua after him brought the people, not yet a single nation but an alliance of tribes, to the Promised Land, but it was left to each of the tribes to secure possession of the land assigned to it. During this period of conquest, the period of the Judges, we discern an oft-repeated dynamic at work. Settling in their new-found land, the people forget the Exodus and the covenant the Yahweh-God made with them, and they begin to go after the strange (foreign) gods of their neighbors. This is inevitably followed by their being oppressed by foreigners. The people under oppression repent their infidelity, and the Yahweh-God raises up a liberator from among them (the famous Judges of Israel), a charismatic leader who engineers the liberation of his people from oppression. At the death of the liberator/judge, the people lapse once again into following pagan ways and the whole process starts up all over again.

This painful process revealed to Israel both the fidelity of the Yahweh-God and the fact that the liberation process begun at Exodus was to continue.

But it would be successful only if the people remained faithful to the covenant and continually strove to be Kingdom-people. Eventually, it became apparent that if the various tribes were to achieve full liberation in the Promised Land, they would have to unite under a single king. That way they could have the economic and cultural benefits of a centralized administration. So it was that the Yahweh-God once again raised up leaders to further the liberation process. This time it was the kings who were to bring the people to greater freedom.

Under King David Israel became a single nation, but Israel prospered because of David's victories over its oppressors. David's administration was supported by his own wealth, the taking of slaves from the people he conquered, and by the taxes collected from the conquered peoples. Under his son, Solomon, things began to go sour. He undertook massive public projects and ran a lavish court, without increasing revenues by foreign conquest. As costs began to exceed income, as the royal bureaucracy grew immense, it was inevitable that the Jews themselves would begin to be oppressed. As the people were pressed into forced labor on the royal projects and administration, food production fell, small farms could no longer produce as much for lack of adequate labor, taxes increased and more and more family farms had to be sold to meet the debts, and suddenly within the bosom of Israel, the original Exodus-people, there was an oppressed and exploited subclass. The monarchy that was to have continued the work of liberation became itself the source of oppression. One must understand the message of the great prophets of Israel against that background.

The prophets were the social conscience of Israel, reminding the people of the Exodus and their covenant with the Yahweh-God, calling them back to the ways of righteousness and justice. Nothing can take the place of a full reading of the prophets, but to make our point, perhaps we can cite a text or two. Isaiah (3:13-15) speaks of the Yahweh-God's displeasure at the rampant injustice in Israel:

> Yahweh rises from his judgment seat, he stands up to arraign his people. Yahweh calls to judgment the elders and princes of his people: "You are the ones who destroy the vineyard and conceal what you have stolen from the poor. By what right do you crush my people and grind the faces of the poor?" It is the Lord Yahweh Sabaoth who speaks.

A familiar theme reiterated often as in this passage from Amos (8:4-6):

> Listen to this, you who trample on the needy and try to suppress the poor people of the country, you who say "When will New Moon be over so that we can sell our corn, and Sabbath, so that we can market our wheat? Then by lowering the bushel, raising the shekel, by swindling and tampering with the scales, we can buy up the poor for money, and the needy for a pair of sandals, and get a price even from the sweepings of the wheat.

Finally, and again from Amos (5:21-24):

> I hate and despise your feasts. I take no pleasure in your solemn festivals. When you offer me holocausts ... I reject your oblations, and refuse to look at your sacrifices of fattened cattle. Let me have no more of the din of your chanting, no more of your strumming on harps. But let justice flow like water and integrity like an unfailing stream.

In reflecting on the prophetic preoccupation with earthly justice, Rabbi Heschel was moved to ask:

> Why should religion, the essence of which is worship of God, put such stress on justice for man? Does not the preoccupation with morality tend to divest religion of immediate devotion to God? Why should a worldly virtue like justice be so important to the Holy One of Israel? Did not the prophets overrate the worth of justice?

He then went on to anwer his own questions (*The Prophets,* Jewish Publication Society of America, 1955, p. 198):

> Perhaps the answer lies here: *justice* is not merely a human value, it is God's part in human life, *God's stake in human history;* it is in relations between man and man that God is at stake. People act as they please, doing what is vile, abusing the weak, not realizing that they are fighting God, that the oppression of man is affronting the divine. The universe is done. *The greater masterpiece still undone,* still in the process of being created, *is history.* For accomplishing his grand design, God needs the help of man. Man is and has the instrument of God, which he may or may not use in consonance with the grand design. Life is clay, justice the mold in which God wants history to be shaped. The world is full of iniquity, injustice and

idolatry. The people offer animals; the priests offer incense. But God needs mercy, righteousness; *his needs cannot be satisfied in the temples, in space, but only in history—in time.*

God's will is not so much that we engage in religious exercises that affirm his sovereignty and greatness, but that we work for the realization of the ancient dream, and that justice flow like the rivers. Justice is God's stake in human history, because it is the primary prerequisite for the Kingdom. As our account has shown, *all moral evils are at bottom injustices,* which rend the fabric of human community, exploit and abuse our fellows, and violate our relational nature by refusing to choose solidarity. Widespread injustice prevents our world from incarnating and bespeaking the presence of the Yahweh-God of faith.

Justice is not merely a human convention or a utopian dream; it is, as Rabbi Heschel observed, "God's stake in human history." It is a transcendent demand, our God's primary concern. Were it not for our Jewish roots, we Christians might never have known that. Indeed, one can wonder whether, until quite recently, we really did know it. It is estimated that about one hundred million Jews have been killed since the advent of Christianity. After the Holocaust, many of our Jewish sisters and brothers can no longer believe in a God, not even in the Yahweh-God of Israel. But the Jews were chosen to become a great nation in Abraham and a gift and blessing to the nations of the earth, not because Abraham knew how to build altars and temples, but as Genesis says, "...in order that he may charge his children and his household after him to keep the way of the Lord by doing righteousness and justice" (18:18-19). So the dream began. The quest for justice is, therefore, never a purely secular affair. It has its roots in the biblical tradition, which continues in our day to seek to create a dwelling place for God in human history.

The Faith That Does Justice

But have you noticed? In this country, people who attempt to create a dwelling place for God in human history usually end up in jail or are assassinated. We have great freedom of religion in this country, but there seems to be an unwritten law that the separation of church and state requires us, as the price for that freedom, to see to it that our religion remains by and large a private matter. See what happened when the Catholic bishops of the United States started to question the country's nuclear policy. There were rumored threats that to continue on such a course would cost the Catholic Church its tax exempt status. The message was clear. Churches are to concern themselves with the private, individual sins of their people, and not concern themselves with the social sins of the nation, thereby calling into question the institutional arrangements of the country. The Christian churches are free from government harrassment so long as they preach what Brendan Lovett calls a "privatized and trivialized gospel." *We can believe anything we like so long as it does not have adverse repercussions on the current system.*

For far too long we have obliged and gone along with that debilitating understanding of Christianity, but after Viet Nam, the My Lai massacre, and Watergate, many American Catholics seem willing to return to a more robust sort of Christianity, one more in keeping with the ancient biblical tradition. That bodes trouble ahead, the kind of trouble prophetic people of every age have encountered when they stood up for justice. To date, the results have been meager, but the consciousness of American Catholics is being raised to see injustice as the cruelest moral evil and as the central issue for believers. Every diocese and every parish in the country is supposed to have a Committee on Peace and Justice, which also obviously includes concerns about the arms race and nuclear war, the most insane of all possible injustices. Catholic youngsters are being educated to see "peace and justice" as the top priorities of their faith. The worm is, if ever so slowly, turning.

This means that Christian faith and the American brand of capitalism are on a collision course. This puts American Catholics in a delicate predicament. As Bill Callahan has so astutely observed ("Alive and Believing for the 1980's," *Chicago Call to Action,* Evening of Reflection, April 9, 1980):

> The real test is whether affluent, educated Catholics can bend their own self-interest to join in the empowerment of poorer people within

this nation and around the world—the sense of the First World "letting go," the theology of relinquishment, or will we, even within the Roman Catholic community, brush aside the social teachings of our church, which have not often been preached widely because they are far more radical than we are *and deeply threatening to the way of life we have lived.* It is not clear whether this challenge can be effectively met; there is little witness of it in the past.

Judging from the reaction to the bishops' statement on nuclear war among grassroots Catholics, Callahan is certainly correct in wondering whether we have what it takes to answer the challenge of our faith in the 1980s. If we cannot even agree that nuclear war is unthinkable and totally contradictory of Christian values, how shall we ever be able to face *the* issue in relation to justice in this country. I mean, of course, the moral legitimacy of national and multinational corporations. Once the churches seriously question the moral validity of our economic institutions, it is not at all clear that they will be able to gain the support of the majority of their own memberships. When that occurs, we shall better be able to discern who among us are really supporters of the ancient dream, and are Kingdom-people.

Perhaps it is time for those of us who have arrived at mid-life and are planning our retirements to consider this justice issue a bit more carefully. Given our commitment to the Lord and to the dream of his Kingdom, can we really devote all of our time to our own pleasures and interests on the theory that we've "earned" it? How would we begin to justify that approach to our retirement when so many of our sisters and brothers in this country are being crushed by intolerable injustice? Would not such a totally self-serving retirement call the authenticity of our faith commitment into question? Even though our generation was brought up to think of sexual offenses as the "real" sins, so much so that we tended to overlook injustice, we need not continue with that same mindset until the end. What a wonderful witness to the Kingdom we would be to our young people if they saw us suddenly getting active in the peace and justice issues! What a turn-around it would be if they had to come to bail us out of jail for a change, and over a peace and justice issue at that. Retirement might just be the opportunity we need to complete our spiritual journeys in a truly meaningful way. It is a time of greater freedom for us. Could we not make it a time of greater freedom for the poor and oppressed among us as well? Of course, there are limits to be faced in the struggle against injustice. We know that full justice will only be achieved with the coming of the Kingdom, so however deep our commitment, we must be aware that we cannot fully succeed. But if Calvary and failure are our appointed lot in our struggle with the principalities and powers, then it is more than ever imperative that we make that journey together in the company of friends and believers. Let us act for justice in such a way that when we fail in our chosen cause, our world will be forced to say of us, "It is not right that so good a people in so noble a cause should have failed." For it is only if we live our lives that way that we shall be justified in saying at the end, like the Lord, "Father, we did all we could. We can do no more. It is now in your hands and in the hands of those women and men of faith who come after us." By so doing, we shall have fulfilled our vocation as Kingdom-people. We shall have struggled to the end against moral evil, and we shall have left our world better than we found it.

SUGGESTED READING

Daniel Berrigan, *Love, Love at the End,* Macmillan, 1968.

John Haughey, *The Faith That Does Justice,* Paulist Press, 1977.

Robert Hutchinson, *Hunger in America,* Twenty-Third Publications, 1982.

Daniel Maguire, "A 'New' View Of Sin," *Catholic Update,* St. Anthony Messenger Press, August 1981.

Robert McClory, *Racism in America,* Twenty-Third Publications, 1981.

Elsa Tamey, *Bible of the Oppressed,* Orbis, 1982.

L. John Topel, *The Way to Peace,* Orbis, 1979.

Walter Wink, "Unmasking The Powers" in *Sojourners* Oct. 10, 1978, pp. 9-15.

CHAPTER THIRTEEN

Forgiveness
and Reconciliation

Our journey through "morality and its beyond" has been arduous and painful, challenging some of our most cherished beliefs and practices. None of the issues treated were given the kind of complete consideration they deserved. Rather, an attempt was made to initiate new ways of thinking about the moral problems facing the adult faith community, ways rooted more directly in human experience and in the ancient dream of the Kingdom, and more in keeping with our post-Vatican II perspective on faith. It is only a meager start, but we hope others will refine, correct, and develop further the positions taken here. In that spirit, I think it is fitting to end this book by returning again to the primary message of the Yahweh-God to humankind. As we noted in an earlier chapter, that message is:

> Sure you died, *but you rose again,* and in my eyes you are a new creation! In my presence, you are entirely new without any guilt what-

277

soever. It's gone—it's forgiven—I love you. If you had a bad experience last year, forget it. If you've been going through bad times—it's over now. You can be your best self because *I am with you,* and I shall never, never abandon you

That is such unalloyed good news that it is hard to understand why the human race has so consistently resisted it, and why the church finds it so difficult to proclaim it. I guess we find it just too good to be true.

Leo Mahon tells a marvelous story of a woman who came to confession to him years ago when he was stationed in Central America. It captures the human dilemma in coping with things like unconditional love and forgiveness. After the introductory "Bless me, Father," the woman began to list her sins. First on the list was "I put celery in my husband's salad." Leo interrupted her, assuring her that was no sin. But the woman responded, "Oh Father, you don't understand." Then she set Mahon straight. "You see, Father, my husband is the most loving, most gracious, most forgiving man alive. He is a saint! He never complains. He is always generous and giving, it drives me wild. Father, do you know how hard it is to live with a saint? Well, the other evening I couldn't take it any longer. I was making dinner. My husband hates celery. So I made his salad and loaded it with celery. And do you know what happened, Father? When we sat down to dinner, he never said a word. He never complained. He sat there chatting pleasantly as he ate the whole salad. Father, he is such a good man. I can't stand it.''

We can all identify with the woman in the story, and perhaps we even have a similar story, wherein we lash out at the truly good people with whom we live because we are uncomfortable in the presence of such virtue. Some of us may even have some stories to tell about how we reacted that way to the Yahweh-God or to Jesus because we become so uncomfortable in the presence of love. We all know the discomfort felt by the older brother in the Prodigal Son story, but our experience tells us that the younger son must have been having mixed feelings too when faced with the absolute and unconditional love of his father. It is great to be forgiven, and it is great to know that the one we've hurt has forgotten, but it is not easy for us to forget, to stop feeling guilty, and to start feeling good about ourselves again.

Psychologically, the Monster-God has at least that going for him. He loves us only when we're good, and when we're bad he imposes penalties which, when paid, make us feel that the slate is clean, that we've been able to do something about making amends. Faced with unconditional love and forgiveness, we seem unable to do anything about it, and so have some difficulty regaining our feelings of adequacy and self-respect. Besides, such love also makes us more aware of just how unloving we remain. Knowing no other way to cope with the situation, many Christians reject the Yahweh-God's primary message and take refuge in the Monster-God because that initially "feels" better. Then, in an effort to justify such a move, they resort to a theology that says that our repentance is a precondition to God's forgiveness, which blunts the Yahweh-God's primary message to us by making his forgiveness conditional. Is there not a better way to assuage our psyches than by denying and rejecting God's revelation of himself? I think there is.

In order to see that, we have to get straight the dynamic relationship that exists between forgiveness and reconciliation. It is our misunderstanding of that that allowed us to teach against faith that God's forgiveness is conditioned on what we do. Interestingly enough, despite the fact that we went to confession in order to be forgiven, we never called it the sacrament of forgiveness, but more accurately the sacrament of penance or the sacrament of reconciliation. Forgiveness—ultimately—is what God does. Penance and reconciliation are things we do subsequent to receiving the gift of his forgiveness. But even if we had named the sacrament correctly, we managed to misunderstand its significance.

This has led to some basic confusions that are the reason so many have stopped going to confession in the post-Vatican II church. It might have been supposed that the new rite of reconciliation introduced in Lent of 1977 was going to remedy the situation, but it hasn't. The reason is because the new rite continues to put liturgical conditions on God's forgiveness, thus contradicting the primary message of faith. As we have seen, the forgiveness of God is available to all and is ours for the taking. The sacrament does not confer forgiveness; it celebrates a forgiveness already given. Of what value or use to Christian life is the sacrament then? The reasons for having the sacrament of reconciliation is that Christians are called to publicly reconcile themselves with one another and with all of humankind as a sign of the coming Kingdom, and that it is a celebration of the fact that out of love the Yahweh-God has made the gift of his forgiveness so readily available to all. Unless and until we have a rite that satisfies those purposes, it does not seem likely that post-Vatican II Catholics will celebrate this sacrament in great numbers.

Having been raised to think of the sacrament as the source of forgiveness, once an adult Christian realizes that forgiveness is given without the sacrament, the natural tendency is to think of the sacrament as unnecessary. It becomes something of a luxury, something we might do at Christmas and Easter, but it offers nothing essential to our everyday lives as Christians. To remedy that misunderstanding, it is necessary to see the sacrament as an integral part of reconciliation, and to see reconciliation as the only appropriate response to the gift of forgiveness.

God's unconditional forgiveness means that there is nothing at all we can do about our own forgiveness. We are forgiven whether we know it or not, like it or not, want it or not. If that creates a pressure within us to want to "do something," we are just going to have to face up to the fact that our forgiveness is pure gift and there is nothing we can do to earn it, merit it, or even be fully worthy of it. What that psychological pressure reveals to us is that having been gifted with forgiveness, there is something we can do, not about our own forgiveness to be sure, but in the light of it.

Having been forgiven by the gracious love of God, we are empowered to forgive one another, to heal one another, so we may truly be one and walk together in peace and solidarity as befits Kingdom-people. If the only way I feel good about myself is to play some role in earning my own forgiveness, then I shall be unable to enter into the process of forgiveness—reconciliation—solidarity required by the Kingdom. I shall remain too centered on myself to accept the gift graciously or graciously to bestow it on others.

That forgiveness—reconciliation—solidarity dynamic reminds me of a scene from the movie *Gandhi,* perhaps the most arresting scene in the whole movie. Having been granted independence, India is aflame with rioting Hindus and Moslems slaughtering one another. In protest against the insanity, Gandhi goes on a hunger strike until death, or until the senseless fighting stops. Weak and near death himself, he is visited by a delegation pleading for him to give up the hunger strike. One of the Hindu men protests that he doesn't want Gandhi's life on his hands too, for he is already "in hell" because, in retaliation for the death of his own child, he had deliberately slaughtered a small Moslem child.

Weakened from lack of nourishment and barely able to speak above a whisper, Gandhi looks at the man with love and compassion for his plight and whispers gently, "I know a way out of hell!" The anguished father asks how. Gandhi urges him to go out and find a small Moslem child orphaned by the rioting, to take the child into his home and raise it as his very own. And then with hushed reverence Gandhi whispers the essential ingredient, "But raise it Moslem!" The distraught man's face brightens ever so slightly as he recognizes the truth in what was said.

The muffled "oh's" and "ah's" from the movie audience that night indicated that we too recognized it as true. There is a way out of the hells into which we get ourselves. There is a way of quieting the awful anxieties of the psyche after we have done evil. There is a way to come to feel good about ourselves even after the worst of falls. How beautiful, how touching, and what a simply marvelous theology. It would seem that those close to God, whatever their religion, can catch on to the truth about him and the way he works in the world.

From the Christian perspective, the sacrament of reconciliation should be viewed then in light of the ancient dynamic with which we are already familiar.

Since the Yahweh-God has forgiven us, endowed us with new life so that now we are spotless in his sight, how can we not forgive our sisters and brothers? How can we not be reconciled with them and to the Yahweh-God's dream of human solidarity? Why, that is truly unthinkable in the light of all that the Yahweh-God has done for us.

We go to the sacrament not so much to confess our sins, which have already been forgiven, but to publicly express our gratitude to the Lord for his gift of forgiveness and new life, and to profess our recommitment henceforth to work for the realization of the ancient dream—all of humankind living relationally at peace in justice and love.

If we think this makes the sacrament of reconciliation less important than the old sacrament of penance, we have not yet recognized how important reconciliation is for both human life and for faith. It is so much easier to think of the sacrament as one of penance, because then I simply read off my list of sins, say I am sorry, agree to work hard not to commit them again, and I am forgiven—provided I say the penance prayer. And I can do all that with only the priest and myself, and in the old days and in some places even yet, it was done in a dark hole, too. It is much more challenging and difficult for me to view the sacrament as one of reconciliation, for its very name requires me to make the human connection to align myself with the Lord's dream for all of humankind. But that is the essential church work. For, as Tad Guzie (*What a Modern Catholic Believes About Confession* Thomas More, 1974, p. 84) has observed:

> The primary function of any Christian community is to be a group of people who accept others and who help others to accept themselves, *no matter what they have done.* The world in its best moments wants peace and reconciliation, and every sincere person in the world wants acceptance and pardon. The Christian church is called by God to be explicitly what the world implicitly wants: a community in which mutual acceptance and forgiveness are a reality.

How could it be otherwise? If the primary message of Yahweh is unconditional forgiveness, then the primary mission of church would be the proclamation of God's words of forgiveness, and the exhortation to be reconciled so that the Kingdom might more fully come. The Catholic Church has always tried to fulfill that mission, but was hampered in really doing so because of its mistaken belief that it had also to be "moral policeman." I have tried to show that this need not be the case, and that the institutional church would better fulfill its mission if it gets out of the morality business and proclaims the God of faith and his dream for the world. By so doing, it will better empower us to be reconciled with one another, and to live in peace and solidarity with all of humankind. For in the end, the best way to promote morality is by mightily striving for its beyond.

SUGGESTED READING

William J. Bausch, *A New Look at the Sacraments,* Twenty-Third Publications, 1983. Esp. Chs. 11-13, pp. 153-201.

Bernard Cooke, *Sacraments & Sacramentality,* Twenty-Third Publications, 1983. Esp. Chs. 17-19, pp. 190-219.

Tad Guzie, *What a Modern Catholic Believes About Confession,* Thomas More, 1974.

Epilogue

You readers who may feel this book has done you harm, I ask your forgiveness. You who have been alienated by it, I assure you that was not my intention. On the contrary, I wrote it in behalf of the dream of human solidarity, as the dedication clearly shows.

D.W.
Summer 1983

Dialogue Questions

1.. Identify some of the things you hold now in moral matters that you once thought you could never espouse. Why did you make the change?
2. How would you distinguish your position from the position of those who simply give up on trying to be moral because it is too difficult?
3. What, if any, *unnecessary* burdens of conscience are you still carrying in adult life due to your early moral training? How has that wounded you as you lived your life? Are you at peace with the Lord about it?
4. Who among the people you know and actually deal with do you consider to be evil persons? Why? Do you think people are basically good, basically evil, or basically neutral becoming good or evil because of their environment?
5. Many say we should not, as Christians, be judgmental of others. What does that mean to you at this stage of your life? Certainly that doesn't exclude our children, does it?

6. What are the contemporary moral issues on which the Catholic Church has taken official stands and with which you disagree? Why do you disagree? What do you think should be done about that disagreement?
7. What do you make of the author's call for a "pastoral morality"? What do you take him to mean by that? Can you give any examples from your own life where this approach might have been helpful to you, but what you got was not?
8. This book is dedicated to those whom the traditional morality we were taught has wounded the most and who, despite those wounds, continued the search for goodness and virtue. Identify the people along the way in your own life journey who seem to qualify as people the author has in mind. Give your reasons why you singled them out.

CHAPTER ONE

A. *The Existential Dilemma*
1. Do you really find ambiguity permeating human life? Explain your "yes" or "no" answer. Hasn't the author really exaggerated the predicament? Most people get along just fine!
2. How do you feel about your own body? Do you consider it friend or foe? (Careful! Remember in some way your body *is* you.) How do you think a senior citizen, a quadraplegic, or a drug addict would answer this?
3. In what situations and under what conditions do you feel most alienated by your body? What do you make of that? Where does sexuality fit in here? Do those experiences make you want to give some credibility to the Platonic view of the human condition?
4. Those making the mid-life passage—how would you answer the preceding question?
5. Share with one another your recollections of how you first came to *know* that you could not avoid death, and your reactions to that knowledge. How did you manage to get beyond it?
6. How does the realization of your death and your human limitations manifest itself in your life right now? What new problems

does it present you with? How are you doing in terms of coping with them? What help would you like to see from your faith community?

B. *A Traditional Interpretation*

1. What do you make of Plato's account of the human condition? It sounds a lot like what many Christians hold, doesn't it? Do you feel like a soul or spirit imprisoned in a body?
2. Is the body to be shunned as the source of evil? After all, it is the source of lots of trouble, e.g. sex, addictions, sickness, disability, and death!
3. What does the author mean when he accuses Plato of excessive spiritualism? And when he says that leads to puritanism? Do you agree or disagree? Why?
4. Isn't it better to be excessively spiritual than to be excessively physical? Explain your answer.

C. *The Ontological Paradox*

1. Do you feel good about yourself? If no, say why not. If yes, don't be bashful; tell us why you feel that way. What is so great about yourself—in your own eyes?
2. From your experience is it true, as the author says, that it is thanks to others that we come to feel good about ourselves? Give some examples from your own life that seem to verify your answer.
3. Any thoughts on the stalemate—I want to be affirmed by others, but they're too interested in having me affirm them to take the time to affirm me. A mess, right? Any suggestions on what to do about it? Can affirmation be forced?
4. What is your own personal hero system? After doing what, do you feel good about yourself and most confident that you *are* special? (It's all right to share that; you are among friends.)
5. When you step back and look at it at this stage of your life, what sort of assessment would you make of your personal hero system? (Adequate, Inadequate, Ignoble, Trivial, Other?)
6. If I'm too heroic or great in the eyes of others, they feel cut off from me. Does that ever bother you? What about feelings of oneness and solidarity with others? From your own experience,

share some moments when the contradiction between your hero system and your need to feel at one with others was the greatest. What did you do? Looking back on it now, how do you feel about it? Would you do anything differently?

D. *The Significance of Coping*

1. From your reading of the chapter, why is it so important to say that we humans "cope" with the things of our lives and don't simply "adapt" to them? What's at stake here?
2. From your own experiences, what has convinced you that human beings are free, at least free enough to be responsible for their actions? Or do you subscribe to the theory that we're all driven, and that therefore everybody's sick and nobody is guilty?
3. Any reactions to St. Paul's and Kierkegaard's looking at us as body, soul, and spirit? Does talking that way help or further confuse you? Explain.
4. Comment on the following:
   a. "Our moments of authentic freedom are real, but they are neither as frequent nor as pervasive as we might wish."
   b. "As spirit we cannot simply live, simply copulate, or simply die. We are called to 'relate' to the things of our lives."
   c. "Spirit is often suppressed by an abortion, men having several self-serving devices for suppressing the embryo of their highest life."

CHAPTER TWO

A. *Evil: a Spin-Off of Life*

1. Do you agree that a world without life would be a world without good or evil and that it would simply exist?
2. Can you think of anything that frustrates vital human needs, desires, and interests that isn't evil?
3. Can you think of anything that frustrates vital human needs, desires and interests that isn't good?
4. If good and evil are always relational, relating to vital human needs, desires and interests, doesn't that make them relative and not objective? Explain.

5. Comment on the list of things the author calls objectively evil:
   a. Death
   b. Pain
   c. Disablement
   d. Deprivation of pleasure
   e. Deprivation of freedom and opportunity
   f. Deprivation of worth or self-esteem.
6. Can you think of anything evil that either isn't one of the six, or leads to one of them? Explain.
7. Doesn't the fact that we sometimes seek one of the six prove they aren't always evil?

B. *The Emergence of Moral Evil*
   1. What do you understand by the phrases "ontic evil" and "moral evil"? Do you generally agree or disagree with the author? Explain why.
   2. Is the infliction of ontic evil ever justified? Give some examples.
   3. Any reactions to the statement that nothing is evil simply because an authority says so, even if the authority of God? What do you make of that?

C. *Immorality and the Human Condition*
   1. What do you make of the claim that we humans cause more ontic evil in the world because of our symbolic selves than because of our animal nature? Give examples to substantiate your answer.
   2. What about the claim that moral evil usually comes from good people thirsting for more life?
   3. Where are you in the classic controversy over the basic orientation of human beings? Are we basically good? Basically evil? Basically neutral? Explain.

D. *Why Be Moral?*
   1. If someone asked you why they should be moral, what would be your answer? Leaving faith aside, what reasons do you give yourself for being moral?
   2. If I am moral merely in order to "get to heaven," isn't that self-interest, albeit spiritual self-interest?
   3. William James said "The nobler things taste better, and that is all

that can be said about it." Do you consider that true or not? Explain.

4. Can you recall when you first had the foundational moral experience? Describe the situation.

5. Name the hero or heroine of a literary work who most affected you and revealed to you the truth of the foundational moral experience.

6. How does one help one's children to have the right "feel" for others? What has worked best in your family?

E. *A Concluding Overview*

1. Do you agree with Kierkegaard that there is no way to prove to anyone that she is "spirit" if she doesn't already know it?

2. What sorts of experiences revealed to you that you were not an animal but *spirit*?

3. Do you agree that experiencing losses makes one compassionate to one's fellows? Couldn't they just as easily make one bitter and withdrawn?

4. Any reactions to the author's assessment of mid-life? What did your mid-life passage reveal to you?

CHAPTER THREE

A. *Sin: Our Earliest Understanding*

1. Recount your own experience of first learning the Adam and Eve story. What affect did it have on you? Was it helpful or hurtful? Any residual effects from that experience still operative in your life?

2. Any stories from your adult life concerning your encounter with those who insist on taking Genesis literally? How do you generally deal with such people?

3. Share something from your own experiences in preparing for or in making your first confession. Did you view it as a kind of spiritual car wash?

4. Comment on the following: "For most people once you get to adult life, the ten commandments are no challenge at all. People can generally keep them standing on their heads—a piece of cake!" True or false? If true, what do you make of that?

5. Where do you stand now regarding the existence of the devil? If you've given up your childhood views on the matter, say why.
6. What's your reaction to the author's suggestion that first confession be put off until the later grades?

B. *Implications and Effects of That Early Understanding*
1. Did the Old Testament Bible stories about how God acts ever frighten you? Explain.
2. Scripture sometimes gives so bad a picture of God that it scares people away. Do you know any such people? What ought we to do about them?
3. When did you come to see God as a loving God, not an angry punisher? How did/do you relate that view of a loving God to the Old Testament stories?
4. What is your reaction to the news that God tests us in this life? Any reaction to the Abraham story?

C. *A Concluding Assessment*
1. What does the author mean when he says that in the "religious" account, Christianity is reduced to a "morality play"?
2. What do you say to people when they say God gave them cancer, or caused the death of a loved one? What ought one say?
3. In your judgment, what was the most malicious remark ever made about God in your presence? What were your reactions? Did you do anything about it?
4. Do you feel there is pressure among Catholics to undo Vatican II? Where is it coming from? Are you for or against it? Explain.
5. Comment on the following:
   a. "We've gone too far—we must go back!"
   b. "We can't go back—we're called to create a whole array of *new* moral, life-giving alternatives."

CHAPTER FOUR

A. *An Exodus Interpretation of Genesis*
1. What do you make of the author's claim that the exodus event is to the Old Testament what the Jesus event is to the New Testament? What does "Exodus" mean to you?
2. Comment on the following remark: "Creation is the first act of

292 / Dialogue Questions

liberation.'' What does the word ''liberation'' mean in that statement? What is its significance?

3. If the God of Exodus-Genesis liberates all of creation from disorder, how did sin (disorder) get into the picture? What do you make of the claim that *we* (humankind) are the source of moral evil in the world?

4. The fundamental sin is the refusal to live relationally; it is the rejection of human solidarity. What does that mean? Any examples of that from your own experience?

5. What does the author mean when he says the Genesis challenge is: ''Can I *choose* to be human?'' ''Can I live my life as a *gift*?'' We're human whether we choose it or not, aren't we?

B. *The Real God of Exodus-Genesis*

1. What do you make of the ''horror-stories'' about God in the Bible? Do you believe that's how God operates with us, engendering fear and threatening reprisals?

2. The author says that the dream of God is that the world be transformed so that it so bespeaks the presence of the God of faith that it will not be a matter of belief but of evidence. What does that mean to you? Have you ever heard the will of God described that way before? What difference does it make for you?

3. ''The God of the Old Testament and the God of the New Testament are identical. The God of the Old Testament is not a vengeful God.'' Any reactions to that claim?

4. Being good or being moral are not enough then for Christians. Why not?

C. *Understanding the Ancient Dream of the Kingdom*

1. ''Saving one's soul and avoiding eternal damnation is too self-centered a version of the Lord's dream.'' Any reactions to that statement? Why is the dream of the coming Kingdom an improvement?

2. The author says he only came to understand the dream of the Lord in mid-life. When were you introduced to that way of viewing things, that the Kingdom is not a place but a state of affairs, when our world exists so as to make God's presence evident?

D. *When God Reigns and His Spirit Rules*
1. When an "individual rules," what is it like?
2. Why is that contrary to the coming Kingdom? We need authority in the church, don't we?
3. The author says the authority of the pope, bishops, pastors and priests does not mean they can say and do anything they like. What are the requirements for them to speak and act authoritatively?
4. What are some of the things said to you "in the name of the Lord" that didn't sound right? What should have been said in those cases to bring them in line with the dream of the coming Kingdom?
5. When God Reigns and His Spirit Rules, It Means the End of Injustice.
   a. Justice is usually taken to mean the fair and equitable distribution of benefits and obligations within a society. But in the ancient dream, justice is not when things come out equal, but when they come out right. Can you think of an example when things came out equal but were not right?
   b. Justice is when things are "right" between us, so it marks the end of destructive and evil relationships, of alienation and division. What are some of the injustices of which you are most keenly aware these days?
   c. When justice prevails, God determines the agenda; we don't. He has already determined the meaning of human life; the rich and the powerful do not have the right to do that. Any examples of people trying to take over that job from God?
   d. When justice prevails, humankind relates in terms of absolute equality—there is no domination among us.
      i. What are your feelings regarding the status of women in the church? In the culture? How do you feel about the ordination of women? Is it really out of the question? Or is it inevitable? Explain.
      ii. How about clericalism and the domination inherent in the present structures? Any flagrant examples of that in your life lately?
      iii. What advice would you give to young people to avoid

such things?

    iv. Could we, in the name of the Lord, adopt simpler life-styles? Any suggestions about how to go about that?

6. When God Reigns and His Spirit Rules, Unconditional Love Prevails.

    a. Love is at the center of things! From time to time, we experience its eruption into our lives. We were living on the surface of life when something happened to remind us of the central truth that love is at the heart of reality. Won't you share such an experience?

    b. Do such experiences always arise from big and important things, or can they be precipitated by simple everyday gestures?

    c. Share a moment from your life when love's moment was clearly perceived by you to be the voice and call of God reminding you that love is what really matters.

    d. How would you distinguish such moments of love from erotic moments? From moments of "falling in love"?

    e. Any reactions to Juliana of Norwich's ecstatic cry: "All will be well. All will be well. All manner of things will be well!"

E. *Morality and Its Beyond*

1. "Something is a *moral evil* because it is an offense against human beings, unjustly frustrating their needs, desires, and interests. Something is a *sin* because it is an offense against God frustrating his desires and interests." Any comments? Why is it all right to say that all *moral evils* are *sins*?

2. Religiously speaking, *sin* is breaking God's law. From the perception of faith, *sin* is breaking with the covenant and the ancient dream. Does it really make much difference which view one adopts? Explain.

3. What's the difference between saying God calls us "to be good" and that he calls us "to be great"? What do you think of the author's claim: "Our God has never told us to be good!"

4. Becker says there is a "crisis of heroism" in the church today and that that is why the young reject it. What do you understand that to mean? The call to be "good girls and boys" doesn't attract the

young; it turns them off. Any suggestions?

5. Why does being a "Kingdom-person" answer our need to be special? (Remember the Ontological Paradox?)

6. How can I be a Kingdom-person when I can't always manage to be moral? Do you know people who are great "signs" of the Kingdom, whose overall lifestyle is great, but who have trouble being moral in one or other area of their lives? What do you make of that?

7. How would you distinguish the people mentioned in the preceding question from those who are playing games with life and are really hypocritical?

CHAPTER FIVE

A. *Obstacles to Our Knowing God*

1. Christians are to personally know the God of love, and then make *that* God and his love known to the world. The author claims that we have difficulty doing that not only because of our sins and failings, but also because of what we were taught early on about God. Any reactions?

2. "The fact is that the majority of Christians have in the past said, and continue in the present to say, things about God which would correctly be judged to be slander or defamation of character in any court in this land." That can't be true, can it? Any examples come to mind that would support this outlandish claim?

3. "God is an invisible being who sits on a throne somewhere up there, watching us, testing us, punishing us if we're bad and rewarding us if we're good. He is the eternally vigilant lawgiver who is no respector of persons, making heavy demands of obedience on all of humankind, threatening them with eternal damnation should they not keep his laws and walk in his ways. That's God as most of the world knows him." What are your reactions to the claim that the world got this horrible view of God from the Bible and from the church?

4. We expect *that* sort of God to emerge from the Old Testament, but how do you feel about Acts 5:1-11 and Revelations 2:21-23?

What's that sort of God doing in the New Testament?

5. When did you begin to suspect that the God of Scripture just couldn't be or do what he was depicted as being and doing in the Bible? Where are you with respect to the fundamentalist revival that is going on worldwide?

B. *The God of Faith*

1. For some strange reason people hang on, almost desperately, to the Monster-god. Why?

2. After reading this section, how would you answer the question: Where is God? If Exodus 3:14 means Yahweh is the One who will be there, where is there? And once you decide where there is, what is Yahweh doing there?

3. Were you shocked to read: "The message of faith is clear. Contrary to what you may have read elsewhere, the truth is that God is so taken with humankind, so smitten with love of us, that he graces us, loves us and forgives us—unconditionally!"? Share your reactions?

4. Why does such a view stick in the throat, as it were, of the institutional church?

5. How would your more conservative friends react to the statement: "No matter what we may have done, we have nothing whatsoever to fear from God."? How did it strike you? Doesn't that make things a bit too easy on sinners?

6. Do you believe that God loves and forgives you unconditionally? Have you really accepted that forgiveness? Or are you still clinging to past sins, continuing to feel guilty about them? If so, one might say you don't believe in the God of faith, but only in the God of religion. How would you react to that?

APPENDIX TO CHAPTER FIVE

1. "Even if it is true that God loves us unconditionally, it is impossible for human beings to love that way!" Any comments on this statement?

2. Are you more loving or less loving because of the church? Has it

coaxed more love out of you than you otherwise might have given? Explain.

3. Kierkegaard questions whether one can love only to a certain degree. And Buscaglia hopes we all have at least one person in our lives who loves us unconditionally. What do you make of what they are saying?

4. We resist the move to unconditional love. We like ourselves as we are, but faith and life itself call us to move beyond our Because-love. How have you experienced that call in your own life recently?

5. It is suggested that the death of a loved one can often be a profound experience of being called to love unconditionally. Has that been your experience? Explain.

CHAPTER SIX

A. *The Church as Gift*

1. What on earth is the author getting at when he suggests that the church get out of the salvation business? This time he has certainly gone too far. Right?

2. Just because it is true that *"God* saves," that doesn't mean that the church doesn't also, does it? The church is necessary for salvation, isn't it?

3. What is at stake in saying that "the church is *given* to the world" rather than that "the church is *needed* by the world"?

4. Gregory Baum says: "The profound things in life are always gifts." Give some examples that would help make his case.

5. Why is it that God's world and God's relations with humankind are marked by unconditional gratuity, whereas the church so often isn't?

6. Comment on the following: "There are no *Christian* obligations, since the whole faith enterprise is from start to finish a gratuity." Can we really take that seriously? What would happen if we did?

7. "Christians must stop viewing themselves as needed and start seeing themselves as *given* to the world." What does this mean? And why does the world so often see Christians as anything but gifts?

8. Padovano says real Christians can be dispensed with by the world because they are not needed, but they cannot be forgotten. They haunt the world. What does that say to you? Any examples of unforgettable, haunting, gifty Christians? What about Gandhi?

B. *Church and the Morality Game*

1. The institutional church too often has been cast in the role of a moral policeman charged with protecting and maintaining social order. What are the effects of the church's accepting that role?
2. What differences does it make whether the church is moral policeman or troubadour of the Kingdom? What would be the effect on the average Catholic? Would there be any more sin in the world if the church gave up its moral policeman role?
3. Should the church stress morality too much, she appears as a harping mother and young people flee from her influence. But should the church preach the Kingdom and God's unconditional love, Catholics would have no real motivation to be good. What should the church do? Why?
4. The aim of morality is to prevent ontic evil. Is that the central aim of the church as well?
5. Which of the commandments are "moral rules" and which are not? How can one tell which are which?
6. Name some things the church has called "moral evils" that are not. Explain your answer. How is it that some of the things called "sins" inflict ontic evil, and others do not?
7. Isn't it arbitrary to say all sins against the sixth and ninth commandments are mortal sins? What determines that?

C. *Church and Kingdom Ideals*

1. What's the difference between a "moral evil" and a "failure to live an ideal?"
2. The author says there are two kinds of Kingdom requirements, Kingdom Rules and Kingdom Ideals. What's the difference? And why is a violation of each called a "sin"?
3. The author says there is an ambiguity about Kingdom Ideals because they simultaneously attract us and frighten us due to the uncompromising nature of their demands. What does that mean? Any examples?
4. Kingdom Ideals are said to be subversive. Why? Could you apply that to the Prodigal Son story? (See Luke 15:11-32.)

D. *Church: Its Essential Ministry*

1. "The institutional church has fallen on hard times." What is your own diagnosis as to why that is so?
2. What is your assessment of the author's claim that this is primarily because "it has not been fully church"? Now what's that supposed to mean?
3. How do you interpret the drop in vocations to the priesthood and the exodus of hundreds of thousands from the Catholic Church?
4. Comment on the following: "It's not that the church is institutional that's the problem, but that it has institutionalized the wrong dream and the wrong ministry. It still thinks it is in the salvation business."
5. "As moral policeman, the church is into a mission and ministry that people not only don't need, but are more and more telling us they don't want." What evidence from your experience can you give for the truth of this statement?
6. Discuss the meaning of each of these traits of church. Church is or should be:
   a. a movement of change;
   b. a movement of truth;
   c. a movement of light;
   d. a movement of freedom.
7. Discuss the pros and cons of this definition of church: "Church is wherever a group of people, believing in Christ, and trusting in one another, are striving to move the world and transform it into the Kingdom."
8. What does it mean to say that the essential ministry of the church that we "have" is to institutionalize the church that we "are"?
9. Do you get the impression that the institutional church really loves and believes in its members? Why? Why not? What happens in your parish when those in charge really love, trust and believe in the people? Give some examples.

CHAPTER SEVEN

A. *The Pastoral Use of Fear*

1. It is claimed that "it is necessary to engender love of God through fear of his chastisements." What is your opinion of that claim?

Can we be sure that fear once induced will lead to love and not something else? What else? Any examples?
2. What does the author mean when he says: "Whatever you say about hell and devils is really something said about God"? Is that really correct? Explain why you think so.
3. In the old days, what was your reaction to the Prayer to St. Michael? As a child, did it frighten you or make you feel secure? Explain.
4. If devils exist and are prowling the world, how does this implicate God in evil, as the author suggests?

B. *"What About Hell, Daddy?"*
1. What are your reactions to the author's story about his encounter with his youngest daughter regarding hell? Do you have a comparable experience from your life? Won't you share it?
2. Have you ever been asked a question in a faith context to which you didn't know the answer, but once you began speaking you found that it was the answer? What do you make of an experience like that? What does it mean?
3. Can you think of any other area of faith where the answer should be "I don't know," but we have a story we tell instead?

C. *We Really Don't Know*
1. Do you believe that devils exist? If not, when did you give up believing in them? Under what circumstances? What do you say about all those Scriptural accounts of devils?
2. What do you make of the author's claim: "All moral evil, without exception, originates with us." If that claim is true, is there any reason to continue to speak of Satan or devils, or have those terms lost all meaning?
3. According to the author, moral evil is like an atomic chain reaction and can get out of hand and beyond control and seem to require superior beings as their cause. Can you give any examples of this happening?
4. What are your adult thoughts about hell? How do they differ from your childhood understanding? Why did you make the shift? Do you believe in hell?

D. *Salvation, Liberation, and Eternal Life*
1. "All descriptions of heaven are anthropomorphic symbolic representations and should not be taken liberally." Comment on this remark from the perspective of your own image of heaven.
2. What do you think it means "to be saved"? To have "eternal life"?
3. Relate your understanding of "salvation" to your understanding of "sin" and the "coming Kingdom."

CHAPTER EIGHT

A. *The Human Connection*
1. Have you ever had real need for a "pastoral person" in your life? Did one show up for you? How did it all turn out?
2. The author in one place says that a "pastoral person":
   a. is patient
   b. does not condemn
   c. does not threaten
   d. is open and caring.

And in another place:
   a. *believes* in the nobility and goodness of human beings
   b. is *sensitive* to the burdens we carry for no other reason than that we are human
   c. *recognizes* that human life is a journey with many stages. Any comments? What would you add to this list? Any subtractions?
3. Who is the most pastoral person in your community? Any stories about her/him you'd like to share?

B. *Traditional Catholic Moral Teaching*
1. If ever, when did the absolute certainty of the church's moral teaching become problematic for you? Under what circumstances did you begin to question that certainty?
2. Identify those official moral teachings you question most. Why? Does it bother you that you're in disagreement with your church? Why? Why not?

3. In your mind, what does it mean to say: "That act is against the natural law"? What does "natural law" mean to you?

4. Did you understand what the author was getting at when he said the church view of natural law was the most crude and primitive of all the ways of understanding it? (Don't give up so easily! It had something to do with whether our nature was fixed and determined or open to further specification *by us!*)

5. What are your reactions when the hierarchical church says its hands are tied, and that it cannot change the traditional teaching on such things as birth control, euthanasia, and divorce? After all, those things are against the natural law!

C. *Portraits of Sin*

I. *Louis Monden on Sin*

1. What is your understanding of Sin I? What is sin on the level of instinct? Have you ever experienced sin on this level? Share what you can of that experience.

2. It is claimed that there are Christians who never get beyond this level. That can't be true, can it? Explain.

3. When did you "turn 21"? Share the experience. What does "turning 21" have to do with the passage from Sin I to Sin II?

4. The author shares one of his more comic confessional experiences. Share one of your more memorable such experiences.

5. What do you make of Monden's Sin III? What does the author mean when he says: "For Monden, that is the most appropriate meaning of the word 'sin' "?

6. Explain the difference between an Object-Choice and one's Fundamental Option. Why is that so important?

7. What is your opinion of Monden's overall view? Of his view of mortal sin?

II. *John Shea on Sin*

1. Comment on the following:
   a. "Sin is the rupturing of relationships."
   b. "Sin contradicts not only God's law, but what God *is*."
   c. "Sin is dominating, manipulative deceit in our relationship with God and with one another.

2. Does *your* experience with sin corroborate Shea's contention that

sin is not blind but has its own momentum and direction, that is, *inward, backward,* and *deathward?* Explain.

3. What did you make of Shea's claim that the opposite of "sin" is not "good" but "grace"? What led him to say that?

III. *Leo Mahon on Sin*

1. What are your reactions to Leo Mahon's "Man/Woman Story"? What did it say to you about the relation between the church and humankind?
2. If the relationship between the church and humankind is supposed to be one of "dialogue," what obstacles to that come from humankind? From the church?
3. "Paganism is the worship of the three lusts (money, sex, power) put together." Any reactions to that statement? What if I only worship *one* of them?
4. What did you make of the claim that the church's primary role is to offer an alternative lifestyle?
5. What were your reactions to Leo Mahon's distinction between "sin" and "sins"? Is your experience of bitterness, especially bitterness with life itself, really that serious a matter? Who is bitter in your family? Over what? How is that bitterness destroying her or him?
6. Comment on: "There is no way to remain bitter and live!" True or false?

D. *A Postscript*

1. Did this chapter strike you as being "soft" on sin? How did the chapter affect you? Has it helped or harmed? Explain.

CHAPTER NINE

A. *Getting Our Heads Together*

1. In general, where do you personally stand with regard to the more liberated sexual mores begun in the 60s? Do you think there is anything positive to be said for that development or is it all negative? Explain.
2. Has "living together" been a problem experienced in your fami-

ly? Who was involved? What were the reactions of family members? Was it ever resolved? How? What have you learned from the experience?

B. *Where the Church Went Wrong*
 1. Read, discuss, and compare I Corinthians 7 and Ephesians 5 in the context of what they say about marriage.
 2. In your own mind, how do you relate celibacy and virginity on the one hand and marriage on the other to the Christian enterprise? In your view, has the church overvalued virginity and celibacy to the detriment of marriage? Explain.
 3. What is your understanding of the author's account of how procreation became central in Catholic thinking about sex? What are your reactions?

C. *Where the Culture Goes Wrong*
 1. Comment on the following:
    a. "Whatever is done sexually between consenting adults, if it inflicts no unjustified ontic evil, cannot be immoral."
    b. "Adults should be left to exercise their freedom in sexual matters unimpeded."
    c. "Marriage is an attempt to clamp social control on sex and to make fun and games serve stuffy values."
 2. "A casual affair is never easy to sustain." Is that true? Why? Why not? What does the author mean when he says "experience reveals that sex is not that carefree"? What evidence do you have from your own experience that what is said is true?
 3. Performing sexually is not so easy, especially when, as human beings, we have one or more of the following things on our minds. Comment on the following reasons generally given for a person's fear of or anxiety over sex:
    a. because it is of the body and the body is of death.
    b. because I must perform and I'm afraid of being inadequate or awkward.
    c. because of its moral dangers.
    d. because I/she might become pregnant.
    e. because it breaks the order and control I have of my life.
    f. because it makes me dependent on another.

    g. because I'm embarrassed about my body; it is not very attractive.

    h. because it is addicting and may become obsessive or compulsive.

    i. because I think it is vulgar and dirty; I'm not at home with it.

    j. because it can so easily become gross, even cruel.

    k. because it demands a level of intimacy that frightens me.

    l. because it is so susceptible to degradation and abuse; it can become pornographic and lustful.

    m. because I perform habitually and the thing has become stale.

    n. because ... (other?).

4. Any reactions to the author's account of the relation between sex and death? Any of your own sexual experiences cast light on that relationship? Won't you share them?

5. After engaging in sexual activity, do you ever feel uneasy because you've been driven by passion or instinct? What do you make of that experience? What do you take it to mean? What does it reveal about human sexuality?

D. *The Meanings of Human Sexuality*

1. What have you learned "in bed" about the "meaning" of sexual relations? What would you tell a young woman or man were she/he to ask you about the real meaning of human sexuality?

2. Why are faith-filled people so reluctant to answer questions like the preceding one?

3. Any comments on or reactions to the division of sexual meanings given in the text? Can you supply examples from the experiences of the group for each sort?

    a. Taking Sex Non-Relationally

       i. Self-Serving and Necessarily Immoral

      ii. Self-Serving and Possibly Immoral

    b. Taking Sex Relationally

      iii. Self-Serving and Self-Giving

      iv. Self-Giving and Self-Serving

       v. Sacrament and Sign of the Kingdom

4. Comment on the following:

    a. "Injustice is more destructive of the Kingdom than sexual

306 / Dialogue Questions

sins."
   b. "God is really not all that worried about who is in bed with whom."
   c. "People have a right to discover the meaning of human sexuality from their own experiences."

E. *Marriage and the Church*
  1. The author says that marriage is an area where the church has made a real botch of things. Agree? Disagree? Why?
  2. In the light of that, the author goes on to call for the church to get out of the "marriage business." What do you take that to mean? Is it a good idea? What do you see happening if it did?
  3. Has the church tried to force non-Christians to live its view of marriage? How could it do that?
  4. "Marriage is a monogamous, exclusive, permanent, indissoluble and formally constitued conjugal union of female and male." Analyze this definition. Any reactions?
  5. If marriage is indissoluble, what do you make of all the marriage breakups going on all around you?
  6. What is your reaction to the fact that priests and religious seem to be able to get out of their commitments but married folk can't?

F. *Marriage as Sacrament*
  1. Have you ever thought of your parish as a "spiritual filling station"? Are there people in your parish who view it that way?
  2. Are the priests in your parish really busy or overworked? What sorts of things occupy them most? Do they begin to feel like liturgy-producing machines?
  3. If sacraments aren't channels of grace—if they don't *cause* grace, what good are they? What's their value according to the author?
  4. Have any young people in your family gotten married lately? Where did the pressure for a "church wedding" come from? Was it a "marriage in the Lord"? If not, what is your assessment of the situation? Didn't that put the priest in a bind?
  5. Discuss the division of marriage into:
    a. marriages
    b. marriages in the Lord
    c. sacramental marriages.

6 Doesn't the pastoral strategy proposed by the author amount to a thinly veiled proposal for "trial marriages"? What does he mean when he says that the proposed strategy is more in tune with the actual rhythm of married life?
7. Should the church get out of the "marriage business" and concentrate on "marriage in the Lord" and "sacramental marriages"? What would be the practical result of such a move?
8. Any reactions to this chapter? How come there is no mention of "love" in this chapter? What accounts for that? Do you think it is because the author overlooked it?

CHAPTER TEN

A. *Individual Sexual Acts vs. One's Life as a Whole*
   1. What were your teachers telling you about erotic pleasure when you were in high school? What view of God did you have at the time? Was his main interest the sixth and ninth commandments?
   2. Describe in as much detail as you can what goes on inside you when you make an object-choice that is not compatible with your fundamental option.
   3. The author says "... only certain sorts of sexual object choices are compatible with a Christian's fundamental option." Where do *you* place that limit as a Christian? What kinds of sexual behavior do you find incompatible with being a Christian? Explain why.
   4. How do you rank the unitive and procreative purposes of human sexuality?
      a. They're both of equal importance.
      b. The procreative purpose is primary.
      c. The unitive purpose is primary.
   5. Comment on the following: "The pill, condoms, and other contraceptive devices are now an integral part of human nature."

B. *Contraception, or Birth Control*
   1. "If an unmarried couple engages in contraceptive sexual intercourse, there is a twofold evil, because they are not married and

because their lovemaking is unnatural." React to and comment on this statement.

2. The author says: "Artificial birth control is rarely, if ever, immoral, but it can quite often be sinful." What on earth does that mean? How can he make such a confusing statement?

3. Comment on the following: "The enemy of Christian marriage is not contraception, but selfishness and indifference."

4. Where are you in the birth control controversy? What public stand do you think the church should take on the matter, if any?

C. *Premarital Sex and Living Together*

1. The author distinguishes three kinds of premarital sex:
   a. Nonrelational
   b. Relational but noncommitted
   c. Relational and committed.
   What do you understand by each of these?

2. Has your family experienced premarital sex by one or more of its members? Which kind was it? What was learned from the experience? Do you feel any differently about premarital sex as a result? Explain.

3. Have the family wounds from the experience healed? Were there any specific measures toward reconciliation that seemed particularly effective? If yes, won't you share them?

4. Is your overall evaluation of premarital sex more of a plus or a minus? Explain. What is your reaction to the author's treatment of the matter?

5. What about the author's suggestion for "a liturgy of reconciliation and separation" when such premarital relationships break up? Isn't that going just a bit too far?

D. *Adultery, or Extramarital Sex*

1. What is your understanding of the following: "To call something a 'sin' is to speak of its inherent message to others and of its negative public relations value in proclaiming the Kingdom."

2. "Extramarital sex and adultery are *always* sins," says the author. Why is that so?

3. "Adultery is more of an affront to the Kingdom than is divorce." Evaluate and react to this statement.

4. How do you interpret the author's treatment of extramarital sex? Does it strike you that he is encouraging it? If not, what is his ultimate stance in the matter? How does it differ from your stance?

E. *Divorce and Remarriage*

1. Have you or members of your family had any direct experience with marriage tribunals? If yes, describe your reactions to that experience. How pastoral were the people you dealt with?
2. Do you think the Catholic Church should change its position on second marriages? Why? Why not?
3. Read and discuss Matthew 19:3-9 and Mark 10:2-12. They sound like divine commands, don't they? What practical difference do you see resulting if they're taken as ideals?
4. What is your opinion of second marriages? Should they be allowed? Under what conditions?

F. *Homosexuality*

1. Comment on the following remark made by a serious Christian: "God is proving what he thinks about homosexuality by sending them AIDS (Acquired Immune Deficiency Syndrome). It is his way of punishing them."
2. Are any of your family members homosexuals? What was the reaction when that became known? Has the family been supportive of the homosexual in its midst, or have they persecuted her or him in the name of the Lord?
3. Do you personally know any homosexuals? Of those you know, how many fit the cultural stereotype that:
   a. Male homosexuals are effeminate, and female lesbians are masculine.
   b. Male homosexuals tend to be child molesters.
   c. Homosexuals are by nature promiscuous and incapable of stable permanent relationships.
   What do you make of the situation revealed by your experience?
4. The author says, "One can be a sign of the Kingdom regardless of one's sexual orientation." Where are you on that issue? Doesn't that make it a bit too easy for homosexuals?
5. What difference does it make whether we call homosexuality a

"sexual inversion" rather than a "sexual perversion"?
6. Have someone look up the Scripture texts on homosexuality for the group to see if what the author says is true, namely, that idolatry is the abomination, not homosexuality.
7. What does it mean to say that the norms for homosexual sex are exactly the same as for heterosexual sex? What are those norms?
8. Saying that there is nothing in principle preventing homosexuals from having a "marriage in the Lord" or even a "sacramental marriage" is going too far, isn't it?

G. *Summing Up*
1. What is your overall impression and reaction to this chapter? Is it rightheaded? Or off the wall?
2. What is your understanding of the significance of saying love and sex are processional?
3. What would happen if the church gave up being moral policeman and simply started to "up-hold" the Kingdom ideals? Would that make matters worse? If so, how?
4. What should be the church's attitude toward those who fail to live up to its lofty ideals?

CHAPTER ELEVEN

A. *The Yahweh-God and Killing*
1. Generally we hold persons sacred and are against killing them. But sometimes it is necessary! Where are you with regard to: killing in self-defense? Killing in a just war? Capital punishment?
2. Which of the following best captures your attitude:
   a. All killing (of persons) is immoral.
   b. All killing of innocent persons is immoral.
   c. Killing is never good, but whether it is immoral or not depends on the circumstances.
   d. Christians should *never* kill; it's against the fifth commandment.
3. Aquinas says we are never allowed to kill ourselves under any circumstances because God alone has dominion over life and death.

The author challenges that. Where are you?

4. Did the Abraham story ever bother you? What are your reactions to the author's understanding of that troublesome Old Testament account?

5. What do you make of the traditional view that it is all right to kill if God commands you to?

6. Is life a "gift" from God? Or do we hold it only as stewards? What difference does it make, just so long as we have life?

B. *Euthanasia, or Mercy Killing*

1. The author says there are three basic positions regarding the termination of innocent human life. They are the *fundamentalist, liberal,* and *radical* views. Are you clear on what each holds and how it differs from the other two? Explain.

2. Which of the three views comes closest to your own position? Have you always held the view you hold now? If not, share what made you change your position.

3. If we can assume the divine prerogative over life and death in matters of self-defense, just war, and capital punishment, why can't we in matters of mercy killing?

4. Do you consider "mercy killing" to be murder? Why? Why not? (Careful, your answer is an implicit statement about God and how he works in the world.)

5. Any reactions to the position of St. Thomas More?

6. Have you had an experience of someone in your family "living beyond the time of their death," or "when health care itself became the source of dehumanization"? What did the experience teach you? Did it alter your view of euthanasia? Explain.

C. *The Abortion Debate*

1. Share your own position regarding the current abortion controversy. Is it an issue about which you are deeply and passionately moved? Or is it an issue about which you are largely indifferent? If the latter, are you a male?

2. If you experience "moral shock" or "profanation" with regard to abortion, what about it so moves you? Do you have any "feel" for the profanation felt by those holding the opposite view?

I. *Abortion: The Legal Issue*

1. What is your assessment of the Supreme Court decisions on abortion? The author seems to think the Court did all it could under the circumstances. Any reactions to that?

2. Do you think the government should enter the abortion issue? What are your reactions to proposing a Constitutional Amendment to ban abortions? Do you agree such a law is virtually unenforceable?

II. *Abortion: The Moral Issue*

1. Have you or any members of your family ever had an abortion? Was the "morality" of the act any sort of factor in the decision at the time? How do you feel about it all now? Any regrets?

2. What can the author possibly mean when he says we don't know when abortion *becomes* a moral issue?

3. In your family, parish, neighborhood, and city—how credible is the Catholic Church on the abortion issue? What do people say about that?

4. Catholics often just assume the fetus is a person from the first moment of conception. Where are you on that? What were your reactions to the fact there seems to be evidence to the contrary? Did you understand the argument? If not, perhaps someone in the group could help by explaining it.

5. In pregnancies due to rape, what do you understand the church's official position to be in the matter of abortion? Do you agree or disagree? Why is the phenomenon of twinning significant in such cases?

6. The author claims that it is the communally-funded experience of women that to abort early is not to destroy *personal* human life. Is that a correct assessment about where *most* women are today? Where are you on that issue?

7. Using your imagination, say what you think would be the effect if pregnant women had transparent abdomens. Do you agree with the author that it would have a significant effect on how people viewed abortion?

8. Any reactions to the position that it is a good rule of thumb to hold that fetuses should be held inviolate once they "look like

us" (which occurs in the twelfth week or at the end of the first trimester)?

III. *Abortion: The Faith Issue*

1. If abortion is so contrary to the Kingdom, what ought we do about it? Concretely, what sorts of things should believers be doing?

2. "The outrage and profanation we feel over abortion must be tempered with compassion for those caught up in the harshness of life, without resources, without loving support, without faith, just trying to survive. Were we in their shoes, can we say with certainty that we'd act otherwise?" Any reactions to that statement?

3. Has your experience with "pro-life" people been mostly positive or mostly negative? What do you make of the author's claim that many of them are angry or bitter?

4. Is graciousness really that important to the Christian life? How would you define graciousness? If we were all to become gracious, wouldn't we lose or give up our prophetic roles?

Chapter Twelve

A. *Unjust! Who Me?*

1. What do you make of the allegation that because the economic system works for us (while at the same time oppressing others) we have clear consciences and can raise lovely families? That's not really fair to say about us, is it?

2. How do you react to the claim that all luxury and superfluous wealth arise only because the system is defrauding someone somewhere? Any examples?

3. According to Leo Mahon, the decision to live our lives for others is a decision that must be made and remade by every Christian. Have you ever made that decision at any point in your life? If so, share the story of the first time you did so. Have you ever had occasion to remake that decision? Share the story of the most recent such episode, if you will.

4. Why are American Catholics so timid about the justice issue? Do

you agree that it is an important bit of "unfinished business" in our spiritual journeys? Explain.

5. And what about justice? When will you be free enough to *really* face that issue?

B. *The Real Moral Evil: Injustice*
1. When it comes to sins, how do you rank the "sins of the flesh" with the "horrors of injustice"?
2. Discuss the following types of sin:
   a. Sins of doing
   b. Sins of no-doing
   c. Personal sins
   d. Social sin
3. According to the author, what is a "mortal sin"?
4. What does it mean to say, as the author did, "There is nothing at all wrong with our hearts. It is our heads that are the problem."
5. Many cannot see the moral evil of *social sin*. They say: "That's business, that's just the way it is!" Give some examples when injustice was rationalized in that or a similar way.
6. Social sin exists on three levels. Give some examples from your experience of injustice on each level.
   a. First Level—Injustice is done to a colleague or co-worker.
   b. Second Level—A story is told to show either why the injustice had to be done, or that it really wasn't unjust.
   c. Third Level—Thanks to the story told on the second level, a false group-consciousness is formed whereby the group actually condones the injustice and calls it justice.
7. How is it that the stories and symbols of Exodus, Jesus as Liberator, and the Coming Kingdom change the way we view the world and allow us to "see" what would otherwise be invisible? Any examples? (Has reading this book changed your view of the world and of sin and moral evil? You might want to discuss how that has happened.)
8. What are the results of looking at the American economic system in a critical and gospel way? How can Jews and Christians accept that system approvingly? How have you managed to do so all these years? Any second thoughts?

C. The Prophets of Israel in Perspective

1. We rarely, if ever, think of Scripture in economic terms. What was your reaction to the account of Israel under its first kings, David and Solomon? Did the account help you understand the outrage of the prophets in a better way?
2. Rabbi Heschel calls justice "God's stake in human history." What does that mean to you?
3. Heschel also says, "God's needs cannot be satisfied in space but only in time—in history." What came to your mind when you first read that? Relate that to the theme of the ancient dream, the coming Kingdom.
4. Comment on the following:
   a. "All moral evils are at bottom injustices."
   b. "The quest for justice is never a purely secular affair."
   c. "God's will is not so much that we be engaged in religious exercises, but that justice flow like the rivers."

D. The Faith That Does Justice

1. "In this country, people who attempt to create a dwelling place for God in human history usually end up assassinated or in jail." Abraham Lincoln; Martin Luther King, Jr.; Dorothy Day; Bobby Kennedy; Daniel Berrigan—can you think of any others?
2. How real is our "freedom of religion"? What about the assertion that "we can believe anything we like so long as it does not have adverse repercussions on the current political system."?
3. What was your reaction to the bishops' statement on nuclear war? How did you feel about the negative vibes and implied threats coming from the government? Do you think that religious leaders should stay out of such matters?
4. "Churches should concern themselves with the private and individual sins of their people and not concern themselves with the social sins of the nation." Agree or disagree? Why?
5. The author thinks there's trouble ahead if we adopt a more robust Christianity, one more firmly rooted in the biblical tradition. What are your reactions to that? What does separation of church and state mean to you?
6. Does your parish have a Peace and Justice Committee? Is it vital

and active or merely perfunctory? Any suggestions as to what should be done about it?

7. "Once the churches seriously question the moral valdity of our economic institutions, it is not at all clear that they will be able to gain the support of the majority of their own memberships." What is your view of this matter?

8. Concern for peace and justice are "deeply threatening to the way of life we have lived." That has been the story until recently; do you see any change in that attitude in your parish? In your diocese? In yourself?

CHAPTER THIRTEEN

1. Has the reading of this book been arduous and painful? Has it challenged some of your most cherished beliefs? (Which ones?) Was it worth the effort? Explain your answers.

2. What is the Yahweh-God's primary message to humankind? Do you find that good news or bad news? Say why you think it the one or the other.

3. Why do we humans find it so difficult to accept forgiveness as a "gift"? Why, after we're forgiven, do we still cling to the guilt and have difficulty feeling good about ourselves again?

4. What does the author mean when he says the right order of the dynamic is: Forgiveness - Reconciliation - Solidarity?

5. When was the last time you went to confession? Why did you stop going? Have you ever gone under the new rite? What do you think of it? Are you comfortable with it? Have you ever received communal general absolution?

6. If you don't go to the sacrament to be forgiven, why go? What does the author mean when he says reconciliation is the appropriate response to forgiveness?

7. Share your reactions to the *Gandhi* story.

8. Why is the sacrament of reconciliation so important in working for the Kingdom?

10. Comment on the following:
   a. "There *is* a way out of the hells we get ourselves into."
   b. "In the end, the *best* way to promote morality is to strive mightily for its beyond."

Index

"Morality and Its Beyond places within everyone's reach an excellent tool for discussion on modern moral issues and the alternatives of Christian response.

"What he has already done for the household church and the understanding of salvation, in *Redemptive Intimacy,* he extends now to the practical functioning of that church."

Donald J. Headley
Chicago Catholic

also by Dick Westley . . . .

Redemptive Intimacy:
A New Perspective for the Journey to Adult Faith

This book is a call to faith for mature Christians; a call to return to the "faith" of their forebearers — not their religiosity. Describing Christianity/Catholicism as a "faith" not a "religion," Dick Westley insists that all are called to intimacy with God, the very heart of the Christian message. Specifying fear as the origin of "religion," he challenges today's Christians to reject religiosity and to guard against the infallible signs of this malaise as a false view of God.

"A retelling of the Christian story in faith categories that goes back to the Jewish roots of faith, exploring spirituality today and considering the fullness of the call to all for intimacy and serenely walking with God."

Spiritual Life

"Solid contemporary theology is communicated in personal terms."

Commonweal

Also available from your local bookseller or directly:

Twenty-Third Publications
P.O. Box 180
Mystic, CT. 06355
(203) 536-2611